THE

PREINDUSTRIAL

CITY

The

Preindustrial

City

PAST AND PRESENT

By Gideon Sjoberg

THE FREE PRESS
A Division of Macmillan Publishing Co., Inc.
New York

Collier Macmillan Publishers
London

THE FREE PRESS
A Division of Macmillan Publishing Co., Inc.
866 Third Avenue, New York, New York 10022

Collier Macmillan Canada, Ltd.

Library of Congress Catalog Card Number: 60-10903

FIRST FREE PRESS PAPERBACK EDITION 1965

printing number

12 13 14 15 16 17 18 19 20

PREFACE

So TO END a ten-year journey. Looking back, it seems that the further I have traveled, the further I have strayed from the traditional pathways in American sociology. But hindsight leads me to believe that it could not have been otherwise. For I have come to entertain grave doubts concerning many generalizations in sociology and have attempted some reformulation of these.

Ostensibly this is a book about cities. Yet it is much more, for through the medium of the preindustrial-urban center I have sought to analyze the structure of preindustrial civilized societies. In turn we seek in the preindustrial city and its society, now retreating from the world scene, a standard for measuring—and, consequently, understanding—the impact of industrial-urbanization, a truly revolutionary force in this the twentieth century.

Anyone who hazards to place his own work in perspective is beset by pitfalls. Yet this much can be said. Most sociology today focuses upon industrial-urban societies, above all the United States. Reflecting upon the problems inhering in a mature industrial-urban complex, sociologists tend to be preoccupied with contrasting the "real"—in the realms of social class, bureaucracy, and the like—with the "ideal" norms and values. Yet such a frame of reference will have little utility for scientific observers of the transformations wrought upon traditional systems by the encroaching industrial-urbanization. For this we must hark back to an older, more strictly European tradition, some of whose representatives, however, survive in the American sociological fraternity. Here the concern is contrasting the past with the present—for example, as in this study, the preindustrial city and the society that supports it with the industrial city and its society.

Admittedly a generalizing study of this sort encounters special problems. One is how to deal with the spelling of foreign names and terms when divergent usages abound. I have attempted for each cultural area or region to follow the general practice of specialists therein, but this has not always been possible. Then too, it is difficult to regularize the names of authors of, say, Chinese descent. Generally speaking, I have used the form employed by the author himself, even though this has led to some inconsistency in the citations.

Acknowledgments: it is easy to know where to begin. With my wife, Andrée F. Sjoberg. A scholar in her own right, she temporarily set aside her current research in linguistics and anthropology to assist in this venture. She is, as indicated, co-author of Chapters II and III. But her contributions do not end there. As a linguist, she has written on such languages as Uzbek and Telugu and has command of the major languages of Europe, including Russian, a fair knowledge of Sanskrit, and some familiarity with Arabic and several languages of India not mentioned above. Her special skills opened up to me previously unknown realms of social data. Moreover, our friendly, though sometimes heated, arguments over specific issues, continuing into the wee hours of many Texas mornings, illumined many difficult areas. In the end, I marvel at her patience when I consider that she is temperamentally unsympathetic to sociology and what she considers its evasive generalizations. Thus, I bear full responsibility for the theory and its failings.

I also wish sincerely to thank Pat Blair, Leonard Cain, Jr., and Richard Colvard for reading selected chapters, particularly for calling attention to some unclear thinking on my part. And I am most grateful to Badruddin Sharafi, whose discerning comments and objective analysis of his own pre-industrial-urban milieu clarified many a sticky problem. Then too, may I note that a grant from the Graduate School, University of Texas, freed me from teaching duties during one summer (1958), making it possible for me to devote more time to this venture.

Finally, I wish to thank the following publishers for permission to quote from their copyrighted materials: E. J. Brill; Cambridge University Press; Jonathan Cape Ltd.; Clarendon Press (Oxford); Columbia University Press; Thomas Y. Crowell Company; J. M. Dent and Sons Ltd.; Dodd, Mead and Company; E. P. Dutton and Company; Harper and Brothers; Henry Holt and Company; W. W. Norton and Company; Oxford University Press; Princeton University Press; Receuil de Travaux d'Histoire et de Philologie (Louvain); The Ronald Press Company; Tower Bridge Publications.

CONTENTS

CHAPTER I

INTRODUCTION

THE CITY and civilization are inseparable: with the city's rise and spread, man at last emerged from the primitive state. In turn, the city enabled him to construct an ever more complex and, we would like to believe, more satisfying way of life. Some scholars regard the city as second only to agriculture among the significant inventions in human history. We shall not quibble over the proper ranking due the urban community in man's storehouse of great inventions. It is sufficient to recognize that it is worthy of intensive treatment.

We propose to describe and analyze the social and ecological structure of the preindustrial, or non-industrial, city. That this is the first such effort is astonishing, given the existence of cities of this type from early antiquity down to the present day. Most emphatically, this is not just a historical study, nor is it directed solely to the urban sociologist. It has pertinence for any social scientist concerned with the structuring of complex societies. In fact, knowledge of the preindustrial city and of the society that enfolds it—standing as they do in dramatic contrast to the modern industrial-urban community and society—illumines these latter, not only in areas where industrial-urbanization is well advanced, but where it is just now emerging.

Only recently have an appreciable number of American sociologists evidenced interest in the comparative analysis of cities and societies. Sociologists have too long been steeped in the positivistic tradition that stresses fact-gathering and absorption in particulars at the expense of broader generalization. And the demands of various bureaucracies in America for the assistance of sociologists in resolving their particular, and sometimes unique, social problems merely accentuate this trend. Such inner-directedness seems likely to continue as sociology's contributions in this area are increasingly recognized.

Sociologists, especially of the urban variety, are apt to dismiss as sheer speculation the works of the traditional comparativists—Hobhouse, Spencer, Sumner, and even Max Weber.[1] Admittedly these writings can be criticized on a variety of counts. Many of the propositions they present demand reformulation; others must be discarded outright in light of recent findings. But to reject in the process the comparative approach—particularly when treating large-scale social systems—is to ignore a compelling fact. Just as the generalizations of the older comparativists frequently fail us today, many of the recent generalizations of sociologists derived solely from evidence in American society, and then for only a short time-span, are certain to prove inadequate and must ultimately be abandoned. Granted that much cross-cultural comparison necessitates "loose" theories or hypotheses, it has the major advantage of imparting meaning to a complex set of data and serving as a corrective against the ethnocentric bias that inheres in so much intrasocietal research. If sociology is to justify its self-concept as a "science of society," it must establish propositions that have cross-cultural validity.

Nowhere is the need for comparative analysis more apparent than in the study of the city. Many propositions, once widely accepted as true, are coming to be recognized as excessively culture-bound. Consider the concentric zone theory of ecology originated by Burgess and elaborated upon by numerous writers.[2] According to this view, cities generally arrange themselves into a series of well-defined circular zones, one within the other, the focal point of them all being the central business district. Our chapter on ecology demonstrates that cities of the preindustrial type display quite a different spatial arrangement. Or take the generalizations of many sociologists concerning organizational units such as the family. Among some writers it has been fashionable to attribute the emergence of the conjugal family that is the norm in present-day urban America to the urbanization process per se. Such a narrow view could not have developed in a climate that stresses cross-cultural research. The conjugal unit, as the family form toward which urbanites strive, is a consequence of industrial-urbanization; it most decidedly is not the ideal pattern in the preindustrial city. In succeeding chapters we shall have occasion to discuss the weaknesses of a number of other generalizations now popular in American sociology.

Of course, not all urban sociologists have been indifferent to the comparative approach. Sorokin, Zimmerman, and Galpin in their review of the history of rural-urban studies suggest that interest in this area can be traced far back into antiquity; however, they consider Ibn Khaldûn, the fourteenth-century Arab social theorist, "the founder of rural-urban sociology."[3] But the sixteenth-century Italian, Giovanni Botero, seems to us the first truly comparative urban sociologist. In his work, *Greatness of Cities,* Botero offers some penetrating observations, albeit highly impressionistic ones, concerning the relationships between social power and the rise and development of cities that contemporary social scientists may still find pertinent and challenging.[4] Unfortunately, his insights were not improved upon by scholars in the immediately succeeding centuries. Although writers since Botero have somewhat haphazardly dealt with aspects of individual cities, or with cities in particular societies, for really substantial contributions to comparative urban research we must await the late nineteenth century and the emergence of the sociological discipline, more narrowly defined. Among the early sociologists who studied cities cross-culturally Adna F. Weber and Max Weber loom paramount.[5] Adna Weber's comparative work on urban areas, primarily demographic in character, concentrated upon the expansion of urban communities in nineteenth-century Europe. Max Weber, much more enterprising, and drawing upon his impressive fund of knowledge, gained some important insights into urban social organization. Although his study of cities was a fragmentary one, and his perspective diverges from that of the present writer, Max Weber's influence upon this book is nonetheless apparent.

In recent years, Kingsley Davis[6] has led the field in the comparative analysis of cities. He and his co-workers, however, have focused their attention upon the demographic aspects of the urbanization process. Such other American-based scholars as Philip Hauser and Bert F. Hoselitz have also advanced our knowledge of comparative urban social structure and ecology.[7] Their writings manifest a growing uneasiness concerning generalizations about urban life based solely upon data from American society—generalizations that unfortunately are widely accepted in current sociological literature. Our study of the preindustrial city, embodying a comparative approach on a global scale, pushes the re-evaluation process still further and seeks to revise many thought-ways in urban sociology and in related fields as well.

Statement of Purpose

Our aim is to describe and analyze the structure of the city, both in historical societies and in surviving literate non-industrial orders, before its transformation through industrialization. We also seek to provide background data on the origins of city life and the growth and spread of cities around the world.

Our principal hypothesis is that in their structure, or form, preindustrial cities—whether in medieval Europe, traditional China, India, or elsewhere—resemble one another closely and in turn differ markedly from modern industrial-urban centers. Most writers have failed to distinguish the industrial and pre-industrial types. As a result, the data on preindustrial cities negate many popular sociological generalizations based solely upon evidence from modern industrial American communities.

The most non-industrial cities today are those like Andkhui and Mazar-i-Sharif in Afghanistan and Katmandu in Nepal, where the populace continues its preindustrial mode of existence quite unaffected by industrial forms. Still largely preindustrial cities abound in other parts of Asia, in North Africa, and in sections of southern Europe and Latin America.

Not only do preindustrial cities survive today, but they have been the foci of civilization from the time of its first appearance in Mesopotamia in the fourth millennium B.C. The "ancient" cities of Athens and Rome, familiar to almost every school child, are in actuality relatively late creations and merely two out of a vast number scattered over much of Eurasia and North Africa around the beginning of the Christian era. Even when Europe entered the Dark Ages and city life waned over much of the continent, the Eastern Roman Empire and Spain experienced a vibrant urban life. Contemporaneously, cities were flourishing in Meso-America, North Africa, and Asia.

To return to our main thesis: preindustrial cities everywhere display strikingly similar social and ecological structures, not necessarily in specific cultural content, but certainly in basic form. Admittedly the idiosyncratic values of any given culture do induce some unique urban patterns. But all too much emphasis has been given to the aberrant, especially by writers imbued with the humanistic tradition.[8] In many instances, elements that are assumed to be unique to particular cities or peasant communities are not so at all.[9] Strictly speaking, the unique can be established only in contrast to predetermined universal reference points.

We seek to isolate for preindustrial cities structural universals, those elements that transcend cultural boundaries.

These cities share numerous patterns in the realms of ecology, class, and the family, as well as in their economic, political, religious, and educational structures, arrangements that diverge sharply from their counterparts in mature industrial cities.

The industrial-urban center is the standard against which we contrast the preindustrial city; the succeeding chapters continually emphasize the differences between these two types of communities. Unlike many historians, our intent is *not* to compare the preindustrial cities of one historical epoch with those of another within the same society. Nor are we concerned with contrasting the non-industrial cities of one time period, on a global scale, with similar cities from another era. Rather we are comparing the typical preindustrial with the typical industrial city. Failing to state explicitly just what is being contrasted leads to much unnecessary confusion in social science literature, a situation referred to on a number of occasions in this work. By making our reference points explicit we have sought to avoid misunderstanding.

Awareness of the numerous shared features of preindustrial cities lends clarity to the structural arrangements not only of industrial cities but of those currently undergoing industrialization—those partly preindustrial, partly industrial. Conspicuous in the writings on underdeveloped countries, a literature now assuming notable proportions, is the attempt by many social scientists who lack any real comprehension of the traditional social structure to delineate the contours of social change that stem from industrialization. Without a yardstick for measuring this change such efforts are doomed to failure.

Some will take exception to the foregoing, contending that preindustrial civilized societies are quite well understood given the rather numerous studies of peasant villages. But though the peasantry forms the bulk of the population in these societies, the focal point of activity is the city. The vital institutional apparatus is urban, not rural. It is the city dwellers who have staffed the key positions in this type of social order, who have perpetuated the society's learned heritage. Rural-urban contrasts, though differing from those in industrial societies, are observable in most fields of social activity. The failure of numerous writers on so-called "agrarian" societies to distinguish between the rural and urban areas makes suspect their generalizations as to life in these societies.

Having reviewed this study's purpose and potential significance, we now examine its theoretical framework.

Theoretical Orientation and Clarification of Terms

For analytical purposes we distinguish three types of societies: the folk, or preliterate, society; the "feudal" society (also termed the preindustrial civilized society or literate preindustrial society); and the industrial-urban society. Only the last two contain urban agglomerations: the preindustrial and industrial cities, respectively.

To achieve this typology of societies, and consequently of cities, we take technology as the key independent variable— i.e., associated with varying levels of technology are distinctive types of social structure. Technology both requires and makes possible certain social forms. This viewpoint does *not* commit us to technological determinism, however, for recognized is the impact upon social structure of other variables—the city, cultural values, and social power—all of which can affect the patterning of technology itself. Nor do we, like sociologists of the "ecological school," conceive of technology as part of the "biotic," or subsocial realm.[10] Technology is not some materialistic, impersonal force outside the socio-cultural context or beyond human control; technology is a human creation par excellence.

Technology, as employed in this study, refers to the sources of energy, the tools, and the know-how connected with the use of both tools and sources of energy for the production of goods and services. Industrialism is that type of technology that utilizes inanimate sources of energy for driving its tools; associated with it are implements and know-how of a much more complex form that those in non-industrial systems. In industrial cities (subsystems of the industrial society) electricity, steam, nuclear fission, etc. supply the power that for so many millennia were provided by animals and human beings. We could consider energy itself as the key variable for distinguishing between the main types of cities and societies.[11] However, technology in the broader sense is a more satisfactory medium for explaining the structure of the preindustrial city and its society.

The technological variable is highly useful for differentiating among folk, feudal, and industrial societies, as well as more specifically between preindustrial and industrial cities. The folk, or preliterate, order's technology is an exceedingly simple one, and cities are absent. Only a few of the simpler folk societies—those that lack any stable food supply and utilize the crudest of implements—survive today; South America and New Guinea harbor some of these. Yet they were quite numerous only a few centuries ago. Most of the preliterate groups that have persisted into the twentieth century—some in West Africa, for example—are of the more advanced type that possess food production and storage techniques enabling them to support some full-time non-agricultural specialists. But even these can be distinguished from typical feudal societies by their lack of literacy and other key traits.[12]

Although the folk society is typically self-sufficient, contrary to Redfield's contention it is rarely isolated.[13] It is debatable whether any society is truly isolated, for every in-group requires an out-group, even if it be merely symbolic; otherwise societal integration can not be maintained. However, folk societies are relatively more isolated than feudal orders and these in turn are isolated to a greater degree than industrial-urban systems. The self-sufficiency and relatively greater isolation of the folk order, combined with its typically small size, lead to norms that are highly prescriptive in a wide range of activities—i.e., few alternative courses of action are available to members of the system.

The lack of a food surplus, itself a function of the little-developed technology, permits a modicum of specialization of labor. Most persons are directly engaged in the struggle for existence and, especially in the simpler preliterate orders, must labor unremittingly and more or less exclusively at the tasks of collecting and preparing food so that they can survive. Specialization of occupational roles is—beyond the limitations imposed by biological factors such as age and sex—at a minimum. Thus Holmberg[14] found among the Siriono of eastern Bolivia little division of labor between men and women; both sexes engaged in food collection and in tasks such as cooking or basket-making when extra hands were required. This paucity of specialization obviously inhibits the development of a class system. Even in a more complex folk society, one that supports a few full-time specialists, not enough persons are liberated from the day-by-day struggle for subsistence to permit the development and utilization of such a complex tool as writing.

The typical folk society is, then, a small, self-sufficient, preliterate group that lacks any real division of labor (save for the limits imposed by biology) or a class system and is therefore highly homogeneous. The technology not only requires this type of social structure but prohibits the development of alternative forms. As implied above, the more complex preliterate society stands in a sense somewhere between this and the feudal or preindustrial civilized order.

Turning to the feudal society, we must qualify our use of this term. The denotation "feudal" seems more satisfactory than the epithets "gentry," "agrarian," "Asiatic," or "traditional," employed by various writers, but it can be misleading. Historians will take issue with our usage, for they often apply the term "feudal" to a particular set of relationships, notably those between lord and vassal, that obtained in medieval Europe and in some Asiatic societies. Still, a perusal of Coulborn's work,[15] for example, reveals inconsistencies even in this usage. We consider the "feudal society" of historians a special case of our own.

Adoption of this label is hazardous too because of the special meaning attached to it in the popular press and in social science literature.[16] Some define as "feudal" any social system they deem undesirable. We attach no moral connotations to the term. Marxist writers also regard feudalism as a special stage in an inevitable evolutionary process that all societies undergo. For them, the four stages of urban development are the slave-owning city, the feudal city, the capitalist city, and the socialist city.[17] Economic organization, *not* technology as we define it, is the variable underlying their classificatory scheme. Their perspective differs radically from our own.

Despite these drawbacks the term, "feudal society," more clearly and concisely than any other, depicts the type of social order under discussion.[18] But to avoid misunderstanding, we introduce two synonyms: "preindustrial civilized society" and "literate preindustrial society." Regrettably, the first-named suggests a "barbarian-civilized" dichotomy within social orders, and the second implies that the society's population is largely literate, which it decidedly is not.

Enough of this discourse on semantics. The feudal society, vis-à-vis the typical folk order, has a more advanced agricultural technology that produces sufficient food surpluses to support large non-agricultural populations. In all instances this technology includes the cultivation of grains. It also embraces (except in ancient Meso-America, discussed in Chapter II) animal husbandry, large-scale irrigation works, the plow, metallurgy, the wheel, and other devices that multiply the production and distribution of agricultural surpluses. Nevertheless, the feudal society is almost entirely dependent upon animate, i.e., human and animal, sources of energy.

This more advanced technology operates in conjunction with (it both requires and makes possible) a complex social organization that is typified by a "leisured," literate elite or upper class. In all instances feudal orders contain cities. Relative to the total population, urban residents are few, but the presence among them of the elite makes the city's inhabitants significant far beyond their numbers.

The term "city" has been utilized in varying fashions. We see it, in contrast to a town or village, as having greater size, density, and heterogeneity and including a wide range of non-agricultural specialists, most significant of whom are the literati. The formation of the latter is, as will become clear in Chapter II, crucial for assigning a beginning date to city life.

Unlike the folk society, the feudal order has a well-defined and rigid class structure and a clear-cut division of labor according to age, sex, and occupation. A small, privileged upper class commands the key positions in the political, religious, and educational structures and exercises rather autocratic rule. The existence of writing fixes tradition and strengthens cohesion among members of the literate group, enhancing the latter's control over the society. The bulk of the populace consists of the lower class and outcaste groups who dwell in the city or in the rural communities. As to the ruralites, these often include, besides the farming peasantry, pastoral nomads, e.g., in the Middle East and Central Asia, or fishing villages, as in Japan.

The upper class sets the pace for the total society. It alone can maintain an extended family system, acquire formal education, and fulfil all the ideal religious norms. In general, the upper class shuns economic activity, one organized in the city along guild lines. These and other structural patterns are elaborated upon below and shown to be functionally related to the technological base.

The city is a subsystem in the feudal society, and as such must be contrasted with the rural community and seen as

part of the broader social order; we seek to avoid any identification with a "city-limit" sociology.

The industrial-urban society, in contrast to the feudal order,
utilizes inanimate sources of energy, a complex set of tools,
and specialized scientific know-how in the production of goods
and services. As a result the greater portion of the industrial
society's populace dwell in cities.

The industrial technology requires, and at the same time
supports, a structural apparatus that diverges strongly from
the feudal type in its ecological, class, familial, economic, political, religious, and educational aspects. The class system is
a highly fluid one that emphasizes achievement rather than
ascription, and social power is diffused throughout the city
and society. Associated with the ill-defined class system is a
small, flexible, conjugal family unit as the ideal norm. In
turn these patterns are interwoven with a large-scale, rational
economic structure characterized by a complexity in the division of labor far exceeding that in the feudal system and
requiring highly trained specialists recruited according to universalistic criteria. The proliferation of skilled specialists implies the existence of mass literacy and an educational system
that emphasizes science.[19] Moreover, in this social order the
norms, even religious ones, tend to be permissive rather than
prescriptive. These and other structural patterns are the guide-
posts against which we contrast those in the feudal city and
society. In this process we seek to avoid comparing the preindustrial order specifically with the United States, being
mindful of the structures that are typical of industrial-urban
communities in general.[20]

Throughout we adhere to a structural-functional viewpoint,
perhaps the dominant theoretical orientation in American sociology, ever cognizant of the methodological problems involved in imputing functions to structures (although the
validity of such imputation is greatly enhanced by cross-
cultural analysis). Yet we seek to avoid some of the pitfalls

inherent in this approach, particularly an overemphasis upon integration, by introducing the concept of "contradictory functional requirements." For within the preindustrial (or industrial) city, various structural arrangements may be at odds with one another; some strains in fact appear to be intrinsic to the system. With the aforementioned perspective such conflicts are more readily discerned.

To sum up: technology is the variable we employ to delineate folk, feudal, and industrial societies. A crucial segment of the feudal order is the preindustrial city whose social structure we examine in its functional relationships to the existing technology. We recognize other variables or factors as pertinent in the analysis of cities, however. Each of these—the city, cultural values, and social power—is the focus of a particular school of thought in sociology. We need now to relate our own analysis to these various theoretical perspectives.

Existing Theoretical Orientations[21]

It has been usual for American urban sociologists to consider the city as the key independent variable for explaining certain social phenomena. Wirth's article, "Urbanism as a Way of Life,"[22] is a landmark in the urban field. He takes the city—defined by its relatively great size, density, and heterogeneity (we add to these other criteria)—as the determinant of various social phenomena. Redfield, too, utilizes the city as the crucial variable in his *Folk Culture of Yucatan*,[23] although for him heterogeneity and lack of isolation are the distinguishing traits of the city.

To Wirth, and to a degree Redfield, urbanism as a way of life is typified by secularization, voluntary associations, segmented social roles, and poorly defined norms: it is a world of tenuous social relationships. Implicitly, or explicitly, the city is contrasted with the rural community or the folk society.

It is significant that to Wirth the effects of urban development are distinct and independent of those stemming from cultural values or from industrialization.

The limitations of this approach are becoming increasingly apparent. Both Wirth and Redfield neglected to examine much of the organization that is the city. The impact of large-scale bureaucratic enterprises upon the social activities of urbanites as well as the persistence, even in slum areas, of intricate webs of social relationships have been largely ignored by writers of the Wirth and Redfield persuasion (or earlier that of Park). This overemphasis upon secularization, disorganization, etc., with a consequent neglect of the organized aspects of city life, no doubt reflects the ethos of the 1920s and 1930s when the American city was reeling under the effects of the great waves of immigration and World War I, to say nothing of the Great Depression. Not only is this preoccupation with disorganization overdone even for industrial cities, but a study of preindustrial cities reveals that urban life can be highly organized indeed.

Another shortcoming of Wirth's approach, one that is still more apparent in Redfield's early writings, resides in the logical structure of the folk-urban comparison. Redfield saw the folk society as a closed system. But the urban community with which he contrasted it is only a partial system; it can not survive without its hinterland. He was, then, contrasting a whole with a part. This conceptualization also blurs the significant distinctions between folk societies and peasant communities, a fact that Redfield came to recognize in his later writings.[24] We of course compare total systems—folk, feudal, and industrial societies—and set in contrast the rural and urban communities within feudal and industrial societies.

With respect to rural-urban differences, many of the generalizations resulting from the early influences of Wirth and Redfield, among others, reflected in today's sociology textbooks, require a thorough overhauling. Numerous patterns on the American scene are erroneously thought to hold for other societies as well, when in fact many of these rural-urban differences are typical only of industrial-urban, not of feudal, societies. Although industrial and feudal orders reveal some of the same kinds of rural-urban divergencies, there are others to which we shall refer that are peculiar to preindustrial civilized societies.

Implicit in the foregoing is that Wirth and sociologists of like mind have failed to recognize that the city is in many respects molded by the social system of which it is a part. Unfortunately, this school of thought has found support in, and derived sustenance from, writers of the Pirenne[25] persuasion, who visualize the medieval European city as having achieved social and political independence of the traditional order it was seeking to destroy. But such a generalization, except perhaps for a narrow time-period and a restricted locale in western Europe, is untenable for feudal societies in general. For the analysis of certain kinds of problems, the city, shaped as it is by the enfolding socio-cultural system, whether preindustrial or industrial, must be taken as a *dependent* rather than an independent variable.

Wirth also viewed the effects of the city as independent of industrialization. Again, had he been more cognizant of the cross-cultural scene—of cities functioning upon a technological base other than the industrial, as well as those operating within the context of divergent value orientations—his theorizing with respect to the impact of the city would, in all likelihood, have taken a decidedly different tack.

Despite our criticisms of the Wirth school of thought, we recognize that the city is a factor in "determining" selected types of social phenomena. The city does differ from the rural community, though not necessarily in the manner some writers claim, and is therefore useful as an explanatory device. Certainly cities are the foci of many strategic societal activities. Here reside the leaders, for an urban base permits the fuller and more effective wielding of social power. No doubt the urban milieu is essential for the development of certain kinds of social organization. And it is a positive force for generating certain types of social change. As the center of intellectual activity it is the situs of much innovation. And Hoselitz[26] sees the expansion of cities as a stimulus to technological change, industrialization included. A comparison of preindustrial and industrial cities should clarify just what is the city's impact upon social organization and technology.

A second theoretical orientation in urban studies—a product of such writers as Firey, Kolb, and, earlier to a degree, Max Weber[27]—is one that stresses cultural or social values in accounting for the ecology and social structure of cities, including the patterning of technology. These writers do have a telling point to make. Undeniably, cities in varying cultures —e.g., Italy or India or China—diverge in some facets of their ecological and social structures. Differences appear among cities operating upon a similar technological base: technology does not explain all facets of urban life. Only distinctive value orientations can account for certain dissimilarities among cities in varying cultures.

But this approach poses problems too. One involves determining precisely the relationship of values to social structure; certainly no one-to-one correlation obtains. Moreover, all too many social scientists are content simply with highlighting the differences among social systems and, lapsing into a crude form of historicism, are prone to assume uniqueness where such does not exist. Only to the extent that structural similarities among preindustrial cities over the world are isolated can the influence of cultural values upon city life be perceived. Our approach, then, is not disjunct with that stressing cultural values. On the one hand, the structural categories set up for preindustrial cities make the effect of cultural values discernible; conversely, a firm awareness of the impact of cultural values, a recognition of the range of variability among cities, enables us to isolate the common structural features of preindustrial (or industrial) cities. All the while delineating these universal structures, we recognize that they may be elaborated in various unique fashions in specific cultural settings. On the other hand, where similar structural arrangements appear among cities in differing cultures, certain shared values seem to support these. In preindustrial cities, therefore, we have a common set of values cutting across otherwise divergent cultural boundaries, both determining and being determined by the technological order. A similar situation holds in industrial cities.

Another major school of thought in urban sociology takes social power as the prime variable in accounting for particular urban ecological and social structures.[28] Historically as well as in the modern world, power structures, especially political ones, have unquestionably played a decisive role in molding cities. Social power on the local, societal, and extra-societal levels influences the expansion and location of cities, their internal ecological arrangements, and their social structure as well. Some patterns can not be explained simply by reference to technology or to values. For example, the forcible movement of Natives from the central areas of South African cities means that the values of this group are giving way before those of the Afrikaners, who command the positions of social power in the society.

We make considerable use of the factor of power in the ensuing chapters to explain why the earliest cities arose and spread (and declined). And, it is apparent that social power has played a prominent role in the development of industrial cities as well—in Japan, the Soviet Union, and elsewhere. Other theoretical orientations can be employed for analyzing cities, among them, those that take demography and the economy, apart from technology per se, as independent variables. But these are not particularly suitable for dealing with the problems we have posed. Some economic factors, say depressions and prosperity, though of value for analyzing changes in industrial cities, have little relevance for understanding preindustrial cities, which literally are in a perpetual state of depression.

Thus, although technology is our chief mechanism for explaining differences between preindustrial and industrial cities, we utilize the variables of the city, cultural values, and social power in accounting for special facets of the preindustrial city. They themselves influence technology, the interrelationships being most complex. Only by assaying the role of these other variables can we determine with relative assurance the social contribution of technology in shaping the urban community!

Methodological Note

The difficulties posed by a study of this kind are not simply theoretical. Some knotty methodological issues emerge, our solutions to which are necessarily tentative. First, we have a few excellent studies by sociologists and anthropologists— e.g., Le Tourneau's work on Fez, Morocco, and Miner's field study of Timbuctoo[29]—and some economists and geographers have provided valuable field work materials. But research of this sort is grossly insufficient. To overcome this limitation the writer has sought to consult a wide variety of sources. Space permits a listing of only a small number of the works consulted; the materials we cite are for illustrative purposes and do not pretend to provide complete documentation for the generalizations. They merely suggest the kinds of data that can be tapped.

Prominent among the source materials are historical works —essential for our treatment of the rise and spread of cities, but useful as well for the analysis of the preindustrial city's ecology and social structure. Another fount of data are the autobiographies of residents of traditional cities. Those on China have proved of particular value. Too, some of the accounts of travelers, diplomats, and missionaries to preindustrial cities yield valuable data. Social scientists are in fact largely beholden to travelers and resident Westerners for much of their knowledge of Chinese cities in the late nine-teenth and early twentieth centuries. The author was informed by one Sinologist that these are richer sources of data on traditional Chinese cities than are most of the works of Chinese scholars themselves, especially where information on the urban lower classes is desired. Travelers and resident Westerners, too, have provided extensive materials on tradi-tional cities like Lhasa (Tibet) and Seoul (Korea). In ad-dition, over a period of years the author has discussed with students on American campuses from preindustrial-like cities in Asia, Latin America, and southern Europe the functioning of their own cities. This study of "culture at a distance" has served as a check upon the author's formulations derived from written sources and has sensitized him to certain social pat-terns he might otherwise have overlooked in the literature.

Yet adequate data are wanting on certain major civiliza-tions. Surprisingly, one of these is traditional India. Through-out India's history, Hindu scholars have shown little interest either in recording events and compiling histories or in de-scribing aspects of their own social order. Many of their writings are of a religious-philosophical nature—to an even greater extent than in most preindustrial civilized societies. Then too, the British who had an excellent opportunity to describe in detail the structure of preindustrial cities in India chose not to do so; though some writers studied tribal groups or peasant villages, the city received little scholarly attention. Even Lhasa, the so-called "Forbidden City," is far more metic-ulously described than such a city as Benares. We have more data on Seoul than on Benares, or any other preindustrial city in India.

In actuality historical data on most preindustrial civilized societies tend to be inadequate in one way or another. They treat only limited facets of life in the city, emphasizing the religious and political activities of the elite while ignoring almost entirely the vast bulk of the city's inhabitants. Our solution has been to emphasize the materials available on relatively recent feudal societies and their cities and then extrapolate from these back to antiquity—employing always the concepts of contemporary social science. Utilizing data on more recent societies as an aid to interpreting the past is a procedure followed by such historically oriented social scientists as Eberhard and Schrieke.[30]

Our emphasis upon more recent materials is related to another problem: that of evaluating much historical data, especially those in secondary sources. Often, historians who should know better fail to make it clear that for the most part the sources upon which they rely for their reconstructions of the past are chronicles of just a small segment of the preindustrial city's population; rather they exhibit a strong tendency to generalize to the total populace from the data at hand. Some, like Sansom,[31] make a point of emphasizing the restricted nature of their data, but many others do not. Furthermore, some writers on early cities tend to assume that because a particular pattern of activity is not mentioned in the sources at their command, it therefore did not exist. But there are instances where a certain pattern should theoretically—i.e., judged by the data from similar societies—have existed. Here is another rationale for our approach. By emphasizing the later preindustrial cities, for which the data are more complete, we can more readily form a "correct" conception of those preindustrial cities for which data are either lacking or subject to diverse interpretations.

Another difficulty in using historical data is the desire of the literary historians to "make history live" to the extent that they may be guilty (from the biased view of the scientifically oriented social scientist) of overpersonalization of their data —even of romanticism. Often, for purely ideological reasons, they insist that such and such a pattern existed—even where no evidence appears in support of it. Classical Athens thus is seen by some writers as a truly democratic order, and the magnificence of its public buildings is extolled, with little note taken of the humbler aspects of the city.

A further problem in the utilization of much historical writing is that often just what is being compared is never explicitly stipulated. Authorities on traditional China or medieval Europe refer to "periods of great urban expansion"—but "great" in terms of what standard? Their point of reference is almost invariably some other preindustrial period—not the industrial epoch—a legitimate orientation so long as author and reader understand one another. Our perspective avowedly contrasts the preindustrial city with the industrial one.

We must also comment on our use of the "constructed type." It is "objectively probable," and as such has the advantage of being more closely related to empirical reality than the ideal, or fictional, type, which is usually a composite picture of certain "unique" features of the phenomenon being studied. Although not all preindustrial cities demonstrate every structural pattern that we isolate, at least a few cities do. To abstract what is "typical," we consider only those traits for which empirical evidence is available from cities in a number of disparate cultural settings. We have, then, taken a very broad spectrum of cities in a variety of cultures and have isolated the general from the particular. This will strike some as blatant oversimplification. Yet the principle of Occam's razor lies at the heart of all scientific analysis. Even the intensive study of a single city in a given culture could never exhaust reality; all scientists, so too all humanists, necessarily are selective in their research. We have, on the other hand, sought to keep faith with reality through our use of the constructed type, and we postulate no perfectly knit system but allow for inherent contradictions in the social order.

Some scholars might prefer using just a few cities as the basis for their generalizations. We have rejected this strategy because of the dangers of relying upon a small number of cases; there lurks the ever-present possibility that these may prove to be atypical or unique. Of course, the materials are far more plentiful on some cities than on others. This has led us to concentrate heavily on some of the better-documented cities: Seoul, Peking, Lhasa, Mecca, Cairo, Fez, Florence, or Bokhara. But we have consulted studies on a wide range of communities in order to enhance the accuracy of our generalizations.

NOTES TO CHAPTER I

1. For a discussion of the early comparativists, see Harry Elmer Barnes (ed.), *An Introduction to the History of Sociology* (Chicago: University of Chicago Press, 1948).

2. Robert E. Park, Ernest W. Burgess, and Roderick D. McKenzie, *The City* (Chicago: University of Chicago Press, 1925), Chapter II.

3. Pitirim A. Sorokin, Carle Zimmerman, and Charles Galpin, *A Systematic Source Book in Rural Sociology,* I (Minneapolis: University of Minnesota Press, 1930), 54.

4. Giovanni Botero, "The Greatness of Cities" (trans. Robert Peterson, 1606), in Giovanni Botero, *The Reason of State and The Greatness of Cities* (London: Routledge and Kegan Paul, 1956).

5. Adna F. Weber, *The Growth of Cities in the Nineteenth Century* (New York: Macmillan, 1899); Max Weber, *The City,* trans. and ed. Don Martindale and Gertrud Neuwirth (Glencoe: Free Press, 1958).

6. See, e.g., Kingsley Davis and Hilda Hertz Golden, "Urbanization and the Development of Pre-Industrial Areas," *Economic Development and Cultural Change,* III (October, 1954), 6-26.

7. Philip M. Hauser (ed.), *Urbanization in Asia and the Far East* (Calcutta: UNESCO, 1957); Bert F. Hoselitz, "The City, the Factory, and Economic Growth," *American Economic Review,* XLV (May, 1955), 166-84.

8. According to one widely accepted view, the humanist deals with the intimate and the particular, whereas the social scientist deals with the general and the abstract. See John Fairbank, *Chinese Thought and Institutions* (Chicago: University of Chicago Press, 1957), pp. 3ff.

9. Thus, for example, Marvin Harris, *Town and Country in Brazil* (New York: Columbia University Press, 1956), attributes many traits of the community he studied, chiefly the urban orientation of the upper class, to so-called "Mediterranean patterns of culture." These traits, however, extend well beyond this cultural boundary.

10. Amos H. Hawley, *Human Ecology* (New York: Ronald Press, 1950).

11. Fred Cottrell, *Energy and Society* (New York: McGraw-Hill, 1955).

12. The utility of writing as a point of demarcation between the feudal society and its cities and the primitive order is discussed in Chapter II.

13. Robert Redfield, "The Folk Society," *American Journal of Sociology,* LII (January, 1947), 293-308.

14. Allan R. Holmberg, *Nomads of the Long Bow,* Smithsonian Insti-

tution, Institute of Social Anthropology, No. 10 (Washington: Government Printing Office, 1950), pp. 25, 27, 41-2, 50.

15. Rushton Coulborn (ed.), *Feudalism in History* (Princeton: Princeton University Press, 1956). This book, though widely accepted, is from a sociological viewpoint open to strong criticism. The term "feudal" is used throughout in varying fashions. Coulborn does define "feudalism," however, as: ". . . a method of government in which the essential relation is not that between ruler and subject, nor state and citizen, but between lord and vassal" (pp. 4-5). Yet elsewhere in the book he discusses the lord as ruler and vassal as subject. Coulborn has not distinguished this narrower kind of society from our more general feudal societal type, although perhaps such a subtype could be established.

16. An exceedingly aberrant usage is found in Arthur M. Ross, "Do We Have a New Industrial Feudalism?" *American Economic Review*, XLVIII (December, 1958), 903-20. He equates feudalism with an immobile labor force.

17. See, e.g., "Gorod," *Bol'shaya Sovetskaya Entsiklopediya*, XII (2d ed.; Moskva: Gosudarstvennoe nauchnoe izdatel'stvo, 1952), 172ff.; SH. A. Meskhia, "Iz Istorii Gruzinskogo Feodal'nogo Goroda IX-XIII vv.," *Akademiya Nauk Gruzinskoi SSR, Institut Istorii, Trudy*, II (1956), 131-52.

18. Other social scientists employ the term in much the same way we do. See, e.g., Ralph L. Beals and Norman D. Humphrey, *No Frontier to Learning* (Minneapolis: University of Minnesota Press, 1957), p. 10.

19. Just as the mere existence of literacy constitutes a dividing line between folk and feudal societies, so too mass literacy, including lengthy formal education, serves as one convenient device for separating feudal and industrial societies.

20. In this book on the preindustrial city it is necessary to work out the common patterns for industrial cities as well, for purposes of contrast. Although we diverge from other authors in some important respects, we utilize the materials of such social scientists as Bert F. Hoselitz, "Social Structure and Economic Growth," *Economia internazionale*, VI (1953), 52-77, and Kingsley Davis, "Social and Demographic Aspects of Economic Development in India," in Simon Kuznets *et al.* (eds.), *Economic Growth: Brazil, India, Japan* (Durham, N.C.: Duke University Press, 1955), pp. 293ff.

21. For an elaboration of these issues, see Gideon Sjoberg, "Comparative Urban Sociology," in Robert K. Merton *et al.* (eds.), *Sociology Today* (New York: Basic Books, 1959), pp. 334-59.

22. Louis Wirth, "Urbanism as a Way of Life," *American Journal of Sociology*, XLIV (July, 1938), 1-24.

23. Robert Redfield, *The Folk Culture of Yucatan* (Chicago: University of Chicago Press, 1941).

24. See, e.g., Robert Redfield, *Peasant Society and Culture* (Chicago: University of Chicago Press, 1956).

25. Henri Pirenne, *Medieval Cities*, trans. F. H. Halsey (Princeton: Princeton University Press, 1925).

26. Hoselitz, "The City, the Factory, and Economic Growth," *op. cit.*

27. Walter Firey, *Land Use in Central Boston* (Cambridge: Harvard University Press, 1947); William L. Kolb, "The Social Structure and Function of Cities," *Economic Development and Cultural Change*, III (October, 1954), 30-46; Max Weber, *op. cit.*

28. See, e.g., William H. Form, "The Place of Social Structure in the Determination of Land Use: Some Implications for a Theory of Urban Ecology," *Social Forces,* XXXII (May, 1954), 317-23, and Leo Kuper *et al., Durban: A Study in Racial Ecology* (New York: Columbia University Press, 1958).

29. Roger Le Tourneau, *Fès: Avant le Protectorat* (Casablanca: Société Marocaine de Librairie et d'Édition, 1949); Horace Miner, *The Primitive City of Timbuctoo* (Princeton: Princeton University Press, 1953).

30. Wolfram Eberhard, "The Formation of Chinese Civilization according to Socio-Anthropological Analysis," *Sociologus,* VII (1957), 99; B. Schrieke, *Ruler and Realm in Early Java,* Indonesian Sociological Studies, Part 2 (The Hague: W. van Hoeve, 1957), p. 291.

31. George Sansom, *A History of Japan to 1334* (Stanford: Stanford University Press, 1958), p. 195.

CHAPTER II

CITIES—THEIR BEGINNINGS*

ALTHOUGH this is not a history of preindustrial cities and our typology does not emphasize those of antiquity, some appreciation of their venerable past is essential. In this chapter we consider the various world regions that may have given rise to cities independently of urbanizing influences from without. The precise number of these centers of origin is still being disputed, as are the general preconditions of urban life, the dating of the earliest cities, and the characteristics of these. We now examine the first two issues in the order named; we then take up the earliest emergence of cities in each of the supposed centers of origin and, in the process, elaborate upon all of the aforementioned problems. The succeeding chapter surveys the spread of cities out of these original centers and discusses briefly the patterns of urban growth and decline over the world.

How Many Times Were Cities Independently Invented?

This question has generated intense controversy among historians, archeologists, and anthropologists. Some of the argumentation stems from the sparseness of data, but it also

---

* Co-author, Andrée F. Sjoberg.

contains overtones of the long-standing debate between the extreme diffusionists,[1] who belittle man's inventive ability, and the vast majority of experts, who take a more generous view of man's capacity for ingenuity. The latter agree that cities were invented twice at the very least—in Mesopotamia and in Meso-America—but they differ among themselves as to whether urban living was also independently developed in the valleys of the Nile or the Indus or the Huang Ho: in other words, two, three, four, or five times in all.

That cities appeared first in the Near East, specifically in the Mesopotamian river basin (or adjacent areas), is generally accepted today. Apparently a few centuries later, city life was constituted in the Nile riverine area of Egypt and, not long after that, in the valley of the Indus, present-day West Pakistan. Whether the complex of traits making for urbanization in the Nile and Indus valleys was invented locally or borrowed from Mesopotamia is a point of debate. The controversy over whether the earliest cities in China, those in the Huang Ho (or Yellow River) valley, were independent creations is particularly acute today, intensified as it is by modern nationalistic trends.

But a rigid diffusion-invention dichotomy is untenable. Most probably some critical traits of urbanization were diffused to other areas, here to be combined with still other elements and/or refashioned in unique ways by the recipients, but undoubtedly some key traits that led to the development of cities were independently invented.

As to cities in the Americas, only the most fertile imagination (at the present state of knowledge) can conceive of these as products of diffusion from the Old World. Meso-America and Mesopotamia, then, are the two regions which most scholars would agree developed city life independently. But more of this below. First the preconditions of urban development must be detailed.

Preconditions of City Life

The prerequisites for the emergence of cities are: 1) a favorable "ecological" base, 2) an advanced technology (relative to the pre-urban forms) in both the agricultural and non-agricultural spheres, and 3) a complex social organization—above all, a well-developed power structure. Apparently all of these conditions had to be fulfilled before that complex entity we call the city could first arise.

With respect to the first requirement, the ecological, the world's earliest cities seem to have arisen in regions where climate and soil were highly favorable to the development of plant and animal life, so that relatively larger populations could be supported, even with the existent technology, upon a small land area. This technology, though advanced over that in the typical preliterate society, was quite simple by modern standards. The favorable environment, then, served to supplement the narrow technology. Also vital to urban growth and survival is an adequate water supply. In most of the regions where city life may have arisen spontaneously, the nature of the water sources—especially the periodic flooding of the river valleys—was such as to make large-scale irrigation feasible despite the relatively scanty storehouse of technology. The earliest cities in Meso-America, of course, lacked the means, indeed the necessitude, for any but modest irrigation ventures. Nonetheless, here, as in the other cradles of urban living, the hydraulic resources, in one form or another, were sufficiently stable to provide for the year-round needs of urbanites.

Apparently also essential for urban development is an ecological situation conducive to repeated contacts among peoples of divergent cultures, in turn permitting a constant accretion of social and technological skills in an area. The augmented food supply and the ease of transport offered by the larger river valleys of Asia and North Africa undoubtedly attracted thereto diverse groups who introduced new traits, which, conjoined with those extant in the region, stimulated technological and social development and, consequently, urbanization. Here again Meso-America appears at first glance to be a deviant case. But closer inspection reveals that this zone forms a corridor traversed by peoples passing to the north in Mexico and south to Central America and beyond, a situation that enabled the inhabitants in or near this through way to draw upon the new skills and knowledge these visitors might have possessed.

But the exploitation of any "favorable" environment requires substantial advances in technology and in social organization. Environment merely imposes barriers to human action; it is not an active agent—in and of itself it can never engender cities and civilization.

The second fundamental requirement for city life is an "advanced" technology in both the agricultural and non-agricultural spheres. Progress in agricultural technology was essential—not just in farming implements but in the crops themselves. The controversies as to where agriculture first arose—whether it was in the river valleys of the Near East, or in the upland or oasis areas of this region, or possibly even in Southeast Asia—need not concern us here. What is significant is that a sizeable food surplus (over and above the reserve needed for sustenance between harvests) is required before cities can emerge; imperative is a relatively advanced technology, one that can multiply greatly the agricultural yield and thus free some persons from primarily agricultural pursuits, or from "extractive" activities such as hunting, fishing, and collecting. These can then devote themselves to tasks necessitating special skills and training beyond those involved in food production—such as the handicrafts—or to activities that demand considerable time for planning, contemplation, and learning—such as government or scholarly pursuits requiring literacy.

Chief among the technological advances that set the stage for urban living was the domestication of grains—wheat, barley, and others in the Near and Middle East and northern China, and maize in Meso-America. The importance of grains is not to be minimized: as a concentrated food that can be stored with facility over long periods, they make possible a year-round food supply for urban populations; supplemented by other plant and animal foods, they form an excellent dietary staple. Other technological developments associated with the emergence of the earliest cities of North Africa and Asia are large-scale irrigation works, animal husbandry, metallurgy, the wheel, and in some cases the plow.[2] Metallurgy meant better tools, both agricultural and industrial, and using animals in cultivation and to transport goods on their backs or by pulling wheeled vehicles meant greater efficiency for agriculture and for the transport of produce to the city. Improved transportation media facilitated access to metal ores, essential to manufacturing in the city. And the expanded trade among cities and between rural and urban places encouraged interpersonal contacts, stimulating innovation as well as permitting some degree of specialization among regions in the kinds of goods produced. But the nexi between technology and urban living are complex: the development of specific technological items was in large measure made possible by the concentration of peoples in permanent settlements (first villages and towns, later cities), and, as indicated, the creation of large, permanent urban communities demanded a relatively advanced state of technology.

Except for the cultivation of grains, the array of technological items just remarked upon was absent in the earliest cities of Meso-America. Still, anthropologists and cultural historians have erred in assuming that the early Maya and other urban peoples around them lacked any advanced agricultural techniques (except for very limited use of terracing in the southern Maya zone).[3] Granted that the plow, the wheel, metallurgy, and pack or draft animals were all missing in early Meso-American civilization, the technology was quite well advanced in one significant respect. For the Indians of the region had a unique and superior kind of plant, maize[4] —one that did not demand large-scale irrigation ventures or metal tools or domesticated animals to pull plows or other devices for its cultivation. Moreover, it was capable of producing more than one crop in a year. It could be grown in a wide variety of physiographic areas—from the tropics at sea level to the higher mountainous regions. Indeed, in the Yucatan lowlands generally devoid of surface water because of the immediate underground drainage of rainfall, in the thickly forested tropics, or upon mountain slopes, advanced agricultural methods like large-scale irrigation and plowing would not have been feasible had they been developed. Taking into account the low degree of effort expended in its cultivation, as compared with other grains, maize—a technological item, a source of energy—provided a greater yield than the grain crops that supported the earliest cities of the river valleys of the Middle East and China. Interestingly, some of the so-called "deficiencies" of the Meso-American technology may have worked to the immediate, though not the ultimate, advantage of the civilized peoples of the region: there were no large domesticated animals to consume a significant portion of the grain harvest, nor did a large segment of the population have to engage in supportive activities such as constructing and maintaining sizeable irrigation works. The Maya, particularly, overcame some of the environmental limitations and their own supposed technological deficiencies through this superior staple crop and so were able to sustain for a time some brilliant urban centers. One can not deny, however, that the lack of true metallurgy, the wheel, and other items of technology ultimately set limits to the expansion of the Meso-American cities.

The third precondition for the emergence of the earliest cities was a well-developed social organization, particularly in the political and economic spheres. Before urban living could be achieved, the economic system had to reach a point where manufactured goods could be distributed within and among communities and, above all, the agricultural surplus moved in a fairly steady stream to larger settlements, there to be stored and/or distributed to the non-agricultural populace. And the activities of various occupations, some of which demanded a degree of specialized knowledge and training, had to be integrated so that certain complex tasks—say the mining, transport, and refining of metal ores to supply the urban metal workers—could be performed. Thus there must be a ruling group—necessarily small because of the meager surplus available—with sufficient social power and skills to direct the activities of others.

Social power often takes precedence over economic pursuits: certainly social stability must be maintained if the economic system is to function effectively. In the earliest cities a political structure had to exist to obtain, through taxation or tribute, a food surplus from the peasantry to support the urban non-agriculturists, most particularly the power elite itself. For peasants have not always willingly produced surpluses and relinquished them to the urbanites. These points will be elaborated upon in later chapters.

We have commented briefly on the preconditions for urbanization: a favorable ecological base and, especially, an improved technology and a complex social organization (relative to those in the preliterate world). With these preliminary points in mind, we turn to an examination of when and where cities first arose.

The Earliest Cities—Mesopotamia

Most authorities today agree that cities evolved first in the Mesopotamian region or in the areas immediately adjacent to it. Yet the dating of the world's earliest cities is still a point at issue. In large measure it depends upon the criteria one employs to define the city. Sociologists who follow Wirth take size, density, and heterogeneity as the traits that distinguish the city from the rural community. But these are insufficient. We add the requirement of a significant number of full-time specialists, including a literate group, engaged in a relatively wide range of non-agricultural activities. Applying all of the above criteria, we find that cities first arose about the middle of the fourth millennium B.C.

The controversy over defining the urban community and the dating of the earliest cities is highlighted by the arguments of scholars over the findings at Jericho (in present-day Jordan), one of the oldest permanent agricultural settlements thus far excavated, apparently pre-dating Jarmo in Iraq. In the early levels Kenyon[5] found well-developed mud houses and evidence of walls with fortifications; apparently on this basis (little is known of the social organization, and writing is absent) she classified it as urban. She first assigned radiocarbon dates of shortly after 8000 B.C. for the beginnings of "civilization" in Jericho, but under the attack of Braidwood later conceded that new evidence might lower this to about 5000 B.C.[6] Wheeler,[7] commenting upon Kenyon's materials, accepts a date of earlier than 6000 B.C. for the existence of Jericho as a "town" and equates Jericho with "urbanization." At one point, Wheeler sees urbanization as preceding civilization, at another, as equivalent to civilization. He takes as the chief elements of civilization, a settled community of a size sufficient to support non-agricultural specialists, and public works that imply an organized and durable administration. Although he views these traits as preconditions for the development of writing, he does not consider writing a necessary component of civilization.

V. Gordon Childe,[8] commenting on this controversy, takes to task Kenyon and Wheeler, and the editor of *Antiquity* to boot, for their loose application of the terms "urbanization" and "civilization" (which we find troublesome too). Childe contends that in addition to size, heterogeneity, public works, and so on, writing is essential to the categorization of the city, implying as it does the existence of a highly specialized non-agricultural group that has the necessary leisure to develop such a complex skill. Above all he sees the use of a writing system as the single firm criterion for distinguishing the city, the nucleus of civilization, from other types of early settlements.[9] We agree. The existence of writing implies a literati, which in turn requires for its propagation some method of formal education, a supporting political apparatus to ensure its hegemony and continued sustenance, and merchants, artisans, and a variety of servants to provide needed goods and services. Not that the criterion of literacy resolves all the difficulties in classifying communities as urban or not. But if the criteria of Wheeler and even Wirth were faithfully applied, we would falsely categorize as cities (and this implies civilization) some of the large villages of, say, Neolithic Europe, or Africa and Polynesia, or the Pueblo Indians and the Northwest Coast tribes.

Our definition relegates to a marginal or transitional status the Inca communities that most anthropologists stubbornly insist were urban centers, foci of civilization. Admittedly the Inca had a relatively complex social structure and apparently were in the process of developing writing, having achieved some mnemonic devices for record-keeping. Nonetheless, they still lacked any conventionalized set of symbols for representing sounds or concepts other than numbers. As a consequence, some key structural elements of the city were absent, including a formal educational system and a scholarly elite. Actually the Inca seem to have had a less complex social structure than the traditional Dahomey, Ashanti, or Yoruba in Africa, which we must also class as "quasi-urban." All of these were complex folk orders that were perhaps on the way to becoming feudal, or literate preindustrial, societies—just as the early cities were relatively simple compared to the later, more fully developed feudal cities from which we have abstracted our type.

The problem of criteria is of more than mere academic interest to sociologists. Davis,[10] one of the few sociologists to address himself to this problem, states that the first cities appear to have arisen sometime between 6000 and 5000 B.C.; however, later in his discussion he indicates that "true" cities emerged by 3000 B.C. He is unclear as to the criteria he employs in defining the "city," though implicitly he admits that "true" cities began with writing. We, taking writing as our explicit criterion, and following the lead of Childe and others,[11] see city life as probably having developed in Mesopotamia during the last half of the fourth millennium, very soon after 3500 B.C.

Among the earliest cities were Erech, Eridu, Ur, Lagash, and Larsa in Sumer (the southernmost portion of the Tigris-Euphrates river valley area) and Kish and Jemdet Nasr just to the north in Akkad. The steps in the transformation of the older village settlements into cities, a process that consumed many centuries, can be traced in a number of these sites.

At first there were a number of small, politically independent city-states with a similar language, religion, social organization, and material culture; this last included wheat and barley cultivation, bronze metallurgy, wheeled vehicles, and the use of oxen for traction. As Davis[12] notes, the difficulties of communication and transport limited the depth of the surrounding countryside that each of these early cities could control.

Each city was ruled by a king who was considered a representative of the city's tutelary deity and thus its chief priest. Inasmuch as the land that supported the city was considered to belong to the chief god, the farming populace was expected to return to him part of the "surplus" crop; this tribute was held by the city's main temple where it was stored in the granaries attached to it. In all probability it was the chief sustenance of the city's ruling group.

The earliest examples of writing uncovered are records dealing with temple accounts.[13] It is likely that writing was developed in response to the exigencies of administration. At any rate, by the time the early communities became cities, a fairly extensive administrative apparatus had taken shape to channel the flow of the agricultural surplus, to make war upon other communities, and so forth.

In the earliest cities, as with later ones, we find evidence of skilled workmanship, especially in the luxury goods recovered from royal tombs and temples. This suggests that special artisan groups were in the service of the upper class. Merchants evidently imported from beyond the Mesopotamian borders some of the metals and precious stones worked by the artisans. And the energies of numerous laborers—some of whom must have been war captives reduced to slavery—were directed to constructing monumental public edifices. According to Frankfort,[14] one temple (at Erech) was set upon an artificial mound that was 40 feet high and covered an area of about 420,000 square feet.

Turning to the physical aspect of these cities,[15] typically they grew up around a walled precinct containing a temple group devoted to the main city-god and other deities. And at least by the early third millennium most of the community was walled. Houses were jumbled together, forming an irregular mass broken at intervals by open spaces in front of a temple or governmental building. Streets were narrow, winding, and unpaved and lacked adequate drainage. They became the chief repositories of refuse thrown from the houses, with the result that excavations at Ur reveal a continual rising of the street level due to the accumulation of refuse, so much so that many houses whose doorways were left below the street level had to be equipped with higher entrances.

Houses—like temples and palaces—were of fired or simple

mud brick. In Ur ca. 2000 B.C. the better houses, constructed around a central court open to the sky, were plastered and whitewashed. Some contained private chapels. The lower storeys lacked windows onto the street and, viewed from the outside, gave the appearance of a continuous wall, broken only by doorways. Scattered among the houses were small buildings that may have been shops. Also, special sections of the city contained alleys lined with booths, undoubtedly the shops of merchants and artisans. A few chapels were interspersed among these, and a few larger structures that may have been inns for traveling merchants are traceable in the ruins. Near the city's periphery resided the poorest people, as evidenced by hovels of mud and reeds. One section of the outer area, in this instance in Ur, apparently contained the somewhat better dwellings of artisan groups such as smiths.

In all, these earlier cities bear a surprising resemblance to the later iron-age cities upon which we draw freely for the data in succeeding chapters. One ecological feature of these cities—the existence within or near the periphery of a large number of agriculturists—deserves special mention. Undoubtedly, as Frankfort[16] stresses, the population of the early Mesopotamian cities, broadly defined, did include a large number of agriculturists, as did the nascent ones in other regions and many preindustrial centers of later eras. The cultivation of crops in plots within or just beyond the city's "limits" was highly functional in that it facilitated the conveyance of produce to markets in the heart of the city.

The inclusion or exclusion of the agriculturists greatly affects the population estimates for the early Mesopotamian cities and accounts in part for the divergencies in the estimates of various writers. Unfortunately, most fail to state whether or not their figures include these marginal agriculturists. For cities of the late fourth millennium, Childe at one point estimates a population of from 7,000 to 20,000, at another from 8,000 to 12,000.[17] We would suggest figures of from 5,000 to 10,000 for the larger cities of this era (only part-time, not full-time, farmers being included), although solid facts upon which we can base any estimates are lacking.

Of course, somewhat later, in the third millennium, cities were more imposing. Frankfort[18] speaks of Ur as having perhaps 24,000 people, Lagash 19,000, Umma 16,000, and Khafaje 12,000. At the beginning of the next millennium, Ur, according to Woolley,[19] included 34,000 persons in the inner walled city, while "Greater Ur" had perhaps 360,000, a figure that obviously includes some of the surrounding agriculturists. However, both Frankfort and Woolley appear to exaggerate the number of persons per house; consequently their estimates of city size are inflated. Frankfort assumes six to ten in Khafaje and Woolley six in Ur. As the chapters on ecology and the family suggest, these estimates, especially for the urban lower class, are open to serious question.

The Emergence of Cities in Other Regions

We turn from Mesopotamia to trace briefly the growth of cities in the valleys of the Nile, the Indus, and the Huang Ho, and finally in Meso-America, all areas where city life could have originated, although it is likely that the emergence of the earliest cities in some of these regions was stimulated by influences from urban Mesopotamia.

The Nile Valley.[20] While cities were developing in Mesopotamia soon after 3500 B.C., a number of villages, some of them large walled communities, were scattered along the lower Nile and in its delta. The communities of the Nile riverine valley were at this time clustered into a number of politically independent units, each containing large cooperative irrigation projects to harness the annual floods of the Nile and divert the water to agricultural and other uses. Wheat and barley cultivation, domesticated oxen and asses for use in agriculture and transport, and technologies such as copper working and the potter's wheel (though not yet wheeled vehicles) existed by the time cities arose. And from the archeological records we infer an increasing differentiation of social classes and occupational groups. Some of the preconditions of city life had been developing here, as in Mesopotamia, over a long period.

The earliest cities, if we take evidence of a writing system as our key criterion, must have appeared by about 3100 B.C. The texts of a few centuries later allude to the union under Menes, the first pharaoh, of the political units along that part of the Nile that flows through Egypt today. Menes, like the later pharaohs, was considered a deity—and was both political head and chief priest. A strong central government contracted the economic surplus and the labor of the populace. And part of the grain harvest was stored in the city. A hierarchy of officials ranging from the pharaoh and his vizier, and the priests and scribes in the capital, down to the provincial and local administrators is attested to by the documents. The early writings tell of a number of cities—Memphis, This, Heliopolis, Nekheb (El Kab), etc.—most of which have since been engulfed by the rising silt deposited in the annual inundations of the Nile or buried under settlements of succeeding periods. However, at Abydos, a very early capital, the royal tombs provide materials from the beginning of the third millennium.

But unfortunately, until almost as late as 2000 B.C. the archeological record, aside from the writings, consists overwhelmingly of temples and tombs—usually built in honor of the pharaohs—and their contents. Most of the earlier sacred and secular public buildings and dwellings in the cities apparently were constructed of sun-dried (unbaked) brick and timber, or sometimes of wattle and daub, materials that have not survived the ravages of time. And later, when stone was used by the pyramid builders, the residences even of the ruling group were still of perishable materials. Furthermore, few large cities developed because of the practice in early dynastic Egypt of changing the site of the capital, normally the largest settlement, with the ascendancy of a new pharaoh. Added to all this is the relative paucity of excavation in the Nile valley, forcing us to speculate from meager data as to the organization of the earliest cities.

We noted that a few religious structures have survived from soon after the inception of city life. These contain inscribed seals and tablets as well as luxury goods of precious metals and jewels worked by specialized artisan groups; some of the materials used, e.g., copper, must have been imported into the area, suggesting specialized merchant groups. But not until ca. 2100 B.C. did bronze appear. The writings indicate a large body of priests and scribes, who made some significant advances in mathematics, calendrics, and other astronomical calculations.

For the period after 2000 B.C. the remains of cities are more extensive. Thebes, which had existed for some centuries, became a large city in about 1600 B.C. The remains of some multistoried houses survive, along with evidence of a broad "procession" street that ran through Thebes to the temple groups of Karnak and Luxor. Two centuries later, Akhetaten was built as a capital, though it functioned as such for only about fifteen years. Its extensive ruins at modern El Amarna indicate an unwalled city strung along the river bank. We have suggestions of social differentiation—a slum area, a handicrafts quarter, and roughly in the city's center a palace, temples, storehouses for grain, and government offices. Streets were unpaved and no drainage system is evident.

It is the opinion of some scholars that the emergence of civilization in Egypt was not accompanied by any significant concentration of activity in urban centers but rather that, with the exception of the capital, the larger communities were little more than marketing centers for the rural hinterland. Perhaps this is true, but they overstate their case. Woolley writes ". . . not even in the capital, for all its magnificence, was there any real civic life." (He identifies "civic life" with the city-state organization of Mesopotamia.) He notes that the communities of Pharaonic Egypt had market places, shop-keepers, priests, and government officials, but no large-scale "industry" or commerce, and on this basis concludes that ". . . there was nothing that called for the urban organization proper to a city."[21] Woolley's methodology is confusing, though he apparently takes the Mesopotamian city-states as the standard against which he contrasts the early Nile centers and finds that the latter differed in some respects. But this does not mean they were not cities.

But we still have to reckon with a point at issue: whether the first cities of the Nile were an indigenous creation. It is now conceded by most authorities that some diffusion of key traits into the area from Mesopotamia occurred just before or about the time the first Nile cities arose. Some cylinder seals and art motifs and the earliest monumental brick architecture in Egypt are thought to have been borrowed from Mesopotamia; more than this, a strong possibility exists that the basic notion of writing diffused to Egypt therefrom. That some early pictographs in Egypt are followed by a well-developed writing system, apparently without any transitional stage, suggests diffusion of the notion of writing to Egypt. Bromehead[22] even believes that copper-working techniques in the Nile valley were derived from Mesopotamian centers. But although the peoples of the Nile acquired some key items for city-building, they proceeded to develop many of these in their own special fashion, and were responsible for the creation of still others.

The Indus Valley.[23] The next possible center of origin of cities and civilization is the alluvial plain in present-day West Pakistan. Here the remains of two well-developed cities have been excavated—Harappa in the Punjab (the area of the five rivers that flow into the Indus) and Mohenjo-daro, 350 miles to the south in the valley of the Indus. Present evidence indicates that these cities were capitals of an empire that flourished between 2500 and 1500 B.C. Each was of impressive size, covering at least a square mile of ground. But we are not even sure who were the people that developed them. Some writers contend that the Dravidians, whose descendants are found today in southern India, were the founders of these urban centers. The Indus valley civilization was obliterated about 1500 B.C. by invaders, generally assumed to be the Sanskrit-speaking Aryans from the northwest, who introduced into India the Hindu religion and its specific social organization. Inasmuch as these peoples were nomads who destroyed many of the cities that lay across their path, city life did not reappear in India until some centuries later.

The large size of these cities and the abundance of towns and villages point to a highly productive system of agriculture. The remains of embankments to control the riverine floods suggest irrigation of a sort. Wheat and barley were the chief crops. Although "advanced" tools were in use, some writers doubt the existence of the plow.[24] Domesticated animals included oxen which pulled wheeled vehicles, elephants, camels, and horses.

Harappa and Mohenjo-daro show almost complete identity in their material culture, down to a common ground plan that includes a citadel on the western edge of each city. These walled structures are topped by buildings that appear to be of a ceremonial or public character. (Although some religious objects have been found, no clearly religious structures can be identified; here the Indus valley cities contrast with those of Mesopotamia and Egypt where religious edifices unmistakably dominate the community.) The high degree of uniformity that obtains between Mohenjo-daro and Harappa, cities 350 miles apart, as well as to a degree in the smaller communities, suggests that the entire civilized area was united under a single ruler.

It is not certain whether these cities were walled, though there is some evidence of a wall in the earliest levels of Harappa. The main streets, though unpaved, were quite straight and in some instances 20-30 feet wide; however, as expected, most streets were mere alleyways. Buildings were constructed of fired bricks, with sun-dried brick and adobe serving as interior filling.

The better houses were built around courtyards; walls that were almost blank, broken only occasionally by windows or doorways, faced onto the streets. Some homes had two or more storeys and were provided with wells and baths and a complex drainage system, forming a veritable labyrinth beneath the streets, that far outshone any similar ventures in the early Mesopotamian and Nile cities.

Among the artisan groups were potters who utilized the wheel in manufacture, cotton weavers, brick-makers, and metal workers in copper and bronze. Harappa and Mohenjo-daro had workmen's quarters consisting of rows of identical small, two-room dwellings. The former contained a large municipal granary close to which milling was carried out, and the latter boasted a "Great Bath." These rather imposing structures, along with a variety of other public buildings, suggest the existence of a controlled labor force, perhaps consisting of slaves, and thus a complex administrative apparatus which must have functioned to siphon off the surplus agricultural produce and store and distribute it within the cities.

As with Egypt, the possibly independent invention of city life by the Indus valley people has been a vexing issue. But that these communities are a millennium later in time than the Mesopotamian cities and appear to us only in mature form (though further investigation may uncover some earlier stages of urban life in the Indus valley region) has led some writers to assume that various traits like the notion of writing, wheeled vehicles, or citadel construction were introduced into the area from Mesopotamia. The distance between the Indus and the Tigris-Euphrates valleys was not formidable, even in that epoch. And there is evidence of some interchange of seals and other artifacts between the two regions before the close of the third millennium as well as just after 2000 B.C. Yet it must be recalled that the Indus valley script is still undeciphered and has not been successfully linked to that of any other area. And the great staticism in the material culture throughout numerous phases of the development of Harappa and Mohenjo-daro bespeaks considerable isolation of these cities, at least in the millennium after 2500 B.C. Yet the possibility that the Indus valley people borrowed some crucial elements for city-building from Mesopotamia looms large, though, as in the Nile region, these were imparted a special cultural flavor by the recipients.

The Valley of the Huang Ho.[25] The first cities in eastern Asia seem to have been those in the region of the Huang Ho (the Yellow River). But just when these took form is still to be determined, for new data are continually being unearthed, some of which challenge the older theories.

Until recently, the earliest-known urban community in China was thought to be the City Shang (or Yin), whose ruins lie just north of the Huang Ho at Anyang. But a hiatus existed between the dating of the latest Neolithic finds and the presumed founding of the City Shang about the fourteenth century B.C. The fine workmanship in bronze and the well-developed writing system uncovered in this city's remains are mute testimonials to the fact that some centuries of civilization, of urban living, had preceded the city's founding. Traditional Chinese histories, in fact, allude to some earlier cities.

Recent excavations at another site datable from the Shang period, Chengchow (just south of the Huang Ho and about 100 miles from Anyang), seem to bridge this gap. According to the report of a leading Chinese archeologist,[26] the materials uncovered there represent an older stage of Shang culture than those at Anyang. There are traces of simple writing in the early Shang levels at Chengchow as well as indications of occupational specialization and class differentiation. And the rather crude bronze work in these earlier Shang findings contrasts with the superb craftsmanship at Anyang. If the discoveries at Chengchow are indeed those of a city predating that at Anyang, as the evidence seems to indicate, the opening date of city life in eastern Asia is earlier than that heretofore assumed.

Shang civilization functioned upon an agricultural base that included the cultivation of wheat, barley, millet, and perhaps rice. Hydraulic enterprise in the form of flood control measures and canalization apparently served to increase the agricultural yield. Among the domesticated animals were pigs and oxen, and horses were used to pull wheeled chariots.

The apparently well-defined power structure included a hereditary political leader and a nobility much concerned with military matters. The presence of decapitated human sacrificial victims in the royal tombs is indicative of the exalted position of the sovereign, whose domain included a number of walled cities and towns and the peasantry in the outlying farming regions. Various of the ceremonial objects, including numerous divination bones and tortoise shells containing inscriptions, point to a literati, some of whom may well have served in a priestly capacity. And the vestiges of highly decorative work in bronze, pottery, bone, and other media attest to a strongly specialized urban artisanry.

The materials at Chengchow from the Shang period include walls of beaten earth whose thickness at the base varies between about 19 and 55 feet. Outside the walls lie the remains of artisans' workshops. The City Shang—capital at the demise of the Shang dynasty ca. the late twelfth century B.C.—no doubt was walled as well, and the city ruins boast a walled palace at the center, flanked by houses, evidently of wood, set upon earthen platforms. Neither here nor at Chengchow have any religious edifices so far been positively identified.

The genesis of these early cities has engendered debate among Sinologists. Eberhard,[27] for one, argues that China received some relatively advanced items of technology (i.e., advanced relative to those in the earlier folk order) from the urbanized regions of western Asia, a process that set the stage for the emergence of cities in China. After all, the earliest-known cities here were much later in time than the Near

Eastern and Indus valley centers. Although the Shang civilization evinced a quite distinctive over-all cultural pattern, it shared some of its basic forms as well as specific traits with the early cities to the west. Eberhard, observing that early Chinese documents allude to the migrations of foreign peoples into China from the dawn of "history," thinks it not unlikely that nomadic craftsmen, for example, may have introduced technological innovations like bronze casting and chariot-making.

Chêng Têk'un,[28] on the other hand, contends that the Chinese developed their cities from an indigenous Neolithic base with little assistance from beyond. He sees in older Neolithic sites in the general vicinity of the Shang cities evidence of towns with walls of pounded earth, the pottery wheel, and horses—all of which appear in the later urban complex. Still, any extreme inventionist position seems dubious. The earliest Chinese cities shared numerous traits with those in the Middle East and were considerably later in time than the latter, making it difficult to believe that at least some diffusion of urbanizing influences did not occur.

Meso-America. The earliest New World cities were those of the Indians of the Yucatan peninsula and Guatemala and of certain neighboring peoples in Mexico.[29] Recent excavations in this general region, supplemented by radio-carbon dating, are creating all manner of controversy regarding these earliest cities and their dating. However, we know that some centuries before the Christian era several Meso-American groups utilizing a writing system were living in communities some of which we, assuming a somewhat unorthodox position, believe represent an early stage of city life. But by the time of the Spanish conquest many of these communities had reached their zenith: some were already on the decline, while others had long been abandoned.

Earlier we commented upon the apparent divergency of the Meso-American urban centers from the incipient Old World cities in that some traits ordinarily associated with city life were absent; however, we argued that maize, a crop that produced a substantial food surplus with relatively little effort, substituted to a degree for the lack of other technological items. Supplemented by a few other plants and some animal foods, maize formed a most significant proportion of the diet.

Over much of the Meso-American region wherein cities first arose maize was cultivated by slash-and-burn techniques. The land was cleared by cutting and burning the existing vegetation; then the maize kernels were planted with the aid of a digging stick and the plot was weeded periodically by hand. But the burning practices and the increasing weed competition after a few years soon forced farmers to seek new land; this perhaps accounts in part for the abandonment of some of the Meso-American cities, particularly those of the Maya.

As to the ecological and social organization of the earliest New World cities, only that in the Maya communities is known in any substantial detail. We, therefore, draw upon these urban centers for our brief sketch of nascent urban life in the Americas. Tikal and Uaxactun rank among the oldest of the Maya cities so far discovered. The numerous later ones included Chichen Itza, Mayapan, Copan, Palenque, and others. Apparently these communities were the foci of small states that now and again combined into loose confederations. A well-developed elite administered the society from these urban places. Ordinarily the supreme ruler of each "city-state" was drawn from the dominant priestly hierarchy, whose members, at least in later times, were recruited on a hereditary basis. The priestly group, including numerous scribes, worked out rather advanced systems of mathematics and astronomy. Chief among their intellectual developments were a positional system of mathematics that embodied the concept of zero and calculations of the length of the solar year whose accuracy, considering the crude implements employed, is truly astonishing.

A secular nobility made up of military officials and civil officers maintained order in the cities, towns, and villages and supervised the collection of tribute from the farmers to support the urban populations. Other specialists included ordinary soldiers, merchants, and artisans. War captives customarily functioned as slaves.

Concerning the physical aspect of Maya cities, Tikal had its large man-made reservoir, but the most spectacular structures in the ruins of this and other Maya cities are almost invariably the religious and other ceremonial edifices. While small compared with the pyramids of Egypt, these display a highly elaborate and complex decorative art. We also have the remains of "palaces" that possibly were the residences of the priests and other notables. Yet most dwellings, especially those of the poor, were, if we can judge by wall paintings in ancient sites and later historical descriptions, simple thatch-roofed huts that could have left few traces.

Bishop Landa's[30] description of a sixteenth-century Maya city provides some clues as to the internal arrangement of the earlier ones. He observed that in the middle of the town stood the temples and "palaces," in and around which lived the nobles and priests, viz., the ruling elite. Next came the residences of the wealthy and other persons of high prestige, while on the city's periphery were the wood and thatch dwellings of the lower class.

This brings us to a fundamental controversy among Maya specialists. A plenitude of archeologists have argued for a quite low population density in the larger Maya centers, even as late as the Classic period, ca. A.D. 300-900. Some doubt that these were cities at all, although, increasingly, Maya specialists are coming to assume that they were indeed true urban centers.[31] (The consensus seems to be that the larger post-Classic communities were unequivocally cities.) The view that the more imposing of the Classic Maya communities were simply ceremonial foci to which the rural populace flocked on special occasions stems in part from the general failure, at least until recently, to search specifically for habitations beyond the cluster of ceremonial buildings, and of course many sites are so thickly overgrown with vegetation that excavation is exceedingly difficult. Nor are archeologists generally interested in the dwellings of the humbler folk. Writers, moreover, seldom ask themselves: Where did the elite—whom all admit existed—live? We dismiss as sociologically naive the assumption that the ruling group were part-time farmers or that the literati responsible for the intellectual achievements, and even some of the artisans who executed the paintings and elaborate sculptures, were not full-time specialists working at least indirectly for the ruling group. The proportion of skilled to unskilled labor required in the construction of some of the monuments apparently was relatively high.

We hold to the opinion that not only were there cities in the Classic period but these existed as well in the earlier Formative stage, beginning some centuries before the Christian era. Current archeological findings are steadily pushing Maya history backward in time;[32] the larger pre-Classic communities, we feel sure, will eventually be viewed as cities. For the literate elite resident in these centers required for its own support a complex apparatus consisting of administrators, merchants, artisans, and servants. To survive and function effectively, all these persons had to congregate in relatively compact areas—i.e., in cities functioning as administrative, ceremonial, and marketing centers. To be sure, these communities were rather small and contained a number of part-time or full-time farmers; yet they seem to have been cities—cities that apparently were developed by American Indian groups with no assistance from the Old World civilizations.

Although this chapter as well as the succeeding one are far from central to the argument of this work, they provide the setting for the ensuing discussion.[33] Any analysis of early cities is necessarily limited to deductions drawn from scanty data; yet these communities do resemble the later, more complex iron-age cities which serve as the basis for our typology and upon which more substantial empirical data are available.

NOTES TO CHAPTER II

1. A current representative of this group is R. Heine-Geldern. See his "The Origin of Ancient Civilizations and Toynbee's Theories," *Diogenes,* No. 13 (Spring, 1956), pp. 81-99. He derives all civilizations from the early Mesopotamian center.

2. V. Gordon Childe, "Rotary Motion," in Charles Singer *et al.* (eds.), *A History of Technology,* I (Oxford: Clarendon Press, 1954), 210. Childe assumes that the plow must have existed in the Mesopotamian and Indus valleys by the time of the first cities, although this is a deduction from other evidence.

3. Joseph A. Hester, Jr., "Natural and Cultural Bases of Ancient Maya Subsistence Economy" (unpublished Ph.D. dissertation, University of California at Los Angeles, June, 1954), p. 75.

4. P. C. Mangelsdorf and R. G. Reeves, *The Origin of Indian Corn and its Relatives,* Texas Agricultural Experiment Station Bull. No. 574 (College Station: Agricultural and Mechanical College of Texas, 1939), pp. 282-83.

5. Kathleen M. Kenyon, "Jericho and its Setting in Near Eastern History," *Antiquity,* XXX (December, 1956), 184-97. Also see her *Digging Up Jericho* (London: Ernest Benn, 1957), pp. 90-92.

6. Robert J. Braidwood, "Jericho and its Setting in Near Eastern History," *Antiquity,* XXXI (June, 1957), 73-81; Kathleen M. Kenyon, "Reply to Professor Braidwood," *Antiquity,* XXXI (June, 1957), 82-84.

7. Mortimer Wheeler, "The First Towns?" *Antiquity,* XXX (September, 1956), 132-36; Mortimer Wheeler, "The First Towns?" *Antiquity,* XXX (December, 1956), 225.

8. V. Gordon Childe, "Civilization, Cities, and Towns," *Antiquity,* XXXI (March, 1957), 36-38.

9. Of course writing alone is insufficient for distinguishing between rural and urban communities within societies.

10. Kingsley Davis, "The Origin and Growth of Urbanization in the World," *American Journal of Sociology,* LX (March, 1955), 430.

11. V. Gordon Childe, "Early Forms of Society," in Singer *et al.* (eds.), *op. cit.,* p. 49; Robert J. Braidwood, *The Near East and the Foundations for Civilization* (Eugene: Oregon State System of Higher Education, 1952), p. 3.

12. Davis, *op. cit.,* p. 431.

13. Childe, "Early Forms of Society," *op. cit.,* pp. 48, 53; Braidwood, *The Near East and the Foundations for Civilization,* p. 39.

14. Henri Frankfort, *The Birth of Civilization in the Near East* (Garden City: Doubleday, 1956), p. 55.

15. Leonard Woolley, *Excavations at Ur* (London: Ernest Benn, 1954), pp. 175-78, 186, 189; Leonard Woolley, "The Urbanization of Society," *Journal of World History*, IV (1957), 245-46; Henri Frankfort, "Town Planning in Ancient Mesopotamia," *Town Planning Review*, XXI (July, 1950), 99-115; V. Gordon Childe, *Man Makes Himself* (New York: New American Library, 1951), p. 123.

16. Frankfort, *The Birth of Civilization in the Near East*, p. 71.

17. Cf. V. Gordon Childe, "The Urban Revolution," *Town Planning Review*, XXI (April, 1950), 3-17, and Childe, "Early Forms of Society," *op. cit.*, p. 49.

18. Frankfort, "Town Planning in Ancient Mesopotamia," *op. cit.*, p. 104.

19. Woolley, *Excavations at Ur*, p. 193; Woolley, "The Urbanization of Society," *op. cit.*, p. 247.

20. Although we have consulted some field-work reports, the data we present are more readily found in such authoritative surveys as: Childe, *Man Makes Himself*, Chapter VII; Childe, "Early Forms of Society," *op. cit.*, p. 50; Frankfort, *The Birth of Civilization in the Near East*, Chapter IV and Appendix; Woolley, "The Urbanization of Society," *op. cit.*, pp. 236-72; Helene J. Kantor, "Further Evidence for Early Mesopotamian Relations with Egypt," *Journal of Near Eastern Studies*, XI (October, 1952), 239-50; H. W. Fairman, "Town Planning in Pharaonic Egypt," *Town Planning Review*, XX (April, 1949), 33-51; J. A. Wilson, *The Burden of Egypt* (Chicago: University of Chicago Press, 1951).

21. Woolley, "The Urbanization of Society," *op. cit.*, pp. 249-50.

22. C. N. Bromehead, "Mining and Quarrying," in Singer *et al.* (eds.), *op. cit.*, p. 564.

23. Mortimer Wheeler, *The Indus Civilization* (Cambridge: Cambridge University Press, 1953); Stuart Piggott, *Prehistoric India* (Harmondsworth: Penguin Books, 1950); V. Gordon Childe, *New Light on the Most Ancient East* (4th ed.; London: Routledge and Kegan Paul, 1952); Childe, *Man Makes Himself*, Chapter VII; Walter A. Fairservis, Jr., "The Ancient East," *Natural History*, LXVII (November, 1958), 504-13.

24. Damodar D. Kosambi, *An Introduction to the Study of Indian History* (Bombay: Popular Book Depot, 1956), p. 64.

25. See, e.g., H. G. Creel, *The Birth of China* (New York: Frederick Ungar, 1954); Li Chi, *The Beginnings of Chinese Civilization* (Seattle: University of Washington Press, 1957); Chêng Tê-k'un, "The Origin and Development of Shang Culture," *Asia Major*, VI (July, 1957), 80-98.

26. Hsia Nai, "China's Oldest Workshops," *Archaeology*, XI (Winter, 1958), 267-70. This is a summary of an earlier article that appeared in *China Reconstructs*, VI (December, 1957), 18-21. Cf. Chêng Tê-k'un, *op. cit.*, especially pp. 87-92.

27. Wolfram Eberhard, "The Formation of Chinese Civilization according to Socio-Anthropological Analysis," *Sociologus*, VII (1957), 97-112; Wolfram Eberhard, *A History of China* (London: Routledge and Kegan Paul, 1950), Chapters I and II.

28. Chêng Tê-k'un, *op. cit.*

29. George W. Brainerd, *The Maya Civilization* (Los Angeles: Southwest Museum, 1954); Sylvanus Griswold Morley, *The Ancient Maya*, rev. by George W. Brainerd (3d ed.; Stanford, Stanford University Press, 1956);

J. Eric S. Thompson, *The Rise and Fall of Maya Civilization* (Norman: University of Oklahoma Press, 1956), pp. 58-61; George C. Vaillant, *The Aztecs of Mexico* (Harmondsworth: Penguin Books, 1956), Chapter I. Recent archeological findings suggest that the earliest urban phases of the La Venta (or "Olmec") culture, as with those at Monte Albán, may antedate the first Maya cities. Wigberto Jiménez Moreno, "Síntesis de la Historia Pretolteca de Mesoamérica," in *Esplendor del México Antiguo* (México, D.F.: Centro de Investigaciones Antropológicas, 1959), pp. 1019-1108; Philip Drucker, Robert F. Heizer, and Robert J. Squier, "Radiocarbon Dates from La Venta, Tabasco," *Science,* CXXVI (July 12, 1957), 72-73, and Pedro Armillas, *Program of the History of American Indians,* Social Science Monographs, II (Washington, D.C.: Pan American Union, 1958), 43, 52.

30. Alfred M. Tozzer, *Landa's Relación de las cosas de Yucatan,* Papers of the Peabody Museum of American Archaeology and Ethnology, XVIII (Cambridge: Harvard University, 1941), 62, 171.

31. Gordon R. Willey (ed.), *Prehistoric Settlement Patterns in the New World* (New York: Wenner-Gren Foundation for Anthropological Research, 1956), especially pp. 93-100, 107-14; Angel Palerm, "La secuencia de la evolución cultural de Meso-américa," *Ciencias Sociales,* VI (Diciembre, 1955), 343-70; S. W. Miles, "Maya Settlement Patterns: A Problem for Ethnology and Archaeology," *Southwestern Journal of Anthropology,* XIII (Autumn, 1957), 239-48; Stephan F. de Borhegyi, "The Development of Folk and Complex Cultures in the Southern Maya Area," *American Antiquity,* XXI (April, 1956), 343-56.

32. Miles, *op. cit.;* de Borhegyi, *op. cit.* Also see two recent popular articles: "Secret of the Rain Forest," *Life,* XLV (October 13, 1958), 84-90; E. Wyllys Andrews, "Dzibilchaltun: Lost City of the Maya," *National Geographic,* CXV (January, 1959), 90-109.

33. The reader may wish to compare our survey with that of Rushton Coulborn, *The Origin of Civilized Societies* (Princeton: Princeton University Press, 1959). Coulborn, however, does *not* discuss the rise of cities. Moreover, we take issue with various of his interpretations, particularly his mode of distinguishing between civilized and primitive societies. Dismissing writing as a criterion, he sees civilized societies as differing from primitive ones primarily in that they alone undergo cycles of development (independently of environmental factors). This is murky reasoning indeed! Without written records from preliterate societies we can hardly prove the absence of "cycles of cultural development" therein. Cultural cycles, if such can be said to exist anywhere, would be determinable only after long periods of record-keeping.

CHAPTER III

THE PATTERNING
OF PREINDUSTRIAL- URBAN
PROLIFERATION*

THE SEVERAL possible centers of origin of cities having been exposed, we can proceed to some of the high points
in the expansion of urban life out of these centers. To avoid
entanglement in the vast jungle of historical data, we provide
only a *coup d'oeil* of the main lines of this dissemination, all
the while offering the reader some indication of the number
and extent of preindustrial cities over the course of history
and the differential urbanization of world regions. But our
primary task is to explain the *reasons* for the rise and fall,
and the occasional resurgence, of these urban agglomerations.

Dissemination of Preindustrial City Life[1]

Our survey is organized broadly in terms of wide geographic
areas, the descriptive matter being arranged chronologically
within each region.

The Middle East. Mesopotamia in the centuries following

* Co-author, Andrée F. Sjoberg.

the emergence of the world's earliest cities (ca. 3500 B.C.)
saw the Sumerian and Akkadian city-states engaged in continued struggles for dominance, with Lagash, Umma, Esh-
nunna, Kish, and Ur, each in its turn, gaining hegemony over
others. Soon after 2200 B.C. the city of Babylon was born and
by about the year 1800 had attained supremacy in the Tigris-
Euphrates riverine area. Meanwhile, the Assyrians to the
north, from their capital at Assur, had diffused city life
westward to Asia Minor (Anatolia) and Syria; but around
1700 B.C. they were temporarily displaced in these last-
named regions by other peoples, most notable of whom were
the Hittites, who established new cities like Khattushash-
boghazköy and Carchemish.[2]

In the interim, by 2500 B.C., numerous cities had been
developing to the west of Asia Minor on the isle of Crete,
Knossos and Mallia being the best known of these. And by
1600 B.C. the Mycenaean Greeks established cities such as
Mycenae on mainland Greece and Troy in Asia Minor. But
within a few centuries both the Cretan and the Mycenaean
civilizations disappeared.[3]

In the Nile valley some of the older capital cities—e.g.,
Heliopolis, Abydos, Nekheb (El Kab)—were still thriving
in about the year 2000 B.C., and soon thereafter Thebes,
Akhetaten (Tell el Amarna), Tanis, Heracleopolis, and
Bubastis rose to significance. But after 1400 B.C. urbanization generally languished—except in Kush, toward the upper
Nile, where Meroë grew up—until the fourth century B.C.
when cities like Heliopolis flourished again under Hellenistic
influence, and some new ones were established.

The Syropalestinian[4] area was a hotbed of urban activity
just before 2000 B.C., when a number of small "Canaanite"
city-states were constituted, though soon after 1900 B.C. these
came under Egyptian and Hittite domination. Some of the
important cities of the second millennium in this region were
Tyre, Sidon, Gubla (Gebal, Byblus), Beirut, Hazor, Ugarit,
Jericho, Gaza, Halap (Aleppo), and Damascus. Damascus

is one of the oldest "continuously" inhabited cities in the world today, although its population has ebbed and flowed markedly as it has been laid waste or revitalized under varying masters.

With the collapse of Egyptian and Hittite hegemony in the Syropalestinian region ca. 1200 B.C., some small cities like Jerusalem started on the path to fame under the Israelites. At the same time, Phoenician sea-farers from their urban bases of Tyre, Sidon, Byblus, and Beirut carried city life westward along the Mediterranean shores—to Carthage in North Africa, Sicily, and Spain.

In Asia Minor after about 1200 B.C. numerous cities were created by the Phrygians, Lydians, Thracians, Lycians, and early Greek peoples, and later by the Hellenistic Greeks and the Romans. Miletus, Samos, Ephesus, Sardis, Ankara, Smyrna (Izmir), Laodicea, Tarsus, Pergamum, Antioch (Antakya), and Iconium are only some of the urban settlements that throve before the beginning of the Christian era.[5]

Returning to Mesopotamia, city life during the first millennium B.C. was experiencing ups and downs. The earlier Assyrian city of Assur, and now Nineveh and Dur Sharrukin, enjoyed a brief period of ascendancy but soon crumbled before the Neo-Babylonians who had grown up just to the south. In the sixth century B.C. their capital, Babylon, reputedly was the greatest city in the world for its time. Yet within a few centuries it was abandoned by its inhabitants, who moved to nearby Seleucia, capital of the new Hellenistic rulers in Mesopotamia.[6]

Persia, which had almost no early cities besides Susa in Elam just east of Sumeria, finally gave birth to Persepolis, Pasargadae, and Ecbatana (Hamadan) around the seventh century B.C. During the next century or so the Persians carried city life into what are now Afghanistan and western Turkestan.[7] Indigenous settlements in the area—Kabul, Merv (Mary), Marakanda, and others—developed into true cities under this influence. And just before the Christian era Tashkent, Termez, Bokhara, Khojend, Kandahar, and Herat stepped into the light of history. Most of these Central Asiatic cities we name, though undergoing occasional decline and/or destruction and subsequent resurgence, have had an almost continuous existence down to the present day, whereas others, less well known, bloomed for a spell and then were destroyed.

In addition to the urban developments in Mesopotamia, Persia, and Central Asia, and in the upper Nile (alluded to earlier) during the first millennium B.C., some cities arose to the south in Arabia. It was in the early part of this millennium that communities on the order of Ṣan'aa' and Ma'rib, or those like Mecca and Medina, astride one of the main caravan routes of the time, took on an urban character. In the last centuries before the Christian era southwest Arabia became the jumping-off place for the establishment of certain small cities like Adulis and Axum across the Red sea in Abyssinia.

It was in the latter half of the first millennium, also, that the Hellenistic Greeks set up scores of cities, including numerous Alexandrias, Seleucias, Laodiceas, and Antiochs, scattered about from North Africa to Central Asia. Some of these rather quickly declined, whereas others experienced a further flowering later under the Romans.

At this point some summarizing statements are in order. By the dawn of the Christian era most sectors of the Middle East, broadly defined, were urbanized to a degree. But for a period just before and for some time after, except where Hellenistic and Roman stimulus prevailed, the pace of urbanization slowed considerably. Even to the east, in Persia and western Central Asia, where a series of empires arose, few new cities were constituted until the Sassanians in the third century A.D. built new urban concentrations like Bishapur and revived older ones like Persepolis.[8] For truly extensive city-building throughout the Middle East we must await the explosion of Islam beginning in the latter part of the seventh century A.D.

Within the space of a century or so the now-Muslim Arabs swept over almost the entire region, demolishing the older empires and setting up a wealth of new cities—except in Central Asia, where the older ones apparently were perpetuated under various Islamized rulers. Some of the post-Islamic creations are Teheran, Isfahan, and Shiraz in Iran; Basra, Mosul, and Karbala in Iraq; and Cairo, Fez, and Tangiers in North Africa. Before several more centuries had passed, one arm of Islam extended downward to the Sudan, stimulating the rise of Timbuctoo, Kano, Djenné, etc., and another moved southward along the East African coast, promoting the formation of Kilwa, Mombasa, Gedi, Songo Mnara, and other Arabo-African urban concentrations.[9]

Viewing the Middle East as a whole, we discover that earlier small cities like Mecca, Medina, Baghdad, and Damascus experienced a dramatic upsurgence under the new Muslim empires; on the other hand, some once-strategic centers of the older Persian and Roman domains—e.g., Caesarea, Seleucia, Palmyra, Petra, Ctesiphon, and Susa—sank into oblivion.[10]

In retrospect, we can safely say that most of the Middle Eastern cities today, perpetuating as they do a host of preindustrial-urban traits, owe their beginnings to, or had their urban development strongly accelerated by, the spread of empires propagating the Islamic faith.

Europe. Earlier we alluded to the eruption of a few cities on the European continent around the beginning of the iron age. Some of these were creations of the Greeks who filtered down from the north into the Aegean region and drew upon the city-building knowledge of other Mediterranean peoples. By the eighth century B.C. they had founded urban communities like Sparta, Corinth, Megara, and Byzantium, and the justly famous Athens had broken upon the scene. Concurrently, in Italy the Etruscans[11] had urban centers—Veii, Pisa, Perusia (Perugia), Siena, and others—and they were the ruling group in Rome. Soon the various Greek cities, or city-states, were establishing colonies in Italy, Spain, and Gaul as well as north of the Black sea.[12]

Rome[13] threw off the Etruscan yoke soon after 500 B.C. to become the seat of an empire that pushed the urban frontiers far to the north and west—to England and in western Europe up to the Rhine, in central Europe and the Balkans, and in much of the Near East. Here and there over this expanse the Romans established forts and some small administrative centers. A few of the modern cities of Europe that can trace their urban beginnings—in name, situs, and/or traditions—to Roman stimulus are: York, London, Brussels, Ghent, Utrecht, Granada, Seville, Cologne, Strasbourg, Paris, Toulouse, Bordeaux, Basel, Vienna, Zagreb, Sofia, and Belgrade.

City life declined throughout western Europe after the collapse of Roman rule. Now only in those portions of Europe under Byzantine or Muslim influence did urban life flourish: in the Balkans, Byzantium (Constantinople), Preslav, and Thessalonica (Salonika) were splendrous cities, and Cordova, Granada, and Seville in Spain were soon to achieve wide eminence.

The cities in most of western Europe shrank markedly as their life lines, the trade routes, with the outside world were obliterated by the Germanic invaders. However, a number of Roman cities were perpetuated as bishoprics (small urban centers under the rule of bishops), a cathedral being built within the walls of the old Roman fort. Soon these religious-administrative centers were ringed by settlements of merchants and artisans and were thriving cities once again. Similarly, kings and nobles, mostly lay administrators, established themselves on older Roman sites. Later they built new fortified strongholds, attracting populations around them to serve their needs; thus were laid the foundations of cities like Bruges, Antwerp, Frankfurt-am-Main, Hamburg, Prague, Warsaw, and Buda (the nucleus of the later Budapest). After the ninth and tenth centuries the increasing political stability and consolidation of kingdoms, with the ensuing upsurge of commerce, induced a burgeoning of urban communities all over western Europe. Among the first to achieve prominence in this renaissance were the Italian ones of Padua, Venice, Milan, Florence, Pisa, and Genoa. Most of these became independent "city-states" that functioned as intermediaries in the large-scale trade that came to be pursued between Byzantium and the Near East and the Low Countries.[14]

In the meantime, in the Low Countries and along the Rhine, Roman cities like Ypres, Lille, Ghent, Liège, Cologne, or Utrecht were being resuscitated; in France, Paris and Toulouse had by now revived after some centuries of eclipse.

In northern Europe beyond the bounds of the Roman Empire—Scandinavia, northern Germany, and the Baltic—the first appearance of cities was generally late, not until about the twelfth century, and then occurred largely as a result of the activities of administrators and traders from the north German cities in the Hanseatic League.[15]

With reference to European Russia,[16] city life had its inception in about the eighth century B.C. with the Greek colonies of Olbia, Cherson, and Panticapaeum (the later Kerch) on the Black sea. But the first city-building of any real consequence spanned the centuries between 600 and 1100 A.D., when Itil, Swarp, Kiev, Novgorod, Gnezdovo (near Smolensk), Suzdal, Pskov, Rostov, Vladimir, and a number of smaller urban settlements burst upon the scene. Not until the thirteenth century did Moscow, which had a citadel (the Kremlin) as its nucleus, assume urban proportions. In point of fact, most of the cities prominent today in European Russia are datable from the past few centuries.

South and Southeast Asia. Re-routing our itinerary to the Indian subcontinent,[17] we are confronted with a time-gap of almost a millennium between the demise of the Indus valley cities and the reappearance of urban life, under the aegis of the Aryan invaders, in what are today Pakistan and India. Although survivals of writing from these Aryan cities can be dated no earlier than the fourth or third century B.C., we assume that full-fledged urban communities existed before this time, perhaps as early as the eighth century B.C. In all probability, perishable materials such as palm leaf were used in the early writings, as they were still later in India, and thus have left no tangible remains to archeology. Then too, the observations of Persians who entered the subcontinent in the sixth century B.C. and of Greek invaders a couple of centuries later, indicate that some Hindu cities flourished therein. Taxila (Takshaśila), for one, reportedly had a university that attracted scholars from diverse regions. From these data, combined with later Indian and Ceylonese writings, we conjecture that at least by the sixth century B.C., city life had been revived on the Indian subcontinent. Besides Taxila, cities by the fourth century B.C. include Śravasti, Kaśi (Benares), Champa, Saketa (Ayodhya), Kampila, Kauśambi, Ujjain, Rajagrha, and Paṭaliputra (Patna). At this time the last named, Paṭaliputra, controlled much of the northern Indian region.

Under the Maurya empire, forged at the close of the fourth century B.C., the seeds of urbanization were sown more widely over India, especially to the south (although further archeological excavation may well reveal evidence of cities established there at an earlier date). Within the next few centuries Ajanta and Broach in central India and Kañchi (Conjeeveram) and Virapatnam farther south made their entrance. After the start of the Christian era, however, few new cities took shape, aside from a few small urban sites that glowed briefly under Roman imperial and commercial stimulus, until the era of Muslim rule in India, extending from the Arab invasions of the eighth century to the age of European dominance. Not a few cities today in India, like Hyderabad, Agra, or Lahore, were products of Muslim, including Moghul, empire-building. The older city of Delhi was transformed into a brilliant (i.e., for its time) administrative and cultural center under the new Islamic rulers. Although the latter's domain embraced well-nigh the entire Indian subcontinent, one seat of Hindu power persisted to the seventeenth century as an island in an alien sea. This was Vijayanagar, a city whose opulence inspired several enthusiastic reports by European observers. By the seventeenth century the Muslim empire was evanescing. Now, the new cities that arose—Bombay, Calcutta, Madras, and others—though possessing many preindustrial features, owed their formation primarily to the activities of European colonialists.

Moving southward to Ceylon, we discover that the beginnings of urban life are again a point of controversy. The sacred chronicles in Pali, compiled during the Christian era, would have it that cities existed in Ceylon as early as the fifth century B.C. Yet we have no evidence of writing on the island before the third century B.C. nor contemporaneous descriptions of these communities.

We do know that the ruins of Anuradhapura, a city whose religious edifices apparently exceeded most of the Egyptian pyramids in size, point to a thriving urban life around the dawn of the Christian era. Nourished by a hydraulic system of monumental proportions for its day, this city ruled supreme in Ceylon until the eighth century, when it relinquished its primacy to nearby Polonnaruha and finally was abandoned in the twelfth century or thereabouts. Though Polonnaruha held the reins of power for a time, the bulk of the population was shifting southward. In time Kandy became the dominant urban focus. Yet urbanization to the south never attained the heights that it had in the north, and it remained for the Europeans and their founding of Colombo to reactivate a bustling city life in Ceylon.[18]

By the first century A.D. the Indians had laid the foundations of city life in Southeast Asia.[19] In the succeeding centuries Shikshetra (Old Prome), Halingyi, Pegu, and Pagan in Burma, and Vyadhapura in Cambodia, were the foci of Hindu kingdoms, though Buddhists from India were a power group also. The late ninth century witnessed the rise of a new seat of Hindu empire—the spectacular Angkor urban constellation—whose ruins, including some of the most massive and ornate temples ever built by preindustrial man, lie nestled in the jungles of Cambodia.

After about the fifth century cities flourished in Indonesia under the aegis of Hindu or Buddhist kingdoms. Palembang on Sumatra was pre-eminent among the early cities; Majapahit on Java was an outstanding later one, emerging in about the thirteenth century. But after this, Indian influence declined in the area. By the sixteenth century the dominant cities in Indonesia and Malaya were the seaports of Malacca, Bantam, and Achin, the political centers of new Islamic principalities.

Returning to the mainland we see that the Thai people set up their capitals, Sukhot'ai and Ayut'ia, in the thirteenth century. Several more centuries were to elapse before Bangkok was constituted. Finally, the European colonists of recent centuries were primarily responsible for the formation of some of the cities of current significance in Southeast Asia —including Singapore, Rangoon, and Manila.

The Far East. Moving north to Tibet, urbanization, attributable mainly to Indian and in part to Chinese intrusion, is relatively recent. Lhasa emerged in the seventh century A.D. as the focus of a kingdom, but other cities of Tibet today— Shigatse, Tashilhumpo, or Gyangtse—were much slower to develop, being insignificant until about the year 1600.[20]

In the region later called China,[21] the City Shang, discussed in the previous chapter, was destroyed in the late twelfth century B.C. by the Chou peoples, who then proceeded to spread urban life east and south to the Yangtze River. Here their chief cities during almost nine centuries of rule were Loyang and Ch'angan. But some archeologists hold that also under the Chou, Ch'angsha flourished south of the Yangtze, in present-day Hunan province.[22]

It was under the Ch'in and Han dynasties, the third century B.C. to the third century A.D., that cities proliferated most widely over East Asia. The Great Silk Road, a caravan route to Sinkiang, became studded with oasis cities like Liangchow, Suchow, Khotan (Hotien), Yarkand (Soche), Kashgar (Shufu), and Anhsi. To the south, Canton, Nanking, and Chengtu attained urban status, and the Chinese were instrumental in founding cities in what are now Tonkin and northern Annam. In all likelihood the settlement north of the Yellow River that was eventually to become Cambaluc, and still later Peking, reached urban proportions under the Han dynasty. But among the most prominent of the cities of the Han era was Ch'angan, periodically the chief political center.

For the ensuing centuries historians find relatively little urban development, but just before or about the time of the Mongol invasions cities like Hangchow, K'aifeng, Yunanfu (Kunming)—and Shenyang (Mukden) in Manchuria—took shape. Toward the close of the thirteenth century the invaders, one of whose capitals had been Karakorum in Mongolia, made Cambaluc the political center of their new empire in China, transforming it into an imposing city whose opulence was perhaps over-exuberantly detailed by Marco Polo. By now most of the prominent non-industrial centers of traditional China had been established. Shanghai and Hongkong, however, are largely products of European intrusion.

Urbanization in Korea,[23] though it came about through Chinese influence, was much later than in China. Pyongyang reportedly can be traced to the beginning of the present era, with Songdo arising somewhat later. Not until another millennium had passed did Seoul achieve urban status.

Japan,[24] too, owes its urbanization to diffusion of strategic traits from the Chinese mainland. City life began here about A.D. 400 with Osaka the leading center. The seventh and eighth centuries witnessed a succession of royal capitals— Naniwa, Nara, and Kyoto. This last, capital for almost a millennium, is thought by a few historians to have reached a size unprecedented for cities of the world in the ninth century.

This early period of urban formation was followed by a decline of city life. Then, in the late fourteenth century, there was a resurgence of urban activity as Sakai, Hakata, Ishiyama, and other cities emerged. Some two centuries later the land was dotted with settlements, including thirty to forty "castle towns" like Edo (Tokyo), Hiroshima, and Sendai, containing populations of at least 10,000. Feudal cities apparently reached their maximum growth in the eighteenth century under the Tokugawa regime. By then Edo had become a teeming preindustrial metropolis, and Osaka and Kyoto were not far behind.[25]

Meso-America and Its Environs. We shall not elaborate upon the later dispersion of cities in the Meso-American region, except to observe that while the Maya and neighboring groups like the Zapotecs continued to develop urban centers, peoples to the north and west—the Toltecs and later the Aztecs—were doing the same. But these later cities—Tula, Tenochtitlan (upon whose site Mexico City now stands), Tlacopan, Texcoco, Tlaxcala, and many others—were of relatively short duration.[26] Those that survived the Spanish conquest of the sixteenth century underwent drastic cultural changes, although many of the older preindustrial forms were perpetuated and, in the early period of Spanish domination, new ones added.

In other sections of Latin America as well, the cities established by Europeans have manifested numerous preindustrial traits; still, they deviate to a degree from our constructed type inasmuch as soon after their founding they began to be affected by some degree of industrialization. In the region of the eastern United States, on the other hand, the few early colonial cities that predated the Industrial Revolution were subjected to far stronger industrializing influences—so much so that preindustrial-urban traits were never able to take hold therein.

We re-emphasize: the preceding pages are no more than a sketch of the main lines of urban development. No detailed historical analysis is attempted. Even so, this synopsis is unique in several respects.[27] It traces the spread of cities out of their several centers of origin, and it dramatizes the unevenness of urban development over space and time. City growth has varied perceptibly not just among regions but within them. Some social scientists, caught up in the overemphasis upon Western culture, see the fall of Rome as having led to a general decline of city life. True enough, but in merely one small segment of the globe. While cities were arising in one region they were evanescing in another—so it has been from almost the beginning of urban existence. Some cities once acclaimed have returned to dust, their sagas perpetuated only in obscure chronicles. Why all this flux? Why has urban life arisen? diffused? and declined? The reasons behind these phenomena have not received due attention, and it is to these that we now turn.

Why Cities Have Developed, Spread, and Declined

Technology and social power, though not alone in stimulating urbanization, are the most crucial variables in accounting for the origin and proliferation of city life throughout the world. Just as technology had to progress before settlements could develop into true cities, so too it had to attain a still more advanced stage before cities could invade "remote" or "inhospitable" regions. In turn, of course, the spread of cities was a variable stimulating technological innovation, if in no other way than by providing mechanisms for increasing contacts among peoples with differing skills.

Unquestionably, for cities to expand and diffuse, the level of technology had to be such as to ensure the surplus of food and raw materials necessary to sustain non-agricultural specialists. But although the preindustrial technology advanced to the point that it permitted urban life to diffuse into many parts of the world, it also encountered barriers to city growth.

Preindustrial cities, after all, have not inhabited the tundra or the broad desert regions where today industrial centers hold sway.

Technology. One of the technological achievements that opened the way for the proliferation of cities in the Old World was the shift from copper or bronze implements to those of iron, made possible by the invention of iron-working techniques apparently sometime around 1200 B.C. The increased efficiency and much greater cheapness and availability of iron tools augmented substantially the agricultural yield and the output of manufactures in already urbanized localities. Iron plows were far more durable than the earlier ones of bronze, stone, or wood. With iron, better wheeled vehicles became a reality, in turn facilitating the shipment of food and goods to the city's markets. And a variety of improved tools such as new types of drills, bits, specialized hammers, and effective axes appeared early in the iron age.[28]

In this era of improved technology, cities arose in environments formerly unsuited to urban settlement. Little wonder that Childe[29] observed that urbanization in the first five centuries of the iron age expanded at a greater rate than it had during the previous 15 centuries of the bronze age. Of course, the iron age began at different times in different regions. Childe was obviously referring to western Asia where, as noted, the iron age had its inception roughly about 1200 B.C.; iron-working techniques did not appear in China before about 600 B.C., were still later in Europe, and of course never were part of the pre-Columbian scene in the Americas. Moreover, in sectors of the Near East where political conditions were quite unstable at the beginning of the iron age, particularly in the Syropalestinian strip, urban centers actually declined for a time.[30] Granted that no one-to-one correspondence obtains between technology and urban development, the association is exceedingly high on a long-term basis.

But the term "iron age" connotes much more than the proliferation of iron implements. Associated with it, even in its early stages, were advances in modes of irrigation that consequently enhanced the agricultural yield and increased mechanization in the crafts as evidenced in such contrivances as pulleys and winches and new weaving techniques.[31] Not to be minimized as a technological innovation with far-reaching consequences was the apparently early iron-age development of coined money. Much more amenable to standardization than earlier forms of money, it promoted long-distance commerce and facilitated the marketing process within the city itself. Items of widely differing values could be exchanged with greater facility, as could goods and services. For example, persons engaged in service occupations could more easily exchange their economic product for the material goods they desired. Furthermore the use of coinage fostered economic enterprise involving investment, capital formation, etc.[32]

As a result of a variety of iron-age developments, communication improved markedly. Papyrus, an earlier bronze-age creation, was used more freely after the start of the iron age, and later centuries witnessed the development and spread of the alphabet, parchment, paper-making, and finally printing. An inevitable by-product of these more efficient media of communication was the increased extension of political empire and, concomitantly, urbanization.

Transportation was likewise affected by the technological advances of the early iron age. In addition to the better wheeled vehicles, there were now more efficient sailing ships that conveyed materials over long-distance sea routes. (While some of these vessels relied to a degree upon manpower for their propulsion, their use of sails to tap the available wind, an inanimate power source, constitutes—as with the later windmills and water-mills—a divergency in the preindustrial world from the usual dependence upon animate providers of energy.)

Technological developments had reached a sufficiently mature stage that by the time cities of later antiquity like Athens or Rome took shape, these could derive a portion of their sustenance from relatively distant places: the Greeks from North Africa, the eastern Mediterranean region, and north of the Black sea, and the Romans from all of these and western and central Europe as well. The dependence of cities upon long-distance transport for their sustenance now became an increasingly common pattern in preindustrial civilized societies.

Although in contrast to the present, technology in the preindustrial era advanced at a snail's pace, this period was by no means devoid of creativity; after all, it set the stage for the Industrial Revolution, the end result of many centuries of accumulated knowledge. Certainly the later preindustrial cities were larger, more complex, and in many ways more stable than the earlier ones. As noted, these more full-blown cities serve as the chief basis for our constructed type.

The Power Structure. But we can hardly comprehend urban growth simply in technological terms. Power operating through the social structure accounts for many urban developmental configurations.[33] Although the succeeding chapters treat in fuller detail the relationships of social power and city life, documenting particularly the urban setting of the ruling group, we must, if we are to explain the growth, spread, and decline of cities, comment upon the city as a mechanism by which a society's rulers can consolidate and maintain their power and, more important, the essentiality of a well-developed power structure for the formation and perpetuation of urban centers.

As to the first point, a power group in the feudal society can sustain itself only if its members concentrate in the kinds of settlements we call urban. Often these are fortified places to protect the upper class against local marauders or invading armies. But invariably they are the focal points of transport and communication, enabling the ruling element not only to maintain surveillance over the countryside but to interact more readily with members of their own group in other cities as well as within a city. The congestion that defines the city maximizes personal, face-to-face communication therein, essential if the heads of the various bureaucratic structures—governmental, religious, and educational—are to sustain ties with one another. So too, craftsmen and merchants prosper in the urban milieu, whose density and occupational heterogeneity foster economic activity.

On the other hand, though the city helps to sustain the ruling elite, the latter's continuance, indeed the city's very growth and survival, demand a well-developed power structure. Without an effective political apparatus through which power can be exerted, cities could not derive sustenance from the hinterland. Peasant farmers, for example, rarely produce and relinquish a surplus willingly in feudal societies; thus tribute, taxation, and the like must be exacted if cities are to gain the wherewithal to support their populations. Through their control of the power structure the rulers obtain the largest share of the economic product and live in a style befitting what they consider their rightful heritage. Their dominant position within the society provides them with the means to import goods from abroad, and their urban residence makes such luxury items all the more accessible to them. However, the upper class is not the only segment of society to profit from a well-developed political organization. A stable power structure also enables merchants and artisans more effectively to pursue their supportive activities.

In light of the foregoing, we reason that social power is a prime variable in accounting for 1) the expansion of cities in both size and number, 2) their diffusion into previously non-urbanized or lightly urbanized areas, and 3) their decline (and occasional resurgence). We discuss each of these patterns in the order named, reinforcing our arguments with illustrative materials.

As to the first, our contention is that urban *growth* in societies is invariably highly correlated with the consolidation or extension of a political apparatus, be the result a kingdom or an empire. Of course, Innis,[34] among others, has shown that a society's ability to transform itself into an empire, or the latter's capacity to expand, is associated with the level of technological development attained therein, particularly in the sphere of communication.

The crux of our argument is that as a society broadens its political control it enlarges its economic base as well. City dwellers can then tap the resources of an ever-widening hinterland by draining off the agricultural surpluses of the peasantry and utilizing raw materials such as metal ores that the new domains might have to offer. And a stable political structure —e.g., by keeping trade routes open—permits an active economy. Without doubt, since cities first emerged, their fortunes have been functionally linked to military conquest and/or political stability.

It is hardly fortuitous that the great cities of the preindustrial world have been those within powerful kingdoms or in the heartland of an empire that has spread its tentacles into, and consolidated its domination over, a wide area. The city of Rome reached its apex at about the time the empire was at its peak. Likewise, in India the cities at the focus of the Maurya empire—especially Paṭaliputra—attained their greatest splendor at the height of imperial expansion, and the same can be said of Delhi, Fatchpore, and other leading urban centers of the Moghul empire in later India. Cambaluc and Hangchow in China were dazzling cities at the zenith of Mongol rule. In feudal Japan, cities reached their peak in the eighteenth century under the aegis of the powerful Tokugawa shogunate.

Not to be overlooked are the so-called "city-states" of medieval Europe—Venice, Genoa, Pisa, and others. Some were actually the centers of small discontinuous "empires" that included patches of territory in the eastern Mediterranean: colonies or trading depots that enabled them to dominate the sea-lanes between Europe and the Near East and without which they could not have aggrandized the urban homeland.[35] In like manner, a few of the Greek city-states functioned for a time as "empires." It follows that the denomination "city-state" is a deceptive one, for some of these social orders, say Athens, exercised dominion over a sizeable hinterland that included some far-flung cities.

Political control as a key variable in urbanization is confirmed by the capital city's pre-eminence in both size and over-all cultural influence in the feudal order. As site of the supreme ruler, the societal capital attracts to itself a disproportionately large share of the economic surplus that sustains the elite and those who serve this group—servants, artisans, and merchants, among others. And it is that segment of the ruling group centered in the capital that subsidizes the premier astrologers, artists, and musicians in the society. Men of belles-lettres find in the capital city support lacking elsewhere. In the end, the more imposing the power of the elite and the richer its domains, the more glittering the capital.

Having indicated that an elaborate power structure is associated with city growth, we move on to a related topic— the *dispersion,* or *diffusion,* of cities into previously non-urbanized, or very lightly urbanized, regions.

The extension of the power group's domain, notably through empire-building, is the primary mechanism for introducing city life into generally non-urbanized territories. Not only is urban living thereby fostered in the heart of the mother society, but it is carried ever outward upon the waves of conquest to the very borders of the empire, and perhaps beyond.

That the sphere of urbanization widens as the society extends its holdings should be little cause for wonder. Administrative and military centers are required to control the newly won lands; undoubtedly some of these have been established upon existing village sites. Around these settlements cluster artisans, merchants, and other assorted groups who function to sustain the non-agriculturists. Soon full-fledged cities develop. The military and other governmental administrators seek in urban living to maximize their contacts with one another and to take advantage of the communication and transportation ties with the societal capital; the small, isolated rural community cannot perform this function. Even when roads are built to outlying areas these connect only the most important cities. These urban outposts, moreover, are the channels through which is funnelled the economic surplus remitted to the heartland, there to satisfy the demands of the ruling elite.

The empirical evidence for these patterns is overwhelming. We indicated how the Persian empires of the seventh to fifth centuries B.C. introduced city life into western Central Asia. For example, Toprak-kala and Marakanda (part of whose site later was occupied by Samarkand) apparently became true cities at this time. In India, the first-known appearance of urban settlements in the central and southern zones— Ajanta and Kañchi, among others—was a by-product of the southward advance of the Maurya empire. Likewise in China the dispersal of cities over previously non-urban areas—particularly to the south and west—occurred under the Ch'in and the succeeding Han empire-builders. Now urban centers like Canton and Nanking first came into being, as well as a number along the Silk Road connecting China and the west of Asia.

The various Greek city-states set up colonies over much of the Mediterranean littoral. A few of these new cities were Cumae (whose colonists in turn built Neapolis, or Naples), Zancle (Messina), and Massalia (later Marseilles). Others included Olbia and Cherson on the Black sea. The Greeks, of course, established cities in previously urbanized regions as well—for example, in the late fourth century B.C. Alexander and his heirs were city-builders on a grand scale in the Near and Middle East.

The best-known instance of city-building in regions previously untouched by urban living is that which accompanied the spread of the Roman empire. Roman military conquests gave rise to cities in Gaul, Britain, northwestern and central Europe, and the Balkans, to say nothing of some previously urbanized regions like Spain, North Africa, and the Near East. Many of the cities of western Europe, particularly, seem to have grown up around military forts and were unquestionably administrative centers for the ruling clique.

Preindustrial-urban political systems not only diffuse city life outward as their domain expands, but, as mentioned earlier, they at times stimulate urbanization well beyond their formal political frontiers. This is likely to occur when emissaries like missionaries and, especially, merchants penetrate not-yet-urbanized societies under the aegis of a well-established power structure. Typically, an empire at its apogee contains an ever-growing body of urbanites and an upper class that has waxed more affluent and has increased its demands for a variety of goods. Merchants are thereby encouraged to extend their sphere of operation into more remote regions, with the result that entrepôts and emporia are set up which in turn may be transformed into small urban centers. Such an eventuality, of course, is largely dependent upon the degree of support and protection offered by the political base within the homeland. If nothing else, the far-flung trading centers require stable supply lines if they are to be maintained.

To illustrate this process, we cite the influx of Indian administrators, missionaries, and merchants into Southeast Asia, soon to be followed by the emergence of the first cities in this portion of the globe. So too, Chinese ventures into Japan triggered the earliest city development there. The Scandinavian and Baltic region owed its nascent urban centers to the activities of merchants and civil and clerical administrators who entered this area as representatives of the Hanseatic League ca. A.D. 1100. New cities have been stimulated by empires in already urbanized regions: Roman merchants (in reality members of minority groups in the Roman empire such as Syrians and Arabs), acting as emissaries of the Empire, built emporia in further Asia which resulted, for example, in the development of Arikamedu (Pondicherry) in India out of a small indigenous village.[36]

Thus the political power variable explains urban growth and proliferation to the frontiers and beyond. It also accounts for some cities' *decline*—and occasional resurgence. Just as a city's capacity for growth is dependent in large part upon an elaborate political apparatus, so too, when this is withdrawn the city will shrink or disappear. Especially is this true of societal capitals, the foci of power in the preindustrial civilized order and the chief target, on both military and symbolic grounds, of invading armies. Many cities therefore have been sacked, burned, and captured as their new rulers have burst upon the scene.

The sad decay that awaits some cities is dramatized by Babylon, Nineveh, and Anuradhapura, which lie today in ruins that only hint of a splendor long since passed. And the majestically carved remains at Angkor in Cambodia are mute testimony of a once-great urban complex. How many persons today have heard of Vijayanagar in India? Yet as capital of a Hindu empire in the thirteenth and fourteenth centuries it so impressed European travelers that they were to write of it in grandiloquent terms. Too, the waning of city life in western Europe after the eclipse of Roman power is evidence of the interrelationship between cities and societal power. These West European cities, incidentally, were to reappear after the ninth century in large part as a result of stimuli from the Byzantine and Arab empires, which seem then to have been near their apogee.[37]

Some may contend that we exaggerate the close tie between the submergence of an empire and the demise of its cities, perhaps citing Athens as a negative case. However, the history of Athens strongly supports our hypothesis. Athens did not decline sharply after the destruction of Greek power. Why? Because it was able to attach itself to another power constellation, the Roman empire, which adopted high Greek culture and subsidized Athens as a center of learning. But once Rome fell, the population and influence of Athens steadily dwindled; it was no longer underwritten by the succeeding empires in the region. Athens lay moldering during many centuries until that just past, when the community that perpetuates its name, tradition, and approximate site was made capital of modern Greece. On the other hand the Greek city-state of Byzantium followed a quite different course. Of minor import under Roman rule, with the demise of Rome it became capital of the Byzantine empire (under the name of Constantinople); still later it was the seat of Ottoman rule and, as Istanbul, it remains an important city to this day.

Thus, although cities usually flounder with the collapse of their political superstructure, some may be perpetuated under the new order—as was Athens and Greek cities of the Near East, like Alexandria or Antioch, under Roman rule. And others that experience a decline may undergo a renaissance when the political climate changes in their favor. Numerous urban centers—Jerusalem is an outstanding example—have been developed, destroyed, and rebuilt numerous times throughout their turbulent history, as a direct expression of shifting political tides.

The network of relationships among urban growth, spread, and decline can not be fully explored here. However, one highly significant pattern deserves special mention. This is that cities on the fringes of empire at times break away from the latter and become the bases of operation for the destruction of the mother cities. This process was at work in Europe —although it is rarely perceived by historians—when the so-called "barbarians," actually groups like the Goths who had been partially urbanized and civilized by the Romans, rose up against and demolished Rome. Earlier, in Central Asia the Persians and Greeks, in the course of extending their imperial frontiers, had introduced urban living to indigenous peoples in the region, among whom were various Aryan and Turkic groups. These in turn assimilated within the urban milieu the techniques for driving out their conquerors and constructing empires of their own, including the Graeco-Bactrian, the Parthian, and the Kushanian.

Moreover, scholars appear to ignore the fact that the "nomadic" Mongols had, before their accession to power, been in contact with urban centers—those established by the Chinese and the Turkic Uighurs. Then too, at least part of the Mongol officialdom, including a small literati, resided in cities like Karakorum and used these as their bases for their broad sweeps over Asia. Nomads completely lacking in the accoutrements of urban living could never have instilled fear in the hearts of civilized peoples to the extent the Mongols did.

Subject peoples, no matter how dissatisfied they may be, must acquire a high degree of knowledge of the use of weapons and military tactics, indeed of the administrative process itself, before they can rise up to smite the empire that nourished them. It is the conquerors themselves who, in the urban context, cultivate the skills and leadership capacities of their subjects, the more effectively to administer and exploit the resources of the region, and thereby sow the seeds of their own downfall. (An analogous process is occurring today as the industrial-urban apparatus is diffused from advanced societies to less developed ones; urbanites in the latter are reacting by rising up and "throwing off the yoke of colonialism.") Detailed analysis of the aforementioned and similar phenomena, as they affect the rise and decline of cities, must await a separate treatise.

Other Factors. We have emphasized the role of technology and, particularly, political power as the prime variables in the development, proliferation, and downfall of cities, but we are not incognizant of the workings of other forces. The value system of a people may affect the fortunes of cities. Jerusalem undoubtedly has been perpetuated through time, despite its periodic destruction, because of its symbolic value for Christians, Muslims, and Jews alike. Yet we must be ever mindful that without a series of power structures to support it, even Jerusalem could not have survived.

Environment, also, influences urbanization by imposing

limits upon city growth. Likewise cities have vanished as a result of shifting environmental circumstances. Kish died a peaceful death after the Euphrates River changed its course, leaving it cut off from its water supply, and Pompeii was obliterated in the eruption of Mt. Vesuvius. Nevertheless, on the whole, environment is more a dependent than an independent variable, being amenable in many respects to advances in technology and the prodigious impact of social power.

Turning to a more controversial issue, many readers familiar with the literature on city growth may wonder why we de-emphasize the link between commerce and urbanization. We do not deny that a commercial organization is necessary if a political system is to be maintained, but it is not as crucial for urbanization as most historians have contended; contrariwise, large-scale economic enterprise is highly dependent upon an effective power structure.

Our argument is grounded in a vast body of cross-cultural evidence. Nowhere do cities, even commercial ones, flourish without the direct or indirect support of a well-established state system. We can find no instance of significant city-building through commerce alone. The flowering of cities in western Europe after the ninth century was the result of stimuli from the Byzantine and Arab empires, then at their apogee, which promoted the activities of merchants beyond their frontiers. Too many scholars writing of the Phoenician cities established around the western Mediterranean or the early commercial cities set down by the Muslims in Southeast Asia, such as Bantam and Malacca, have seen merely commercial, or economic, factors at work. They fail to recognize that the Phoenicians at the height of their commercial expansion were lords of the Mediterranean, or that the early port cities in Indonesia and Malaya were the foci of sultanates whose development paralleled the culmination of Islamic empire-construction to the west, e.g., in India, whence these cities derived their early support. Unquestionably, the factor of political power, much more than commerce, is the key to the rise and spread of urban centers throughout history.

This completes our adumbrated sketch of the historical spread of preindustrial cities over the world, intended as a setting for the ensuing analysis of the social structure of this city-type. Our contention is that the basic form of these communities has remained relatively constant throughout many hectic eras of change, although their content may have varied perceptibly. It is to this fundamental ecological and social structure of preindustrial cities everywhere that we now turn.

NOTES TO CHAPTER III

1. Here we can not possibly review the many controversies, particularly over dating, that revolve about the history of cities. Nor can we mention every non-industrial city or document all the sources we have consulted. Our survey is a synthesis and evaluation of data from many diverse works that sometimes differ in specific details and in the interpretation of materials. Disagreements among historians result from lack of data, divergent theoretical perspectives, and the tendency of each to glorify the cities within his area of specialization.

2. Ralph Turner, *The Great Cultural Traditions: The Ancient Cities,* I (New York: McGraw-Hill, 1941); O. R. Gurney, *The Hittites* (2d ed.; Harmondsworth: Penguin Books, 1954).

3. E.g., V. Gordon Childe, *The Dawn of European Civilization* (6th ed.; London: Routledge and Kegan Paul, 1957).

4. Martin Noth, *The History of Israel,* trans. Stanley Godman (London: Adam and Charles Black, 1958); Philip K. Hitti, *History of the Arabs* (3d ed. rev.; London: Macmillan, 1946); Philip K. Hitti, *Lebanon in History* (London: Macmillan, 1957).

5. E.g., David Magie, *Roman Rule in Asia Minor* (Princeton: Princeton University Press, 1950); A. H. M. Jones, *The Greek City* (Oxford: Clarendon Press, 1940).

6. Turner, *op. cit.*

7. R. Ghirshman, *Iran* (Harmondsworth: Penguin Books, 1954); V. A. Lavrov, *Gradostroitel'naya Kul'tura Srednei Azii, s Drevnix Vremen do Vtoroi Poloviny XIX Veka* (Moskva: Gosudarstvennoe Izdatel'stvo Arkhitektury i Gradostroitel'stva, 1950); V. V. Barthold, *Four Studies on the History of Central Asia,* I, trans. V. and T. Minorsky (Leiden: E. J. Brill, 1956).

8. C. E. Van Sickle, *The Political and Cultural History of the Ancient World*, II (Boston: Houghton Mifflin, 1948), Chapter IX; A. H. M. Jones, *The Cities of the Eastern Roman Provinces* (Oxford: Clarendon Press, 1937); Ghirshman, *op. cit.*

9. Basil Davidson, *The Lost Cities of Africa* (Boston: Little, Brown, 1959); Bruce Howe, "Africa," in "A Decade of Discovery, 1948-1957," *Archaeology*, X (Winter, 1957), 242-43.

10. Hitti, *History of the Arabs.*

11. M. Pallottino, *The Etruscans* (Harmondsworth: Penguin Books, 1956).

12. Kathleen Freeman, *Greek City-States* (London: Macdonald, 1950).

13. Harold Mattingly, *Roman Imperial Civilization* (London: Edward Arnold, 1957); Robert E. Dickinson, *The West European City* (London: Routledge and Kegan Paul, 1951).

14. A. A. Vasiliev, *History of the Byzantine Empire* (2d ed. rev.; Madison: University of Wisconsin Press, 1952); Sidney Painter, *A History of the Middle Ages: 284-1500* (New York: Alfred A. Knopf, 1956); John H. Mundy and Peter Riesenberg, *The Medieval Town* (Princeton: D. Van Nostrand, 1958).

Unlike many social scientists, we do not date the beginnings of medieval cities in western Europe from the time they received their charters; these writers assume a narrow legalistic perspective, one aptly illustrated in *La Ville*, Recueils de la Société Jean Bodin, VI (Bruxelles: Éditions de la Librairie Encyclopédique, 1954).

15. Ziedonis Ligers, *Geschichte der Baltischen Städte* (Bern: Paul Haupt, 1948). Also see articles on specific cities in the *Encyclopaedia Britannica*.

16. George Vernadsky, *Ancient Russia*, I (New Haven: Yale University Press, 1943).

17. Sourindranath Roy, "Civic Administration in Ancient India," in *La Ville, op. cit.*, pp. 177-224; A. L. Basham, *The Wonder that was India* (London: Sidgwick and Jackson, 1954); R. C. Majumdar (ed.), *The History and Culture of the Indian People: The Age of Imperial Unity* (2d ed.; Bombay: Bharatiya Vidya Bhavan, 1953); K. A. Nilakanta Sastri, *A History of South India* (London: Oxford University Press, 1955); R. C. Majumdar, *et al., An Advanced History of India* (2d ed.; London: Macmillan, 1950).

18. Rhoads Murphey, "The Ruin of Ancient Ceylon," *Journal of Asian Studies*, XVI (February, 1957), 181-200; Harry Williams, *Ceylon: Pearl of the East* (London: Robert Hale, 1950); Reginald Le May, *The Culture of South-East Asia* (London: George Allen and Unwin, 1954), p. 42.

19. D. G. E. Hall, *A History of South-East Asia* (New York: St. Martin's Press, 1955); Franz H. Michael and George E. Taylor, *The Far East in the Modern World* (New York: Henry Holt, 1956), Chapter IV; Lawrence P. Briggs, "The Ancient Khmer Empire," *Transactions of the American Philosophical Society*, XLI (Philadelphia: American Philosophical Society, 1951), 1-295.

20. Charles Bell, *Tibet: Past and Present* (London: Oxford University Press, 1924).

21. E.g., Glenn T. Trewartha, "Chinese Cities: Origins and Functions," *Annals of the Association of American Geographers*, XLII (March, 1952), 69-93; Herold J. Wiens, *China's March Toward the Tropics* (Hamden,

Conn.: Shoe String Press, 1954); Yu-shan Han, "A Historical Survey of Some Geographical Names of China," *Sinologica,* I (1948), 152-70; and a number of general works on the history of China.

22. Lauriston Ward, "Old World Archeology and Prehistory," in William L. Thomas, Jr. (ed.), *Current Anthropology* (Chicago: University of Chicago Press, 1956), p. 90.

23. Cornelius Osgood, *The Koreans and Their Culture* (New York: Ronald Press, 1951).

24. George Sansom, *A History of Japan to 1334* (Stanford: Stanford University Press, 1958); R. A. B. Ponsonby-Fane, *Kyoto* (Kyoto: Ponsonby Memorial Society, 1956).

25. John Whitney Hall, "The Castle Town and Japan's Modern Urbanization," *Far Eastern Quarterly,* XV (November, 1955), 37-56; Irene Taeuber, *The Population of Japan* (Princeton: Princeton University Press, 1958), pp. 26-27.

26. G. C. Vaillant, *The Aztecs of Mexico* (Harmondsworth: Penguin Books, 1956); William T. Sanders, "The Central Mexican Symbiotic Region," in Gordon R. Willey (ed.), *Prehistoric Settlement Patterns in the New World* (New York: Wenner-Gren Foundation for Anthropological Research, 1956), pp. 115-27.

27. The reader may wish to compare our discussion with Jean Comhaire and Werner J. Cahnman, *How Cities Grew* (Madison, N. J.: Florham Park Press, 1959). However, we question many aspects of this study, particularly the analysis of the data.

28. H. H. Coghlan, "Metal Implements and Weapons," in Charles Singer *et al.* (eds.), *A History of Technology,* I (Oxford: Clarendon Press, 1954), 618.

29. Gordon Childe, *What Happened in History* (New York: Penguin Books, 1946).

30. Noth, *op. cit.,* p. 82.

31. Charles Singer *et al.* (eds.), *A History of Technology,* II (Oxford: Clarendon Press, 1956), *passim.*

32. H. A. Innis, *Empire and Communications* (Oxford: Clarendon Press, 1950), p. 85.

33. The relationship between social power and the rise and decline of cities has been discussed by Ibn Khaldûn, Giovanni Botero, and Ralph Turner. Although we owe a debt of gratitude to these scholars, our formulation seems to be an advance over their efforts.

34. Innis, *op. cit., passim.*

35. Vasiliev, *op. cit.;* F. L. Ganshof, "The Middle Ages," in Ernest Barker *et al.* (eds.), *The European Inheritance,* I (Oxford: Clarendon Press, 1954), 311-511.

36. Mortimer Wheeler, *Rome Beyond the Imperial Frontiers* (London: G. Bell and Sons, 1954), p. 147, *passim.*

37. We remind ourselves that the Roman cities in Europe did not disappear completely during the so-called "Dark Ages." While some sank to the status of small towns, or even villages, being resuscitated only in later centuries, others survived as small cities throughout this period.

A few writers are coming to define the larger feudal "manors" in Europe as small urban communities. We concur. Some of them did fulfil all our criteria for denomination as cities.

CHAPTER IV

DEMOGRAPHY
AND ECOLOGY

Now that the historical background of the preindustrial city has been sketched we can get on with the central task of this work—delineating the structure of this city within its societal setting, stressing always those features that set it apart from the industrial-urban community.

In this chapter we examine the demography, the patterns of location, the functions, and the internal spatial and temporal patterning of preindustrial-urban communities.

Demography

Preindustrial cities in general, especially those of antiquity, have been small; a few of the later ones, though dwarfed by modern megalopoli, have attained substantial size. Admittedly, some predominantly non-industrial cities of the twentieth century with populations of over a million have been subsidized, directly or indirectly, by industrial societies. Nonetheless, certain cities unaffected by the Industrial Revolution may have reached the million mark. Ch'angan in the early centuries of the Christian era, in the view of some historians, embraced a million inhabitants. According to Kracke,[1] censuses of the time suggest that by the year 1100 four urban areas in China contained populations of over a million and that a century or two later Hangchow had well over a million people. Soon afterward, Marco Polo visited China and was dazzled by the magnitude of Hangchow and other cities. In Japan, Edo (Tokyo) perhaps attained the size of a million during the Tokugawa era—although Taeuber's[2] estimate is considerably lower, and it must be recalled that at this time large segments of the nobility of other cities were expected to maintain official residence in Edo and spend part of each year there. Turning to the West, some historians, though a minority, believe Rome may have included a million people within its precincts.

I consider it exceedingly unlikely that the relatively simple technology of the feudal order—with its limited food "surplus" and mediocre facilities for transporting supplies to cities over any appreciable distance—could have long supported centers of a million people. Only in special situations might a temporary burgeoning of the city's population occur. Recent demographic writings reject most of the earlier population estimates for preindustrial centers as exaggerations.

Several factors have contributed to the overestimation of preindustrial city size. One, early European travelers may have wanted to impress the home folks with the grandeur of far-away places they had seen. Thus, an Italian who journeyed to Vijayanagar (India) at its peak described its walls as 60 miles in circumference.[3] And Marco Polo is notorious for his "tall tales" about the cities he visited. Second, it is all too easy to inflate the statistics on cities, even unintentionally, by including the agriculturists who reside close by in small villages. Certainly not all these full-time cultivators can be viewed as urbanites. Third, the older censuses such as those in traditional China are to be interpreted with utmost care: often they counted households rather than individuals, and unless we know the size of households at the time, these figures tell us little about the population of urban areas. Archeologists are faced with similar difficulties when they attempt to estimate the population of cities when they have little more than evidence of dwelling sites to go on. Evidence from more recent societies (discussed later) suggests that preindustrial city families, except among the privileged elite, have been small. Social scientists must recognize the sharp differentials in size between families of the small upper class and those of the abundant urban poor and should not use the elite as the norm for estimating family size in non-industrial cities. Fourth, as noted for Edo, Japan, temporary increases in population, resulting from special institutional patterns or social crises, may occur, but these should be recognized for what they are. Lastly, scholars err in assuming that just because a city has been of vital functional import in a feudal society it necessarily has had great size.

Yet in all fairness it must be admitted that some counterarguments carry a measure of conviction. China's highly intensive agriculture and elaborate canal and river transport systems conceivably could have supported some teeming cities, even as early as the Sung dynasty. Murphey[4] observes that Shanghai's food supply, even in the present century, has come from a rather narrow agricultural hinterland connected to the city by a still largely preindustrial water transport system. Perhaps a similar pattern obtained in the past. Nonetheless, I am sceptical of the existence of cities of a million ca. A.D. 1100-1300 in Sung China.

My own reasoning finds substantiation in the recent efforts to minimize the supposedly large size of some earlier preindustrial centers. Russell,[5] in his survey of late ancient and medieval populations in Europe and the Near East, may be too conservative, yet his statistics seem to be in keeping with reality. He believes Rome in the second century A.D. had not a million people, but only about 200,000, that Constantinople under the later Roman empire had 192,000, not the 500,000 or a million suggested by some. Even under the Fatimids,

Cairo in the tenth or eleventh centuries included only 25,000 persons, although Russell concedes that Baghdad before A.D. 1000 probably contained about 300,000 people.

A recent study by Mols on medieval European urban populations supports Russell's conclusions. In Mols' words (translated from the French):[6]

> In reality, there is no parallelism between the importance of a city in the past and an absolute population figure. With its 10,000 inhabitants, Lubeck dominated, in the thirteenth century, over all the cities of northern Europe. Cologne was the uncontested metropolis of western Germany. However, it does not appear to have had much more than 15,000 inhabitants at that time. . . . In the course of the two centuries between 1350 and 1550, the first place among the cities of Brabant was occupied successively by Louvain, Brussels, and Antwerp. However, their population figures were modest: 20,000, 40,000, 80,000 in the period of their great splendor.

Recognizing the tendency of earlier writers to overestimate the size of cities, we still must concede the existence of some large preindustrial-urban concentrations in Asia. Edo, even by conservative estimates, attained a population of 500,000 during the Tokugawa era and the cities of Kyoto and Osaka were not far behind.

In summary we can state with some assurance that preindustrial cities of more than 100,000 have been sparse, at least until the late nineteenth and early twentieth centuries, when they came to be subsidized by industrial societies. Even preindustrial centers with populations between 25,000 and 100,000 have been relatively uncommon. Numerous preindustrial cities of consequence have undoubtedly sheltered little more than 10,000 and perhaps only 5,000 persons. Size alone is never an index of a city's historic role.

Over-all, it is doubtful that preindustrial cities have typically comprised more than 10 per cent of the total populations of feudal societies; in some instances the figure may be less than 5 per cent. Most people are farmers, closely tied to the land, who support themselves and a small elite through their own labor and that of a few domesticated animals. This kind of technology simply does not permit any extensive surplus.

Though we have little reliable information on the size of preindustrial cities, still less is available to us on other demographic patterns. Migration into and out of urban areas certainly has occurred, but its extent and nature can only be surmised by extrapolating from data on existing preindustrial orders. Generally, feudal orders display much less social and spatial mobility than do industrial ones. Nevertheless, preindustrial cities—partly because of the vicissitudes of war, periodic famines, and especially, the devastating epidemics— depend upon in-migrants for much of their population growth. We should not underestimate the impact of such catastrophes upon preindustrial city life and its demographic structure.[7]

Throughout history, people have traversed vast distances as a result of war or natural disasters, or in the course of trading activities, and urban centers, rather than rural ones, have been the prime receptors of these long-distance migrants. Cities, therefore, exhibit more striking ethnic diversity than the surrounding countryside.

Apparently in most feudal societies men move to cities from rural areas in greater numbers than do women; the latter's actions are more restricted and their opportunities for urban employment more narrow. Certain mining centers and trading posts, like those along the main caravan routes, have been heavily populated by males.

We intimated that mortality rates in feudal cities have been high: the toll taken by disease, war, and starvation has been upped by other natural disasters that preindustrial urbanites can not cope with. Still, life expectancy was lower in the past than in preindustrial-like cities today; in turn the average life-span in the latter is appreciably shorter than that of the industrial city's inhabitants.

We can not assume, however, that death rates have been higher in the cities than in the villages. As we later emphasize, the largest families in feudal orders have been encountered in urban, not rural, communities. Moreover, data of a tenuous sort suggest differential mortality rates among classes: death rates soar higher in the lower class than in the upper stratum. Yet outstanding fertility differentials are not discernible among classes (and perhaps not between rural and urban communities). Birth control measures, with some exceptions, being nil, families in all strata are prone to have as many children as possible, but because the upper class has a greater survival potential, its progeny are generally more numerous.

Location

Inasmuch as various facets of urban location were dealt with in the two previous chapters, we shall tarry but briefly on this subject, systematizing our observations and elaborating where necessary.

The salient factors in urban location are environment, technology, the economic structure, the power structure, and cultural values.

Environment sets limits to urban location but never determines it. The existence of barriers is a function of the technological base: the more backward the technology the more numerous are the areas inimical to city life. In the feudal world urban living has been unfeasible wherever food and water are difficult of access and where the terrain poses problems for cultivation or transport. Yet throughout the history of preindustrial civilized societies, technology has advanced, though at a languorous pace, enabling cities to spring up in environments that earlier could not have nourished them. The world's first cities, given the technology of the time, could hardly have arisen in central Tibet, where not until the early part of the Christian era did Lhasa make its appearance, or even on mainland Greece, which became sprinkled with flourishing urban centers relatively late in history: here better sailing ships and an improved agricultural technology, among other considerations, made city life feasible.

Related to environment and technology are economic factors. Although what constitutes a "break" in transportation is partly a function of the technological base, we must recognize that the expansion of many cities can be traced to the concentration of people at key sites along trade routes. Cities may arise at transfer points in the movement of goods or persons—i.e., from land to water, or vice versa, or at relay points on overland trade routes. Istanbul, at the nexus of the Mediterranean and Black seas and seated astride the overland routes between Europe and the Near East, has profited much from its position, serving for almost three millennia as a prime trading center. Cities all along the Mediterranean littoral grew significantly as maritime commerce was intensified. On the other hand, those urban centers situated on the overland routes from China to eastern Turkestan or from western Turkestan to Arabia owe much of their prominence to their role as relay stations in the transfer of goods from one caravan to the next. Long-distance trade could not have crossed the vast expanse of Asia without such oasis communities as Tashkent, Samarkand, or Yarkand, stopping-off points for a variety of economic transactions.[8]

But we tend to minimize, though not dismiss, economic factors, lending, as before, stronger emphasis to technology and social power. The pages of history are replete with examples of the primacy of social power in determining both urban location and growth. After all, even granting the limits imposed by the environment, technology, and economic factors, alternatives do appear in the placement of cities, and it is here that power considerations may loom all-important.

Social values come to be interwoven with social power in complex fashions. Values, as the handmaiden of social power, led to the shifting of the sites of the capitals of early Egypt. With the accession of the new pharaoh the old capital customarily was deserted and temples and tombs (pyramids) were erected in his honor at the site of his choosing. As the chief seat of administration, the site or its environs soon became a bustling city as it attracted ever larger numbers of people. Another dramatic illustration of the link between cultural values and power in urban location is the traditional use in Japan of geomancers for the selection of an auspicious site for a new capital. According to Sansom,[9] this was the chief reason for the specific location of the site upon which arose the new capital of Kyoto in the eighth century.

We have also seen how values—religious or otherwise— attach to certain cities and become a potent factor in their continuation or repeated resurgence upon the same general site. Probably for this reason Peking has functioned on and off as the societal capital during many centuries. Surely values have been the prime factor in the continuance of Benares (earlier Kaśi) since the incipience of Hindu cities in India and in the frequent rebuilding of Jerusalem (and its destruction by antagonistic groups) over several millennia.

Functions

The question of functions is interwoven with urban location. The key functions of preindustrial cities are political (both administrative and military), economic, religious, and educational. No city serves only one function to the exclusion of all others, but even so cities come to play special roles.

Here again the factor of power looms paramount. Political centers geared to administrative and/or military functions are unquestionably the dominant cities in the society. Concerning administration, we have already suggested that the elite must be urban-based to sustain its power position. The nature of the city serves to sustain communication among the elite and thus aids the administrative process; the urban centers, moreover, are the focal points of contact with outlying portions of the realm. It is hardly surprising that societal capitals, first and foremost, and after that the provincial and local ones, dominate all other cities in the feudal order. Few strictly non-political cities have achieved prominence. At times the capital cities rank supreme among the economic, educational, and religious centers. Contrast this, incidentally, with the pattern in highly industrialized societies where the leading commercial or industrial communities, for example, are often non-political centers. In the United States, New York, Chicago, Los Angeles, Detroit, and other leading metropoli are not capital cities.

The pre-eminence of capital cities in feudal orders derives from the restricted nature of the economic surplus; the powerful elite, resident in the strategic political centers, can command the largest share of goods and services, not just those required to fill man's basic "needs" but luxury items as well. Because the societal capital, especially, attracts to itself the "best of everything," it inevitably emerges as a leading commercial center. And because the political bureaucracy is so interwoven with the religious and educational ones, the society's capital is likely to become a leading educational and religious center.

Cities serve not only politico-administrative functions but military ones as well: the two of course are almost inseparable. The ruling group must command military power if it is to maintain dominance over the populace within the society and protect itself from attack from without. It is hardly accidental that many cities have grown up around fortresses, as did Moscow around the Kremlin, or Mycenae around its acropolis. Thus the city is at the same time a focal point of enemy attack and a haven for the elite in time of danger.

Another outstanding function, aside from the political, is the economic one. Of course, as suggested above, the economic function is carried out effectively only within the context of a supportive power structure. Within the preindustrial society some cities thus supported emerge as primarily commercial or manufacturing centers or both, and they may specialize within these functions.

Within the feudal order are small cities or market towns that serve as transfer points for produce that eventually finds its way to the large cities. Their populations may fluctuate greatly during the course of a week, swelling enormously on special market days—when farmers pour in from the outlying areas to sell their goods to the local townspeople or to traveling merchants who have put in appearance—only to be drastically reduced during the rest of the week.[10] These local marketing centers are vital links between the peasantry and the larger cities.

In contrast to the small market towns stand the commercial cities that serve as intermediaries in "international" commerce. The medieval Italian "city-states," political centers in their own right, functioned as the prime vehicles in the trade between the Byzantine and Arab empires and northwestern Europe. Nineteenth-century Canton filled this role in East Asia on a massive scale, and the caravan cities along, for example, the Spice Route in Arabia and Syria—e.g., Petra and Palmyra—owed much of their prominence to the part they played in moving goods over long distances.

Some cities have achieved fame for their specialization in particular handicrafts.[11] For example, Muslim Delhi was known for its brocades and other wares in gold and silver and for its ivory work. Other Indian cities like Benares and Bangalore have attained renown in part for their fine silk weaving. The Chinese city of Chefoo has been celebrated for its pongees and laces, and rather superior porcelain was produced at Chingtechen (Kiangsi province). Turning to the Near East, Damascus has been famed throughout the area and in Europe for its swords, and its name has been bestowed upon a special kind of cloth, damask, originally produced there; another kind of cloth, muslin, derives its name from Mosul, where it supposedly was first developed. In Central Asia Bokhara was distinguished for its prayer rugs and Samarkand for its paper-making; it is apparently from the latter that the art of manufacturing paper diffused to Europe. Venice, Pisa, and Palermo ranked high among medieval European cities for their silk-weaving establishments. Recently, in fact, the European cities of Delft and Limoges, which lent their names to distinctive types of chinaware, famed over the Western world in an earlier era, have sought to revive these handicraft arts.

Because of the dependency of cities upon effective economic and political organizations, none has specialized solely as an educational or religious center; nevertheless some are more outstanding in these spheres than are others, achieving renown as the foci of pilgrimages or of intellectual pursuits.

Mazar-i-Sharif in Afghanistan, Karbala and Najaf in Iraq, Kyoto in Japan, Lhasa in Tibet, and San Juan Compostela in Spain, have all attracted multitudes who perform there special religious rites. But more prominent than any of these are cities on the order of Benares, Mecca, Jerusalem, or Rome. Though religious centers abound in India, none rivals Benares, which has long reigned supreme. The goal of many a Hindu is to visit it, there to bathe in the sacred Ganges, and for the orthodox an ultimate blessing is to have one's ashes scattered into the river at Benares. One of the chief pillars of Islam is the obligation to journey at least once to Mecca, the birthplace of Mohammed. Through the centuries it has attracted untold numbers of pilgrims from the farthest corners of the Muslim world, from Morocco to as far east as the Philippines. Jerusalem, symbolically more eclectic, has been a sacred city for a number of peoples—Jews, Christians, and Muslims.

Many pilgrimage centers are renowned as seats of learning, for in preindustrial civilized societies education has typically been religiously oriented. Benares and Mecca are two that have achieved eminence as university centers. But other cities, not considered as "sacred," have been famed for their religious studies: e.g., Cairo with its al-Azhar University, and Cordova and Bokhara, which once attracted intellectuals from myriad parts of the Muslim world.

Mentioned so far are the political, economic, religious, and educational functions of cities. Some urban places, usually leading political capitals, also serve as "cultural" centers for art, music, and literature: the court and the elite are the ones who subsidize this activity. Communities rarely, if ever, are resort cities per se; the "leisured class" is too minute to support them. Non-industrial cities exhibit much less specialization of function than do those in industrial societies; in the ensuing chapters we find that this reflects the limited technology.

Spatial Arrangements

If industrial man could remove himself temporarily from his milieu, with all its comforts and conveniences, and set himself down within a non-industrial city, he would immediately perceive the dramatic contrast between its physical complexion and that of the modern industrial metropolis. We first discuss some salient features of the cityscape that would strike his eye, then consider specific land use patterns.

A General Overview. Typically, all or most of the city is girdled by a wall. Inside, various sections of the city are sealed off from one another by walls, leaving little cells, or subcommunities, as worlds unto themselves. Walled cities have been the generalized pattern throughout the Middle East from North Africa to Central Asia, and in India and China during much of their history. Even certain pre-Columbian cities of Meso-America conformed to this pattern.[12]

Walls, moats, and similar devices have been common as defensive bulwarks, though only partially effective, as evidenced by the numerous once-thriving walled cities now lying in crumbled ruins. And with the advent of modern weapons, they have become obsolete. But the city's ramparts serve other functions, like regulating the activities of merchants and other visitors to the city: watchmen and other agents can readily be stationed at the few points of entry to collect tolls or ward off social "undesirables." And the circumvallated districts or quarters reinforce the segmentation of social groups that obtains in many cities. Minority ethnic groups, especially, may be so sealed off in quarters of their own—e.g., as in Fez —that they have only tenuous relations with the general populace. As with the gates to the city proper, the entrances to the various walled quarters are secured at night, bringing communication among the units to a halt. With the ever-present threat of thieves and other marauders, locking the interior gates provides an added measure of protection for the inhabitants.

Within the walled precincts congestion is the order of the day. Although crowding in the center is alleviated somewhat by the spacious dwelling units of the wealthy, the urban poor, except those on the outskirts, beyond the walls, live closely packed. Given the scanty transport media, people reside and work where they have access to the city's special facilities, and because the technology does not allow many multistoried structures, buildings are set closely together, often immediately juxtaposed, to permit a maximum number of people to partake of the advantages of life within the city walls.

The clumping of buildings is intensified by the narrowness of the streets, mere passageways for humans and animals, though a few permit the circulation of small wheeled vehicles. Two-way auto traffic in most traditional cities is out of the question. Cities in India, the Near East, Tibet, China, and parts of Europe and Latin America still contain streets wherein the pedestrian can touch buildings on either side simultaneously. The "Street of the Kiss" in Guanajuato, Mexico, derives its name from the fact that at least part of it is so constricted that lovers in houses on opposite sides of the street could kiss from the overhanging balconies.[13]

The usual street, as opposed to the few main thoroughfares, is narrow, winding, unpaved, poorly drained, and apt to turn to mud during periods of snow and rain, making transportation slow and uncomfortable. Medieval Paris was notorious in this respect.

The typical street is greatly congested during the day. Here ambulatory vendors hawk their wares, and numerous small shops and stalls front on the street with little or no sidewalk intervening. Indeed, much business is transacted in the street itself. Combine this with the din of children playing, adults gossiping or bargaining, and animals being led to market, and we find life in feudal cities far from placid and uneventful.

Consider the discomforts and dangers of unpaved, congested, poorly lighted, and poorly drained streets in a city wherein public services are almost totally wanting. Garbage collectors and street sweepers are sparse relative to those in industrial centers. The limited technology of the preindustrial city and the dearth of scientific knowledge about sanitation procedures or the very need for these have meant that waste materials are apt to litter the community. Salusbury[14] describes street life in late medieval England:

> . . . butchers and poulterers were by no means alone in their careless disposal of animal refuse; fishmongers and cooks and the ordinary households were all guilty. In Chester (1475) . . . women carrying entrails of animals from the butchers carried them uncovered and threw them out near the gates, to the public nuisance. . . . The private citizen was only too ready to dispose of dead dogs and cats by dropping them into the river or just over the town wall, or even by placing them in any open space . . .

Furthermore:[15]

> The final disposal of filth and rubbish collected from the streets presented a grave problem. The town ditch and the river were used very frequently for this, but in the fifteenth century a greater population made these places less desirable for the purpose, and indiscriminate showering of garbage over the walls and just outside the gates became intolerable.

These patterns, quite generalized in preindustrial cities, have also been vividly described for Lhasa[16] and for Rabat, Morocco, at about the turn of the present century. Concerning

Rabat, Caillé remarks as follows (in translation from the French):[17]

The removal of waste is effected in a very primitive manner by donkey-drivers who load it in the *chouaris* their animals carry. But this service includes only five or six donkeys for the whole city. Besides, it is suspended on holidays and when it rains; also, in winter, the streets of the city often show a layer of liquid mire more than ten centimeters deep. When the waste-matter has been removed it is thrown into the sea; or often it is simply heaped up at the gates to the city, where it forms a veritable cesspool.

And an Indian comments concerning present-day, pre-industrial-like Hyderabad city:[18]

A high majority of the citizens commit nuisance promiscuously in open spaces. . . . Public latrines are few and far between . . . [and] are not kept clean by the scavengers, and it is an annoying sight to see many a scavenger emptying his bucket full at some street corner or under a culvert. . . .

Of course in many cities human waste is collected by scavengers in baskets or other receptacles to be distributed to farmers in the immediate countryside.

In addition to humans, dogs, pigs, birds, or other animals roam about serving as scavengers of the offal indiscriminately thrown into the streets. Though frequently provided with a depression in the center for drainage purposes, streets are more often than not choked with refuse. This explains in part why preindustrial cities have risen continually throughout the ages—some of the ancient ones uncovered by archeologists reveal many layers of habitation, the newer buildings having been constructed upon the refuse of the past.

The problem of sanitation is compounded by the difficulty of obtaining an adequate water supply; little can be spared for keeping streets and houses clean. The aqueducts of Rome were marvelous inventions for their day, but they did not serve the city's tenement areas. In non-industrial cities many households are dependent for their drinking water upon water-carriers. Or a few wells, apt to be contaminated, may serve a great number of homes. Inhabitants of Rabat have used the water conduits for bathing, washing their clothes, and watering their herds. Andkhui, a small urban community in northern Afghanistan, has long depended, for both drinking and cleansing purposes, upon a large water tank teeming with finger-length worms and other wriggling creatures. Facilities in Indian cities are still notoriously inadequate by industrial standards, a protected water supply being unavailable to a large portion of the citizenry.[19]

Under these conditions, and in the absence of a scientific understanding of the causes of communicable disease, the prevalence of epidemics in preindustrial cities, both past and present, should elicit no surprise.[20] Once underway, these sweep through a city like a fire fanned by violent winds, leaving thousands of dead in their wake. In the face of such devastation the inhabitants have little more than their religious and magical beliefs to cling to.

Preindustrial urbanites, at the mercy of the periodic epidemics and subject to the general malaise resulting from the non-salubrious conditions, are also prey to destructive fires. Having at their disposal only the meagerest of fire-fighting equipment, cities like those in Japan, with their closely-bunched dwellings built flimsily of wood, have been ripe for annihilating conflagrations.[21] Even cities with many fewer wooden structures—e.g., late medieval London or mid-nineteenth-century Cairo—have existed under the perpetual threat of fire because of the excessive crowding and the paltry technological means for coping with such eventualities.

The foregoing discussion, though not of central concern to urban ecology, nonetheless serves to capture some of the flavor of preindustrial city life. But let us turn our attention to patterns of greater theoretical interest to ecologists.

Specific Land Use Patterns. This section takes up three patterns of land use wherein the non-industrial city contrasts sharply with the industrial type: 1) the pre-eminence of the "central" area over the periphery, especially as portrayed in the distribution of social classes, 2) certain finer spatial differences according to ethnic, occupational, and family ties, and 3) the low incidence of functional differentiation in other land use patterns.

As to the first, concentrated in the city's "central" area (often coterminous with the physical center, but not necessarily so) are the most prominent governmental and religious edifices and usually the main market. The chief public buildings either crowd around an open square, or plaza, onto which converge a number of streets—as in numerous cities of the Near East, southern Europe, and Latin America—or stand along, or at the end of, a broad, straight thoroughfare— as in Thebes (in ancient Egypt), Vijayanagar, and Peking. Considering the narrow lanes that wind through much of the city, the main plaza or street can be nothing but imposing.

The plazas or main streets serve as meeting places and ceremonial sites for the populace. Into these open spaces flow the citizenry to hear public pronouncements, mass communication media being non-existent, or there they engage in the elaborate processions and pageantry that mark the ceremonial life of these cities.

Both physically and symbolically, the central governmental and religious structures dominate the urban horizon. The Acropolis (or citadel) at Athens contained the chief religious buildings and in its early days served as the royal headquarters. So did the Temenos at Ur. Peking has had as its focus the "Forbidden City," site of the residences of rulers and of the leading temples. But often the religious edifices at the center dwarf the nearby governmental structures. This was the case in pre-Columbian American and ancient Cambodian and Ceylonese cities. The public buildings in many a medieval European city were overshadowed by the main cathedral, as in cities today in southern Europe and Latin America. So too, the typical Muslim city has the chief mosque as its hub, while traditional Buddhist Lhasa radiated outward from its own "Cathedral," the focus of most community activity.

An understanding of these patterns is dependent upon knowledge of the technology and the total social structure. Any explanation of the ecology through a biotic, i.e., non-social, orientation collapses when applied to the preindustrial city, for an exceedingly high correlation exists between the technology, the social structure, and the spatial distribution of the city's inhabitants, and between all these and the urban center's physical appearance. Because we have yet to analyze the social structure, only some of the more pertinent relationships are suggested here.

Because political and religious activities in feudal cities have far more status than the economic, the main market, though often set up in the central sector, is subsidiary to the religious and political structures there. Interestingly, the chief market is apt to be located next to, or nearby, the dominant religious edifice. (In fact, markets and ambulatory vendors tend to cluster about religious buildings throughout the city, apparently to take advantage of the considerable pedestrian traffic these attract.) Nevertheless, the commercial structures in no way rival the religious and political in symbolic eminence; typically these tower above all others and are the most resplendent—the resulting skyline is far different from that of industrial cities where commercial structures tend to loom over all others. These land use patterns refute the still widely accepted proposition of the Chicago school that the "central business district" is the hub of urban living, a generalization fulfilled only in industrial cities, where commercial activities are necessarily more prominent, supporting as they do the complex industrial system.

The preindustrial city's central area is notable also as the chief residence of the elite. Here are the luxurious dwellings, though these often face inward, presenting a blank wall to the street—a reflection of the demand for privacy and the need to minimize ostentation in a city teeming with "the underprivileged."

The disadvantaged members of the city fan out toward the

periphery, with the very poorest and the outcastes living in the suburbs, the farthest removed from the center. Houses toward the city's fringes are small, flimsily constructed, often one-room, hovels into which whole families crowd. (Still farther out, well beyond the city limits, are the summer homes or ancillary dwellings of the elite.)

This general elite and non-elite ecological arrangement can be adduced from archeological finds at Ur, Knossos, and numerous other ancient urban sites. We have historical evidence of it for medieval Europe, and it persists today in parts of Italy, France, England, and other European countries, although modifications wrought by industrialization have for some time been underway. Descriptions of Cairo, Timbuctoo, Aleppo, Fez, Lhasa, Calcutta, and cities in Japan and Indonesia and Latin America all confirm the universality of this land use pattern in the non-industrial civilized world.[22]

Urban sociologists themselves have documented the tendency of the elite to cling to the city's center, the poor being concentrated on the outskirts. Gist[23] observes this for Bangalore, India. The investigations of the Dotsons[24] in Guadalajara, Mexico, reveal that the upper class, traditionally clustered about the central plaza, has only recently been attracted to the suburbs. And Rosenmayr[25] stresses that the traditionally high prestige accorded residence in or near Vienna's historic nucleus is responsible for the low incidence of suburbanization, although he falsely considers this a peculiarly Viennese phenomenon. Like most urban sociologists, these writers have not perceived the generality of their findings, each being content to immerse himself in the culture or society that is his specialty.

How do we explain this distribution of classes as between the central sector and the periphery? Throughout feudal cities, values operate defining residence in the historic center as most prestigeful, location on the periphery as least so. But reference to values alone can not account for the ecological differences between the traditional and the modern urban community. Far more pertinent is technology. For one thing, the feudal society's technology permits relatively little spatial mobility, thereby setting limits to the kinds of ecological arrangements that can obtain. People travel mostly on foot, occasionally on animal-back; only the privileged ride in the human- or animal-drawn vehicles, slow and uncomfortable though these be by industrial standards.

Assuming that upper-class persons strive to maintain their prerogatives in the community and society (here social power enters as a factor in ecology), they must isolate themselves from the non-elite and be centrally located to ensure ready access to the headquarters of the governmental, religious, and educational organizations. The highly valued residence, then, is where fullest advantage may be taken of the city's strategic facilities; in turn these latter have come to be tightly bunched for the convenience of the elite—patterns that are readily revised with the introduction of rapid transit, telephones, and so on. Residence in or near this high-status area reinforces one's social position. This locale is, moreover, the best-protected sector of the city, often enclosed by a wall of its own, whereas residence on the urban periphery is hazardous in time of war or in the face of the recurrent banditry.

The poor, in conformance with the rigid class structure, are kept toward or upon the outskirts and must accept all the disabilities of this location. It is they who travel the farthest to gain access to the city's facilities. Even in this community where time is not highly valued, those in the suburbs, though least able to afford it, often must traverse the greatest distance to reach their place of work. With heavy rain or snow the environs may be cut off completely from the central district as the streets become veritable seas of mud and slush.

Various low-status groups are relegated to the city's outskirts through efforts of the elite to minimize social contact with them. This is most apparent for those workers in malodorous occupations—tanning, butchering, and the like—mainly the province of outcaste groups.[26]

Some lower-class groups settle on the urban extremities so as to supplement their meager incomes and food supply through the cultivation of crops, impossible in the heart of the city. These patterns persist today in Mexico, India, and the Near East, to mention just a few sectors of the world. In turn these farmers at the city's edge are functional to the maintenance of the urban populace, for they make available perishable commodities that the urban community with its poor storage and transportation facilities would be unable to import from remote regions.

Having considered the gross disposition of the elite and lower-class (and outcaste) groupings in the central city and the periphery, respectively, we can examine some of the finer ecological demarcations according to ethnic, occupational, and kinship affiliation that are generally subsumed under the broader class categories.

Subdivisions along ethnic and/or occupational lines are manifested in the preindustrial city in the numerous wards or quarters, well-defined neighborhoods with relatively homogeneous populations that develop special forms of social organization. Bokhara at the turn of the present century allegedly included 217 different residential quarters, many with their own leaders and special paraphernalia for their periodic ceremonial activities.[27]

Segregation by ethnic groups, which in turn are associated with specific occupations, occurs widely in preindustrial cities. The Jews in Europe have had their well-defined ghettos, persisting in some locales well into the twentieth century, and Jewish quarters have long been part of the urban scene throughout the Middle East. Ethnic quarters tend to be self-sufficient entities to the extent that urban living allows, physically and socially separated from the rest of the community. Often they have their own unique social structure—political leaders, schools, etc.—and even some ecological differentiation according to "class" within the quarters. It must not be thought that the Jews are alone in carrying out this role; there have been Muslim quarters in Chinese cities, Christian quarters in Near Eastern cities, and Hindu quarters in the urban areas of Central Asia, to name a few.[28]

Differentiation of land use according to occupation is usual. A special quarter, district, or street is allotted to a particular economic pursuit. Here are grouped merchants dealing in certain kinds of produce or handicraftsmen plying a specific trade. In Fez craftsmen have had shops strung along special streets, whereas a few groups, like potters, have had quarters all to themselves. Gray[29] in his description of Canton in the nineteenth century lists dozens of streets, each restricted to the shops of artisans and/or merchants dedicated to making and/or selling a specific product—paper objects, gongs and bells, pork fat, or betel and cocoa nuts. In a host of pre-industrial cities streets commonly bear the names of their occupational groups—the street of the goldsmiths, the street of the glass workers, and so on. Sometimes just a few blocks may be devoted to one occupation, while another group takes over farther along, with resultant name-changes several times along the length of the street.

This localization of particular crafts and merchant activities in segregated quarters or streets is intimately linked to the society's technological base. The rudimentary transport and communication media demand some concentration if the market is to operate: in this way producers, middlemen, retailers, and consumers alike can more readily interact. How much business could a seller of hides transact in a day if his prospective customers, the leather workers, had their shops scattered helter-skelter about the city? Moreover, the social organization, especially the guild system (see later chapters), itself largely interwoven with the technology, encourages the propinquity of members of an occupation, which in turn fosters group cohesion.

Other dimensions to occupational differentiation cut across the previously discussed elite-non-elite residential gradient. Domestic servants are one lower-class, or outcaste, element, that live in upper-class districts, in quarters provided by their employers, the better to serve their masters. As a further complication, which finds its counterpart in the social structure, merchant groups occupy a wide range of ecological positions. A few well-established businessmen are situated close to the principal markets at the city's core, whereas the least prosperous, including the outcaste foreign merchants, huddle on the urban fringe.[30]

Land use differentiation, aside from that related to class, ethnic, and/or occupational groupings, occurs along family lines. A particular family, or an extended kinship unit, may control a given street, forming a well-defined subsystem. If the family is prominent the street may bear its name, one apt to persist long after all remnants of the kinship group have died or moved away, as evidenced in some European and Latin American cities today.

Although sharp ecological differentiation along certain lines is characteristic of the feudal city, absent are a number of forms of land use specialization so typical of industrial cities. Frequently a single plot of land serves multiple functions in the non-industrial-urban milieu. Religious edifices functioning concurrently as schools are a not-uncommon sight. And markets are likely to be set up on the grounds adjoining the church, mosque, or temple. In medieval Europe a favorite spot for fairs was in or near the city's principal church. Or, we can turn to a description of Bokhara for a colorful portrayal of the multiple uses to which the zone around the religious structure may be put.[31]

Meschidi Namaziya, or Namazi-gah, is a great mosque, with an immense platform before it. . . . Prayers are read in it during the Ramazan and Kúrban; at which periods the public also resort there for amusement.

The whole square . . . is covered, on such occasions, with temporary booths, in which confectioners, vendors of dried fruit, . . . exhibit their tempting merchandize [sic] to the gaze of the crowds which rush to and fro; . . . Behind the tents and the booths, wrestlers show off their feats; races, also, are set on foot; and camels are made to fight.

The dearth of land use specialization is also attested to by the fact that the residential units of artisans and merchants often serve simultaneously as their places of work, the living quarters being behind or just above the shop. The ecological situation wherein a person may reside, produce, store, and sell his wares within the confines of the same structure has been a feature of preindustrial-urban life from the earliest cities in Mesopotamia down to the present day.[32]

To reiterate: the feudal city's land use configuration is in many ways the reverse of that in the highly industrialized communities. The latter's advanced technology fosters, and is in turn furthered by, a high degree of social and spatial mobility that is inimical to any rigid social structure assigning persons, socially and ecologically, to special niches. Moreover, the improved technology and the greater rationality of the economic organization in industrial cities both require and permit considerable specialization in land use. For example, rapid transit enables the urbanite to live far removed from his place of work.

Temporal Patterning

Implicit in the discussion of the spatial ordering of social relationships have been certain temporal patterns. With the poor technology, communication is necessarily slow and movement from one part of the city to another, relative to that in the industrial city, is most time consuming. Travel between cities or between rural and urban communities is a major undertaking, one limited to specialized groups—merchants, administrators, and the like. The preindustrial order requires a certain amount of intercity and intracity mobility, but nothing on a scale comparable to that in industrial cities where the technology demands and makes possible spatial movement in a grand manner. The labor force must be mobile, and scientists and other experts who man the key positions in the system must maintain a great deal of social contact if they are to keep it operating.

The temporal ordering of life within the city merits special comment. Activity proceeds at a slow pace, and the preindustrial urbanite, compared to industrial man, does not think of time as a "scarce commodity," except within broad limits such as days or weeks. The shopkeeper opens and closes his establishment at varying times as the spirit moves him. And keeping an appointment at a stated time is more the exception than the rule. Even businessmen may spend several hours in pleasant conversation before getting down to the matter at hand. All this is quite in keeping with the technology of the city, which typically lacks any precise measuring instruments. Clocks, a recent phenomenon, are mostly confined to the small urban upper class. The average person must observe the position of the sun or gauge time by the pealing of church bells and the like: in Muslim cities the periodic calls to prayer from the mosque orient the actor to the daily tempo of city life. One illustration of the crude time-reckoning technology, from about the turn of the present century, makes these generalizations more empirically meaningful.[33]

In Kabul and the principal cities time is kept by means of a sundial, but though there are tables printed in Persian of the daily difference between solar and mean time, the time given by them is only approximate, for the dials have been constructed for other latitudes, and they are fixed in the direction of the magnetic north instead of the true one.

Under these circumstances, people can hardly maintain rigid, time-bound schedules, even if such were their goal. Admittedly, chronological measurement over days, months, and years is much more precise. All preindustrial cities have had a calendric system, in large part used to standardize the routine of religious ceremonial activity.

Quite a different picture emerges in the industrial city. It demands of its populace extreme consciousness of time and provides the means for such. In industry the wheels must turn at just the right moment; the workers on the assembly line must synchronize their efforts with the tasks of others or costly bottlenecks will ensue. And science, the basis of modern technology, could never proceed without precise measurement of the "time factor."

Another distinguishing feature of the temporal distribution of activity in the non-industrial city is the restriction of so many activities to the daytime. The typical preindustrial city is without permanent artificial street lighting, making passage through the city difficult and dangerous at night. Handicraft activities, for example, have to be carried on during the day, and the work-day varies from season to season depending upon the number of hours of daylight. Of course, on ceremonial occasions torches, or similar devices, may be set up in the main squares, but urban night life on a grand scale is definitely a post-industrial development.

Inasmuch as the ecology mirrors the social structure, and vice versa, the succeeding chapters should clarify the points we have discussed.

NOTES TO CHAPTER IV

1. E. A. Kracke, Jr., "Sung Society: Change Within Tradition," *Far Eastern Quarterly,* XIV (August, 1955), 481-82; E. A. Kracke, Jr., *Civil Service in Early Sung China* (Cambridge: Harvard University Press, 1953), pp. 13ff.

2. Irene Taeuber, *The Population of Japan* (Princeton: Princeton University Press, 1958), pp. 26-27.

3. R. C. Majumdar *et al., An Advanced History of India* (2d ed.; London: Macmillan, 1950), p. 374.

4. Rhoads Murphey, *Shanghai: Key to Modern China* (Cambridge: Harvard University Press, 1953).

5. J. C. Russell, "Late Ancient and Medieval Population," *Transactions of the American Philosophical Society,* XLVIII (Philadelphia: American Philosophical Society, 1958), especially 37-101.

6. Roger Mols, *Introduction à la Démographie Historique des Villes d'Europe du XIVe au XVIIIe Siècle,* II (Louvain: Université de Louvain, 1955), 39.

7. E.g., Taeuber, *op. cit.,* pp. 25ff. We may also infer much from the data presented by Mols, *op. cit.* and by Ping-ti Ho, *Studies on the Popula-*

tion of China, 1368-1953 (Cambridge: Harvard University Press, 1959), Chapter X. Although the latter's materials do not bear directly upon cities, they point to the significance of disasters in feudal orders.

8. W. C. Brice, "Caravan Traffic Across Asia," *Antiquity,* XXVIII (June, 1954), 78-84.

9. George Sansom, *A History of Japan to 1334* (Stanford: Stanford University Press, 1958), p. 99.

10. E.g., Ching-kun Yang, *A North China Local Market Economy* (New York: Institute of Pacific Relations, 1944).

11. E.g., see Edward T. Williams, *China: Yesterday and Today* (5th ed. rev.; New York: Thomas Y. Crowell, 1935), pp. 165-82; Philip K. Hitti, *History of the Arabs* (3d ed. rev.; London: Macmillan, 1946), pp. 529-613; A. Bopegamage, *Delhi* (Bombay: University of Bombay, 1957), p. 53.

12. E.g., see Wolfram Eberhard, "Data on the Structure of the Chinese City in the Pre-Industrial Period," *Economic Development and Cultural Change,* IV (April, 1956), 253-68; J. Sauvaget, *Alep* (Paris: Librairie Orientaliste Paul Geuthner, 1941); Robert E. Dickinson, *The West European City* (London: Routledge and Kegan Paul, 1951); Pedro Armillas, "Mesoamerican Fortifications," *Antiquity,* XCVIII (June, 1951), 77-86.

13. George Woodcock, "Guanajuato," *Mexican Life,* XXXIV (December, 1958), 15.

14. G. T. Salusbury, *Street Life in Medieval England* (2d ed.; Oxford: Pen-in-Hand, 1948), p. 77.

15. *Ibid.,* pp. 90-91.

16. Austine Waddell, *Lhasa and its Mysteries* (New York: E. P. Dutton, 1906), pp. 340, 352.

17. Jacques Caillé, *La Ville de Rabat jusqu'au Protectorat Français,* I (Paris: Vanoest, 1949), 558.

18. S. Kesava Iyengar, *A Socio-Economic Survey of Hyderabad-Secunderabad City Area* (Hyderabad: Government Press, 1957), p. 353.

19. E.g., K. N. Venkatarayappa, *Bangalore: A Socio-Ecological Study* (Bombay: University of Bombay, 1957); Sevak Samaj Bharat, *Slums of Old Delhi* (Delhi: Atma Ram and Sons, 1958), pp. 28ff. Also, recent studies of Baroda, Bombay, Lucknow, Gorakhpur, and Calcutta, mimeographed summaries of which were examined by the author, lend dramatic support to this conclusion. For medieval Europe, see R. J. Forbes, *Studies in Ancient Technology,* I (Leiden: E. J. Brill, 1955), 175-76.

20. E.g., Mols, *op. cit.;* David Herlihy, *Pisa in the Early Renaissance* (New Haven: Yale University Press, 1958), pp. 47ff.

21. R. A. B. Ponsonby-Fane, *Kyoto* (Kyoto: Ponsonby Memorial Society, 1956), pp. 403ff.

22. E.g., Marcel Clerget, *Le Caire: Étude de Géographie Urbaine et d'Histoire Économique,* I (Cairo: E. and R. Schindler, 1934), 265; Horace Miner, *The Primitive City of Timbuctoo* (Princeton: Princeton University Press, 1953); F. Spencer Chapman, *Lhasa: The Holy City* (London: Chatto and Windus, 1938), pp. 167-68; Thomas O. Wilkinson, "Tokyo: A Demographic Study" (unpublished Ph.D. dissertation, Columbia University, 1957), p. 46; Justus M. van der Kroef, "The Indonesian City: Its Culture and Evolution," *Asia,* II (March, 1953), 27-28; Mols, *op. cit.,* p. 37.

23. Noel P. Gist, "The Ecology of Bangalore, India: An East-West Comparison," *Social Forces,* XXXV (May, 1957), 356-65.

24. Floyd Dotson and Lillian Ota Dotson, "Ecological Trends in the City of Guadalajara," *Social Forces*, XXXII (May, 1954), 367-74. Also see Pedro Yescas Peralta, "Estructura Social de la Ciudad de Oaxaca," *Revista Mexicana de Sociología*, XX (Septiembre-Diciembre, 1958), 769.

25. Leopold Rosenmayr, "Anotaciones sobre el Fenómeno de la 'Urbanización Allende de la Ciudad,'" *Revista Mexicana de Sociología*, XX (Septiembre-Diciembre, 1958), 737-38.

26. E.g., Chapman, *op. cit.*

27. O. A. Sukhareva, "Byt Zhilogo Kvartala Goroda Bukhary v Kontse XIX—Nachale XX Veka," *Akademiya Nauk Soyuza SSR, Institut Etnografii, Kratkie Soobshcheniya*, XXVIII (1957), 35-38.

28. E.g., J. Weulersse, "Antioche: Essai de géographie urbaine," *Bulletin d'Études Orientales*, IV (1934), 27-79; O. Olufsen, *The Emir of Bokhara and His Country* (London: William Heinemann, 1911).

29. John H. Gray, *Walks in the City of Canton* (Hongkong: De Souza, 1875).

30. van der Kroef, *op. cit.;* Sauvaget, *op. cit.*

31. Khanikoff, *Bokhara: Its Amir and its People,* trans. Clement A. De Bode (London: James Madden, 1845), p. 120.

32. Dickinson, *op. cit.;* Mary L. Shine, "Urban Land in the Middle Ages," in Richard T. Ely *et al., Urban Land Economics* (Ann Arbor: Edwards Bros., 1922), p. 79; Clerget, *op. cit.,* II, 140; Olufsen, *op. cit.,* Bopegamage, *op. cit.,* pp. 173ff.

33. Frank A. Martin, *Under the Absolute Amir* (London: Harper and Bros., 1907), pp. 91-92.

CHAPTER V

SOCIAL CLASS

ONE of the most striking of the features that set the preindustrial city apart from its industrial counterpart is the all-pervasiveness of its stratification system, above all the rigid class structure. We begin with an overview of class in the feudal city. But because we can hardly comprehend the family, economic, political, and educational structures, discussed further on, without reference to social class, we elaborate at some length upon special features of it in the pertinent chapters.

The Nature of Class

Social scientists concerned with social class have become entangled in a web of confusion, in part attributable to their failure to clarify their theoretical perspectives—including the reference points they utilize to delineate a class system. Because of the differing points of reference they consciously, or unconsciously, employ, they present conflicting pictures of the class patterns of feudal orders and their cities. A scientist, viewing the system as an outsider and using other social systems as his standard of comparison, is likely to come up with a different set of conclusions from those of a person who participates in the daily round of activities in a city and thereby frames a host of minor differentiations so as to stabilize his own actions. Consequently, a scientist who, as a participant observer, takes the viewpoint of the craftsman, merchant, or priest in a traditional Chinese city will discover more gradations in the social scale than one who, assuming a broader perspective, compares its class system with that in industrial-urban centers. Disagreements over the nature of a particular ordering of classes quickly dissipate when writers make explicit their theoretical perspectives.

Our formula concerning class patterns in the preindustrial city and the larger society is achieved by contrasting them with those in the industrial city and society; implicitly the folk order serves as another standard of comparison. We do not compare the class systems of cities in different cultural settings; nor do we examine possible changes through time in the class ordering of any particular city.

For us, a social class is a large body of persons who occupy a position in a social hierarchy by reason of their manifesting similarly valued objective criteria. These latter include kinship affiliation, power and authority, achievements, possessions, and moral and personal attributes. Achievements involve a person's occupational and educational attainments; possessions refer to material evidences of wealth; moral attributes include one's religious and ethical beliefs and actions; and personal attributes involve speech, dress, and personal mannerisms.[1]

Preindustrial cities across cultures display strong consistency in their class structure—in the kinds of criteria that are highly valued and the manner in which these are assigned in determining class position. Thus specific kinds of occupations are rated highly, and these are closely associated with certain kinds of achievements, greater power and authority, the "desirable" possessions, a particular kind of kinship system, and special moral and personal attributes. So too, the kinds of criteria that are devalued are very similar for cities from one culture to the next, and if a person has one lowly valued kind of criterion he is likely to have the others also, although the correlation is never perfect.

As we develop our argument, we shall contend that the preindustrial city is characterized by a bifurcated class structure comprising the elite or upper class, that which manifests the highly valued criteria, and the lower class, or mass populace, that which does not. The elite, though small, forming perhaps less than 5 to 10 per cent of the total social order, dominates both city and society. At the minimum, this literate group comprises the upper ranks of the governmental, religious, and educational bureaucracies. The bulk of the lower-status urbanites and the vast peasantry, two groups that share many traits, form the great commoner, or lower-class, group.

Few feudal societies and their cities are without an "outcaste" group as well. These persons are isolated from both the upper and lower classes, the respectable elements of the social order.

The preindustrial city's class structure, contrasted with the industrial-urban type, is distinguished by its rigidity and lack of mobility. Industrial-urbanization demands and furthers flexibility and looseness in the class system to an extent unheard of in the preindustrial city. Even the relative weighting of the criteria of class—personal attributes, for one—undergoes marked change.

Before launching into an analysis of the upper class, lower class, and outcaste group, we must demonstrate that the dominant element is an urban phenomenon and explain why it exists.

Urban Locus of the Elite

The preceding chapters have more or less taken for granted the urban character of the elite. Yet this pattern goes unrecognized by most social scientists. American sociologists who speak of "peasant societies," our feudal orders, are wont to assume as typical, patterns that are not rural but urban, and then associated only with the literate elite. They impute to the peasantry in traditional China, India, and other societies a way of life that is realized fully only among the upper class, city dwellers par excellence. The large extended family, for instance, erroneously assumed by many writers to be rural, is achievable in its full-blown form only by the literate urban elite.

One reason for the failure to see the elite as urban (though who ever heard of kings living in villages?) is that sociologists, and many anthropologists who should know better, have labeled as "villages," entities that stand between true peasant communities and the larger cities—that actually are market towns or small cities. Those who take Lewis'[2] study of Tepoztlán, in Mexico, as an exposition of the peasant way of life should stop to consider that this community, though rural in its orientation, is nevertheless a market town, and traditionally an administrative center, for a number of surrounding, considerably smaller, communities that are evidently much more rural in character. Some "upper-class" elements appear in Tepoztlán.

Or consider India. Here, for various cultural reasons, the smaller towns may be more "urban-like" than those of similar size in Mexico. A recent book, the *Twice-Born*,[3] describes itself as a study of an Indian village and apparently is accepted as such by many social scientists. Closer inspection reveals, however, that it included 2,417 residents (in 1951) and is a market center for a broad area. Until 1948 it apparently was larger, serving as an administrative center for an extensive region and the site of the ruler's palace. Far from being the nice little peasant village so dear to the hearts of social scientists, it must be counted a town or small city.

To a degree the Indian "village" of Senapur studied by Opler and Singh[4] also illustrates the point at issue. To judge by the writers' statistics, it contained about 1,400 persons, not even a third of whom were full-time agriculturists: most functioned as full-time non-agricultural specialists. Little wonder that this community displays so many urban traits.

Bear in mind that as late as the 1951 census, of all communities in India, those with fewer than 500 inhabitants were the most numerous.[5] It seems safe to conclude that these minuscule communities are more representative of the peasant way of life than are aggregations of several thousand people, especially when these include a wide variety of non-agriculturists and a small elite that in so many ways is more congruent with the upper class in the larger cities than with the rural peasantry. Awareness that market towns and small cities are distinctly non-rural entities—i.e., recognition of what are the extremes of the rural-urban continuum—makes it eminently clear that the upper class can only be perceived as urban, as an element quite foreign to village life.

The failure to define satisfactorily just what is rural or urban has led some social scientists erroneously to assume that because many in the upper class are large landowners, the elite are therefore largely rural. Others, however, have recognized the fundamentally urban nature of this stratum. Concerning upper-class elements in the Middle East, Patai[6] observes

. . . the preference for urban residence (and more precisely, residence in the capital city) by the owners of landed estates. The actual supervision of these estates has traditionally been entrusted to managers, while the landlord and his family lived in the city and had no direct contact whatsoever with the people whose work made it possible for him to live a life of leisure and luxury.

Likewise, the commentaries of Sinologists—Lang, Fei, Fried, and others[7]—support our contention that large landlords, and other elements of the elite, in traditional societies have been preponderantly urban.

Nor do we except the so-called "landed gentry" of medieval and later Europe. The nobility and other privileged families in the cities often maintained auxiliary homes in the country-side as symbols of high status, to which they repaired periodically either to escape the summer heat or for purposes of pleasure. But the European elite have been traditionally urban.[8] Even some of the lesser nobility, as in England, who spent a considerable portion of the year in the country in order to maintain surveillance over their rural holdings were fundamentally urban in their orientation.

Then too, the writings of Pirenne[9] and his followers, who emphasize the bourgeoisie's control over the European city of the late Middle Ages in northern France and the Low Countries, have convinced some social scientists that the nobility of that era were established elsewhere, in rural areas. But this was not the case even during the period of bourgeoisie ascendancy (essentially a short-lived one) in selected cities and was still less so in Europe as a whole or the Middle Ages in general. The fact that the nobility rather quickly regained control of the political apparatus in numerous cities wherein the emergent "middle class" had temporarily displaced them is evidence of their retention of an urban base. Indeed, had the more prosperous commoners wielded as much power in the urban government as some writers claim, there would have been little need for the French Revolution—essentially a revolt against the urban nobility—some centuries later.

We reiterate that throughout the preindustrial civilized world the upper class, and above all the society's ruling stratum, is urban in nature. But it is not enough merely to observe this fact; we must also present the reasons behind it. First, it seems apparent that the elite congregate in the cities partly because these are bastions of defense. Although they receive the brunt of any attack by foreign invaders, they nonetheless afford a degree of protection not attainable in the rural zones. So too, they offer shelter from the bandits that plague the country folk. The small rural community, on the other hand, can not command the resources for large-scale undertakings like constructing an encircling wall or maintaining a military force; as a result it is easy prey for marauders.

But more than this, members of the upper class, to ensure their dominance over the key societal organizations, and to reinforce their self-concept as the privileged group, must concentrate in urban areas rather than scatter a few here and a few there over the countryside. For only the urban milieu provides the means for sustained communication among members of the elite, both *within* and *between* communities.

Residence in a relatively compact area enables the dominant elements—especially the governmental, religious, and educational leaders—to sustain close ties. The high degree of density that characterizes the urban agglomeration permits considerable direct face-to-face contact in this social order where mass communication is non-existent. Without such propinquity, the various administrative officers could not be apprised of each other's actions, nor could the religious and educational heads consult with the governmental leaders. Intensive interaction among officials makes a cohesive policy attainable and enhances the "collective representations" of the ruling group. As noted, even large landlords who do not occupy formal bureaucratic posts seek to maintain an urban base so as to influence the decisions of officialdom and thereby preserve their eliteness.

Inescapably, the intellectuals congregate in the city. For them, access to library facilities, scanty though these be by industrial standards, is absolutely essential, and since only the very wealthy subsidize libraries, these are concentrated in the largest cities. Nonetheless, with the limited use of the written word, learned men depend largely upon interpersonal contacts for the exchange and perpetuation of ideas and information; so it was in ancient Athens and so it has been in a host of other centers of learning. To the cities, therefore, flow those in quest of advanced knowledge.

Urban living is demanded of the elite for purposes of intercommunity contact as well. Officials could never govern a society unless they resided in cities straddling the major "thoroughfares." Intrasocietal communication, rudimentary at best, rarely extends to the remote corners of the realm; "all roads lead to Rome," not to any outlying village.

Localization in urban areas, besides providing protection and multiplying interpersonal contacts, enables the elite to profit from the presence of merchants, servants, craftsmen, astrologers, musicians, and others offering a wide variety of services. It is these who subsidize the elite's sybaritic existence, on a plane far removed from the grinding drudgery of the poor. Eschewing any form of manual work, the upper class gathers around it a large body of attendants to fill its varied "needs."

In turn the sheer presence of the upper stratum in the city enhances the latter's chances of survival and expansion. Commanding the political means to extract the agricultural "surplus" even from a "starving" peasantry, the ruling group uses this to support itself and to maintain the complex urban apparatus upon which it depends.

The more potent the elite, the grander the city. The more services and luxury goods the elite commands, the larger and more specialized can be the urban population that supports the upper class, and the more likely is the privileged stratum in a particular city to expand its membership, either by absorbing some of the city's lower class or by attracting upper-class persons from other portions of the realm.

Of the feudal cities, the societal capital is by far the most imposing. Into it stream the best of the products and the services the society has to offer; to it are attracted individuals who seek to attach themselves in some way to the upper class, or more specifically the ruling element, and thus pick up "a few crumbs from the king's table." In some societies, say traditional Korea, the capital has been the only real cultural center, and anyone who aspires to success must set up residence therein.[10]

The pre-eminence of the capital implies a status hierarchy within the elite itself, based partly upon the relative ranking of one's community of residence. This is most obvious among government officials—the most powerful residing in the capital, with the lesser lights located in the provincial capitals or small administrative centers.[11]

Yet these gradations evanesce when the elite is compared with the heterogeneous upper class of industrial-urban societies. Furthermore, when set off against the feudal city's lower class and the peasantry, it displays a remarkable degree of cultural homogeneity. For the upper class experiences much more social interaction, personally and symbolically, than the rest of the populace; as will be emphasized, its formal indoctrination in the traditional learning, effected through its urban concentration, standardizes its thinking and its lifeways. So in China, throughout the Arab world, in many parts of medieval Europe, and across the cultural and linguistic diversity of India we find far greater standardization of speech, beliefs, and customs among the elite than in the lower class, most particularly the peasantry. Such homogeneity is attainable only because of the urban-centeredness of the upper class.

Why An Elite?

A privileged stratum is absent in the simple folk order. The latter's technology is insufficient to support a true elite: everyone must work at food production in order to survive. In full-fledged feudal orders, on the other hand, the technology and the social organization have developed to the point that some persons can function as full-time non-agriculturists— as rulers, scribes, merchants, or artisans. This group is necessarily small, for the amount of surplus food and raw materials is still so minute that few people can evade the necessity of engaging in some form of primary economic activity. The technology simply can not support a large "leisured" class;

only the industrial order permits this. Here we have one of the most striking distinctions between the industrial and the preindustrial city.

But all this does not tell us why an elite exists in feudal orders in the first instance, a far more difficult issue that has taxed the minds of a number of writers. Wittfogel in his highly publicized book, *Oriental Despotism*,[12] contends that the ruling elite invariably has grown out of the need to manage and control "large-scale" irrigation works. As stated, his notion should hold for the kinds of societies we term "feudal." His argument, derived in part from Marx's observations concerning Asiatic societies, rests upon the assumption that irrigation is essential to the development of a stable food surplus and that this "hydraulic" agriculture requires an administrative apparatus controlled by an elite. Durkheim earlier argued that an increased division of labor requires some specialists to co-ordinate the activities of other specialists. This principle is applied by Wittfogel but on a more limited basis. (An essential part of his argument is that the elite is a "despotic" one, but more of this in later chapters.)

Wittfogel's hydraulic determinism—though appealing in its simplicity—is grossly oversimplified and, as such, has evoked criticism from a number of quarters. We, too, find fault with it. The elite in preindustrial civilized societies does more than merely co-ordinate hydraulic activities. If the society and the city are to survive, the activities of specialists of various kinds —military men, merchants, and craftsmen—must be integrated. If metal ore from the mines is to reach artisans in the city, if the food surplus is to be distributed to urbanites, and so on, some group must command the complex apparatuses of the society. Thus, urban centers—relatively compact aggregations of non-agriculturists—could never have arisen and been sustained were there not an elite to manage and control a relatively wide range of human activities, a point elaborated upon immediately below.

The Upper Class

Although the specific composition of the various classes differs somewhat among feudal societies, depending upon the presence of idiosyncratic values, the similarities are more striking. To some, India may appear as an exception. But the assemblage of castes in Indian cities forms an upper-lower-outcaste triad. The elite, the highly Sanskritized entity, differs little from upper classes elsewhere. Overconcern with caste has blinded some social scientists to the fundamental semblances between this social order and others of the preindustrial civilized type.

The privileged stratum in preindustrial cities and their societies includes at the minimum the officials of the political, religious, and educational bureaucracies. Members of other occupational groups may belong, but the aforementioned are never excluded.

In all feudal realms—traditional China, Japan, India, the Middle East, those in medieval Europe, and so on—political leaders are accorded elite status. Control of the instruments of power and authority is crucial to the survival of the ruling group, especially if it is to defend itself against rival elites in other societies. And through such authority it siphons off the economic "surplus" to support itself and other non-agricultural urbanites. It is erroneous to assume that surpluses are constituted simply as a result of technological forces, although relatively advanced technology is necessary if a surplus is to be produced. Through an appropriate ideology, reinforced by coercion in the form of taxes and tributes, the elite induces the peasantry to increase its production and to relinquish some of its harvest to the urban community. In other words, it must persuade many persons subsisting, relative to industrial standards, on the very margins of existence, under conditions of near starvation or malnutrition, to surrender food and other items that they themselves could readily use.[13] Not only does the upper class function without engaging in physical labor, but it arrogates to itself "luxury" items that enable it to achieve a life style that dramatically sets it apart from the lower class; in turn this ostentation reinforces its power and authority.

A potent element of the elite are the key religious leaders (many of whom also serve as astrologers or physicians). In theocracies, such as traditional Tibet or numerous of the preindustrial civilized orders of antiquity, the political head and the primary religious leader have been one and the same person. Even in societies where the chief priest is not in supreme command, his influence pervades the social structure. Religious leaders are instrumental in providing moral justification for the total social order, including the dominance of the society by a privileged few. Much of the power and authority of governmental officials, in fact, derives from certain "rationalizations" in the sacred literature, for generally only religious functionaries are capable of interpreting these writings. Moreover, most of the norms governing life in the upper class are prescribed in the religious literature.

Many of the religious functionaries double as educators; the entire educational apparatus is difficult to separate from the religious. For the educational system is the mechanism by which the formal religious norms sustaining the elite are propagated; in turn, matters pertaining to religion make up a large proportion of the academic curricula. Remember, the elite alone has access to formal education, one feature that sets this group apart from the illiterate urban and rural lower-class elements.

This interrelationship of the educational, religious, and governmental structures inevitably means that the leaders of each of these hierarchies depend upon one another for support. It is this that makes the exposition of the preindustrial city seem so circular—we always come back to where we started, so interrelated are these phenomena we describe.

Still other occupational groups may gain entrée into the

elite. Landlords commonly form part of the upper class. Some have no other calling. However, political, educational, and religious leaders often double as landholders—either this, or the bureaucracies they command control extensive parcels of landed property. Unquestionably a paramount source of wealth in the feudal order, land is highly immutable through time and during periods of social upheaval; its ownership may ensure one of a continual food supply. Landholding can, moreover, be made a "respectable" pursuit. Peasants being easily subjugated, the landlord evades the necessity of working with his hands to gain a livelihood. And landholding does not commit one to usury and other pecuniary activities or to the heterogeneous social relationships that are responsible for much of the opprobrium directed against business enterprise.

The military, one segment of the governmental bureaucracy, deserves special attention. Some elements of it are admitted into the feudal city's "charmed circle." In Tokugawa Japan the samurai, the military leaders, were definitely of the nobility, as were the war chiefs in pre-Columbian American cities. And the dominant military figures in Islamic cities have been accepted as of the elite. But what about traditional China? Sinologists tend to disagree over whether the higher echelons of the military always ranked within the most privileged stratum.[14] The ideal norms tended to exclude them; yet, as some recent writings observe, they did enjoy high status. No doubt contradictory functional requirements were operating here. In traditional China, as elsewhere, the military role, stressing force, threatened the status of the literati, who based their authority upon their knowledge of the sacred literature. At the same time, the latter were dependent upon the armed forces for protection and had to cater to the leaders of this body, who thereby became at least marginal members of the elite.

A few merchants, though ideally excluded from membership in the elite, manage to achieve high status. Most are unequivocally in the lower class or outcaste groups, however.

As a consequence of their wide interpersonal contacts within the lower orders of society, their necessary recourse to manipulation (as occurs in money lending) as a means of getting ahead, and other factors, they threaten the authority structure of the elite. Nevertheless, they must be permitted to thrive; the city depends upon commerce for its very existence. Yet this opens up the possibility for some merchants of the commoner, though rarely of the outcaste, group to amass wealth and thereby to use this to gain an elite position.[15] But more of this later.

Because of its animately powered technology, the preindustrial city and the society at large lack many of the specialized occupations that enjoy high status in the industrial-urban milieu. The emergence of scientists—including physicists, doctors, and chemists—and a host of other highly educated experts and technicians has been associated with the development of a large "middle class," a phenomenon that, relatively speaking, is lacking in the non-industrial urban setting. Such experts are rarely required, nor could they be supported, in the preindustrial civilized order.

Specific Composition of the Lower Class

The make-up of the lower class differs markedly from that of the elite. First of all, the lower echelons of the religious and governmental structures are part of this commoner group: not all the personnel in the society's strategic bureaucracies are members of the elite. A similar point can be made with regard to the military. The topmost leaders generally are members of the urban upper class, but the ordinary soldier is usually drawn from the lower strata, including the outcastes. As to religious personnel, those who serve the commoners generally lack the highly valued objective criteria of class and are therefore part and parcel of the humbler group.

Crucial elements of this class are many merchants, large

and small, and the bulk of the artisanry, the handicraft workers. (Both merchants and artisans have representatives among the outcastes also.) The preindustrial city's artisans, by the standards of the folk society or the peasant communities in the feudal order, are highly skilled workers; however, their output, compared to that of skilled workmen in the industrial system, is scanty indeed. Nonetheless, through purely handicraft methods they manufacture a fairly wide range of items— shoes, utensils, and other utilitarian products for all ranks of the urban community, and luxury items for the elite that often involve fine, intricate handiwork. Without these lower-class artisans, the rulers could not bask in such splendrous surroundings.

Unskilled laborers form another segment of the urban lower class. The presence in every preindustrial city of these workmen is usually overlooked by historians and others who glorify the skilled craftsmen of the feudal world. Numerous tasks that in the highly industrialized environment are accomplished by machines are here fulfilled by humans. The city teems with servants, burden-bearers, messengers, animal-drivers, ditch-diggers, and others. For persons of the lower class, these occupations, though humble, are not considered truly ignominious; they enjoy a measure of respectability denied to those in typical outcaste pursuits.

The ranks of the city's lower class are swelled by part-time or full-time farmers on the urban fringe. Maintaining close contacts with the urban community, some, though far from all, are functionally marginal members of it, participating as they do in various social activities, particularly those that attract the lower class.

The urban lower class evinces some internal gradations of status, though to a lesser degree than the privileged stratum. The small shopkeeper or the ordinary skilled worker assuredly ranks higher than the unskilled laborer, while the master artisan or the prosperous merchant, if not in one of the outcaste ethnic groups, is a cut above any of these. Even so, too much can be made of the internal distinctions within the upper or the lower class; they pale to insignificance when these two broad strata are contrasted with one another.

Concerning the relations of the urban lower class and the peasantry, these bodies differ in numerous respects; yet, set in contrast to the elite, they share a surprising number of traits. Although the urban lower class is usually a notch above the peasantry, looking down upon the latter as backward and rustic, from a societal perspective the two merge to form one broad, lower-class group.

We revert to a point earlier alluded to, namely that the lower class, especially the peasantry, lacking the standardizing mechanism of formal education and the continuity this provides over space and time, varies from one community to another—in its speech, dress, customs, and beliefs—far more widely than does the elite. Lower-class elements in traditional China—both urban and rural—could barely communicate over any distance, for numerous of the regional vernaculars were mutually unintelligible. While in Indian cities the elite have been linked through a common grounding in the sacred traditions, spanning a potpourri of cultural and linguistic regions, the lower class and outcastes have displayed much less homogeneity throughout the society. With industrialization many of these community and regional differentials evaporate, although, significantly, such processes as "individualization" and intensive occupational specialization induced by the advanced technology create new kinds of diversity among industrial urbanites.

Contrasting Life Styles of the Upper and Lower Classes

Upper-class persons, we earlier remarked, are likely to possess the "correct" kinship ties, to engage in the most prestigious occupations, to evidence the most highly valued possessions and achievements and moral and personal attributes, and to wield a high degree of power and authority. We elaborate upon the factor of kinship in the section on the family, occupation and possessions within the chapter on economics, power and authority in our discussion of political structure, moral attributes in the realm of religion, and special kinds of achievements in the section devoted to education. Here we need only trace briefly the interrelationships among these items before focusing our attention upon personal attributes, singularly obvious markers of social class in the feudal city.

Universally, the upper class engages in mental, non-manual work; the more physically taxing and distasteful—as well as least remunerative—occupations fall to the humbler strata. The preferred pursuits invest the elite with much power and authority, in turn reinforcing its privileged status. In this social order with its still small surplus and limited opportunities for economic expansion, the upper class must employ autocratic measures to preserve its dominance; permitting the "disadvantaged" access to certain "scarce" goods and services would simply undermine its own status.

Eliteness is ordinarily prescribed by birth into one of the proper kinship groups. Upper-class households are larger, embracing a wider range of relatives, than lower-status family units. Maintaining a broad kin group as a single functioning entity requires extensive financial resources and a stable power position. In turn the elite's extended family aids and abets its members' formal education and entrance into the high-status occupations, for these positions are filled primarily by selection according to the particularistic criteria of family or friendship ties. Likewise, in the lower class one's family background largely determines one's future career or life chances.

Returning to formal education, such is attainable only by the elite, demanding as it does considerable leisure and plentiful resources. In turn, higher education is essential if one is to gain entrée into the privileged occupations. Through formal schooling one attains the all-important symbols of literacy and familiarity with the sacred writings, and these enable one to acquire the moral and spiritual attributes that are deemed praiseworthy. The elite alone has the resources of leisure and wealth to fulfil the ideal behavior patterns, especially the performance of the complex rites demanded in the sacred writings. Furthermore, ordinarily only this stratum possesses the means to purchase "luxury" goods—richly furnished homes, expensive jewelry, elaborate clothing, and the like— and to support and cater to certain of the arts. Conspicuous consumption on the part of the elite reinforces its status, helping to transmute its assumed power into authority. We elaborate upon these various patterns and their mutual relationships in future chapters.

Our attention focuses upon the criterion of personal attributes—*manners, dress,* and *speech*—that, more than any other, make apparent the distinctions among classes in the preindustrial city, proclaiming the disparate life styles of each for all the world to see. The unique and all-pervading role of personal attributes in non-industrial cities is generally disregarded by American sociologists, even by specialists on class—probably because these status-markers have so little meaning in industrial-urban communities, most pertinently in the United States.

Strong emphasis is given to *manners* in the preindustrial city, certain patterns of action being prescribed for particular classes and even substrata within these. In traditional Chinese cities a lower-class person has had to give way to any high-status individuals he encounters on the street.[16] Observers in Korean and Japanese cities have noted the different modes of bowing, including the depth of the bow and its duration and frequency, as reflecting the class positions of the persons involved. In all feudal cities—from Cairo to Delhi to Kabul to Tokyo—class and other status distinctions, including those within the family, rigidly determine who sits where in a room, who goes first through a door, who precedes whom on the street, etc.

Descriptions of Tibetan cities record some of the personal mannerisms that have expressed class distinctions. Shen and Liu[17] observe that whenever the high political leaders mount or dismount from their horses,

> . . . riders are to climb down and salute. Pedestrians should stand aside, with their hats in their hands and their tongues hanging out.

Bell[18] describes other patterns in Lhasa that bear upon our point.

> As to how far, if at all, the host goes to meet the guest, that depends on their respective ranks. If the latter be greatly superior, the host will go outside the door of the house and even beyond to meet him. If slightly superior, it will be sufficient to go to the door of his room. If the guest's rank be far lower than his own, he barely rises from his seat.

Some of the ritual reinforcing status differentiations of this sort in preindustrial cities is extremely elaborate and time consuming.[19]

Dress is a still more visible indicator of status in feudal cities. Osgood[20] emphasizes the differences in the day-by-day attire of the commoners and of the upper class (the Yangpan) at the turn of the present century in Seoul, Korea.

> A gentleman of wealth and position wore a long flowing gown with full sleeves of generous proportions over his other clothing, or sometimes several of these robes, one on top of another. . . . High rank and the number of tunics were correlated, some bearing embroidered insignia—a stork or phoenix for civil officers, and an oriental unicorn, a lion, or a tiger for the military leaders. . . . In general, silk was practically restricted to the Yangpan class, both men and women wearing it, whereas the common people had to be content with hemp . . . or cotton. . . .
> A slightly more subtle difference between the classes showed in the hats worn by the men. The gentleman's regular head covering was the most distinctive Korean headdress, with a crown in the form of a truncated cone and a wide straight brim, the whole finely woven and sometimes resting on a stepped pyramidal inner hat of the same material sandwiched in between the brimmed top piece and the head-

band, which was tightly bound around the temples on coming of age and was not taken off thereafter. Such a hat would not survive anything but gentle treatment and consequently was the mark of a man not engaged in physical labor, at least at the time.

The literati of traditional China dressed in keeping with their special status, like garments being expressly forbidden to other persons. Membership in the various Indian castes (in turn subsumed under broad class groups) is often signalized by differing clothing styles. Throughout medieval Europe the lower class was clearly distinguished from the elite by its general mode of dress. Even in Elizabethan England commoners were prohibited by law from wearing clothing fashioned from gold or silver cloth, velvet, furs, and other "luxury" materials.[21]

Permit us to define "dress" rather broadly, and thereby to include the comments of a woman of the elite for a Chinese city of the present century.[22]

In addition to the coolies who actually carried the chair, there was a head coolie who ran alongside the chair. . . . This man's duty was to carry important documents Father was taking with him. . . . Ahead of the chair ran a coolie who carried a red umbrella on the end of a long handle. This umbrella was a signal to all who saw it that an official of high rank followed right behind and that they must make way.

Even at night, disparities in status were illumined, as in Persian cities some decades ago.[23]

Those who do go out carry lanterns, as few cities in Persia are lighted. The lantern shows by its size the rank of the Persian passing. The simple house owner will go out with a small paper lantern of a few inches in diameter, whereas servants of the governor general precede him carrying lanterns of the same pattern, but of two feet in diameter.

As with personal mannerisms, dress may differentiate elements within classes. Occupational groups and religious sects often are identifiable by their garb. In traditional Cairo or Kabul or Bokhara the color of one's turban has proclaimed one's calling. Every complex social order uses dress as a status-marker, but the norms governing social action in this realm are especially rigid and all-pervasive in the preindustrial-urban milieu.

Speech, another personal attribute, is a highly sensitive status indicator in the feudal order. Upper- and lower-class persons employ quite divergent linguistic patterns, as do subgroups within classes; ruralites *vs.* urbanites, men *vs.* women, old people *vs.* young people, and occupational groups too. Korean, Japanese, Tibetan, Chinese, Uzbek, Arabic, Persian, numerous languages of India, various languages of traditional Europe—e.g., Greek, Italian, German, Norwegian—all contain forms that reflect the class structure of the city or society in question.[24]

Upper-class speech everywhere differs from that of the humbler strata in vocabulary and grammar and often in phonology (viz., the sounds employed as well as pitch and stress). The educated elite utilize lexical and grammatical forms that the abysmally poor and illiterate rarely have the opportunity to hear, much less acquire. The speech of the commoners is viewed by the upper class as "vulgar" and ungrammatical. While class distinctions in the realms of vocabulary and grammar may be rather easily perceived by the social scientist, the phonological differences in the speech of the elite and the commoners often go undetected by persons lacking linguistic training, though certainly not by actors in the system. Upper-class speakers of Uzbek affecting to pronounce the numerous Arabic and Persian loanwords in the language in a manner they deem "correct"—though it might not seem such to the native speaker of Arabic or Persian—utilize sounds that strike the rest of the Uzbek populace as foreign. In South India today, educated speakers of the literary Dravidian tongues regularly employ sounds that are absent in lower-class speech. One Tamil-speaking Indian informed me that in his city upper-class persons occasionally taunt members of the lower stratum by asking them to pronounce certain sounds restricted to the educated speech and derive amusement from the latter's awkward efforts to do so. Too, the lower strata in many Mexican cities still employ intonation patterns that set them off unequivocally from the upper class. Though industrialization is rapidly transforming this situation, it so persists that certain Mexican movie stars dramatically alter their linguistic patterns, particularly as regards intonation, as they enact varying class roles.

The upper-lower class distinctions in non-industrial cities are rendered more complex by the presence of different varieties of a language as employed by the educated elite. In Dravidian India, among the Turks in Central Asiatic cities, in cities of Chinese, Persian, or Arabic speech, in ancient Rome,[25] and in numerous other cities, upper-class persons, specifically the educated adult males, utilize two "levels" of a language—a formal style and an everyday, informal brand. Unlettered persons, on the other hand, command but a colloquial type of speech which, as suggested above, is distinct from both the informal and formal styles of the educated in vocabulary, grammatical forms, and, frequently, sound patterns as well.

The elite's formal speech is modeled after the literary, i.e., the standard written, language.[26] It differs from the educated informal tongue in its lexical and morphological features and quite often in its phonology. The distinctive sound patterns employed by upper-class Telugu speakers as they shift from informal to formal speech have been discussed in some detail by Andrée F. Sjoberg.[27] The bulk of the sounds peculiar to the formal speech have entered Telugu through lexical loans from Sanskrit, the sacred, literary language introduced into south India by the Hindu conquerors. When utilizing the numerous Sanskrit loans in formal Telugu the educated Telugu speaker seeks to emulate the "ideal" pronunciation of Sanskrit and therefore employs special phonological patterns; when he shifts to the informal variety of Telugu he drops many of these "Sanskrit" sounds. Similarly, formal Arabic differs from the vernaculars in that many of its grammatical and phonological

forms approximate the language of the Koran, and the speaker
of it is considered an educated man, one steeped in the
sacred literature.

Facility in the use of formal speech, acquired through
formal indoctrination, is a prerogative of the privileged stratum. Being closest to the written language, the formal variety
has come to be relatively standardized over time and space,
whereas the vernaculars, including that of the elite, have
undergone far greater change through the centuries; they vary
appreciably among cities and from one rural community to
the next.

The formal speech of the elite is reserved for use on special
occasions—in public addresses, in the classroom, during worship. As such it sets the upper class apart and lends an aura
of mystery to their activities; the commoners typically do not
comprehend this speech form. In many transitional societies
the formal speech is utilized today over the radio, and to an
extent in the cinema, but a mere segment of the populace is
reached through this means. Internal strains are created as
various people agitate for more democracy in disseminating
information, and this is a necessitude if the industrial-urban
order is to advance.

Besides the distinctions between upper- and lower-class
speech and the frequent existence of formal and informal
varieties of the former, honorifics—special grammatical forms,
chiefly verbs, nouns, and pronouns, that reflect the relative
statuses of speakers—are widely employed by both upper-
and lower-class persons, though the specific usages may vary
to a degree among different strata. Educated Korean speakers
draw upon at least four to five series of honorifics—each of
which has its own distinctive grammatical forms—to express
differing statuses, particularly those of class. In Japanese the
different levels of honorifics even have their formal and informal varieties. Honorifics in some Asiatic languages are
extended to refer to the property of the person in question.
Thus a Tibetan lama writes:[28]

The horse of a higher-rank person had to be addressed in honorific style! Our autocratic cat, stalking across the courtyard on some mysterious business, would be addressed by a servant: "Would honourable Puss Puss deign to come and drink this unworthy milk?"

In Europe honorifics have been less extensively employed, and their impact has been further tempered by industrialization; yet traces of honorifics persist in many cities of Scandinavia, Germany, and eastern and southern Europe. An upper-class person speaking to one of lower status, notably an employee, is likely to utilize pronouns and verbal endings that express the latter's inferior role. Conversely, a higher-ranking person is addressed by forms denoting his superior status.

Apart from the mechanisms of class-differentiation embodied within a language, a not-uncommon pattern in literate preindustrial societies, resulting from some form of cultural or political conquest, is the introduction of a new language, one that sets off the rulers from the ruled. Persian was for centuries the primary language of the elite in cities of western Turkestan and Afghanistan, whereas the urban commoners spoke one of the Turkic languages or Pushtu, as the case may be. At one time Chinese was spoken by the upper class in Korean cities, in the past Danish was the upper-class speech of Norway, and so on. From the societal capital and its court the impact of the new language radiates slowly outward.

By now the reader may wonder about the relevance for urban sociology of this discourse on personal attributes. Apart from reflecting and reinforcing the rigid class structure in the non-industrial city, the nature of personal attributes strikes at the core of much of the theorizing in the field of sociology. Wirth and his adherents more or less assumed that the secondary-group environment that is the urban community is inevitably correlated with unstructured interpersonal relationships, as opposed to the primary group-like orientation of the primitive community or the rural village. But the empirical evidence reveals that many secondary-group relations in the preindustrial city are in fact highly institutional-

ized: one's class position (as well as age and sex) are visible
to all concerned, eliciting well-defined responses.

The distinctiveness of personal attributes in the non-industrial city makes it almost impossible to evade one's class (or
other status ranking), whether in a strange locale or on a
crowded city street. Individual, or group, anonymity is unachievable. In a city where the elite wear fashionable clothing
and the poor mere rags and tatters, dress at a glance advertises one's class position. With respect to speech, the actor is
perennially confronted by others who, through special linguistic forms, either deride him or set him on a pedestal, a
continual socialization process that reminds him of his relative
status and defines for him the acceptable mode of behavior
in any given situation.

Personal mannerisms are of theoretical import inasmuch
as they can be revised only through years of purposeful effort.
In the preindustrial city overhauling one's speech habits is
most difficult of all; the commoner, lacking access to formal
education, can never really duplicate the cultivated speech of
the upper class. The inherent conservatism of language habits
is demonstrated, for example, in European cities. The class
structure of these communities has been extensively altered;
yet some of the linguistic status-markers persist, giving the
actor the impression of greater class rigidity than the high
degree of occupational mobility, resulting from industrialization and urbanization, would seem to indicate.

By way of comparison we glance at American cities, which
have lacked any feudal tradition. Here personal attributes are,
by and large, no longer effective class indicators. One can not
identify with certainty the class position of most individuals
encountered on the street. Consequently, persons of relatively
low ranking can at least occasionally escape the status ordinarily defined for them on the basis of occupation or income.
Unlike his preindustrial-urban cousin, industrial man steps out
of his class temporarily by dining at a plush hotel or attending
exclusive night clubs. Through these periodic excursions up

the social ladder he acquires a greater understanding of higher-class modes of behavior, intensifying his desire to elevate himself and, often, actually enabling him to adopt some of the more desired status symbols.

The haziness of personal attributes, being meaningful as class-markers only at the very extremes, is associated with the considerable social and spatial mobility—required and made possible by industrialization—and the advent of mass education and mass communication, which, among other effects, act to standardize speech habits through a wide range of industrial-urban environments.

The Outcastes

Not to be overlooked in the feudal city's status hierarchy are the outcaste groups. Sharing many of the traits of the lower class, they are socially distinct, nonetheless, a hiatus that is reinforced by their ecological segregation from both the elite and the lower class. The outcastes are part of, yet apart from, the life of the non-industrial city. On the one hand, they perform some functions of utmost significance to the city; on the other, they are continually subject to scorn and ridicule. While the lower class, despite its obviously disadvantaged role, enjoys a measure of respect in the society at large, the marginal groups are often viewed as non-human, as little more than animals, and they have almost no legal rights.

Who are the outcastes? Slaves, those persons who are the property of others, are a component of almost all non-industrial civilized societies, though more prominently in ancient ones, wherein the technology was relatively simple. Slave labor has been employed in the erection of public buildings, irrigation works, and other efforts requiring a large, servile labor force. And a number of preindustrial cities have down into the twentieth century utilized slaves as household servants.

The occupations of slaves and commoners often overlap; yet socially (and legally) the two groups have been clearly distinguished.

Outcastes, other than slaves, include groups like the Eta of Japan, the untouchables (or Harijans) of India, the Hazara Mongols of Afghanistan, various elements in Tibet and Korea, and so on.[29] Most perform those tasks the society considers defiling. Though the composition of this group varies somewhat from one social system to the next, generally included are night-soil carriers, leather workers, butchers, many barbers, midwives, prostitutes, dancers, lepers, etc. Many of these are subsumed under the "mean" people of traditional China, a crucial element of all the major cities.

> The lowest social class of all was the so-called "mean people," a social stratum below that of the commoners. They were few in numbers and were made up of actors, barbers, members of other lowly professions, prostitutes, and domestic slaves. Such people were regarded as being greatly inferior to all others and were excluded from the examinations and therefore from any opportunity to rise in the social scale.[30]

The aforementioned groups, forming *one outcaste type,* are, with rare exceptions, illiterate. *Another outcaste type* includes groups, functioning primarily as merchants, each of which supports its own small literati. Illustrative of these are ethnic minorities like the Jews of medieval European and Middle Eastern cities and the Muslims of Lhasa and various traditional Chinese communities. Because of their domination of strategic aspects of urban economic life, they are better off financially, and to a degree socially, than the illiterate outcastes.

Nonetheless, the outcastes as a whole differ from the upper and lower classes in their kinship affiliations, and in matters of power and authority, possessions and achievements, and moral and personal attributes. Just as the elite insulates itself from the commoners through a distinctive life style, so too an institutionalized set of personal attributes demarcates the outcastes from both of these strata. Outcaste groups employ distinctive speech forms, personal mannerisms, and clothing. Thus the Jews of medieval Europe and the Middle East, the Eta of Japan, and numerous other minority groups in feudal cities have worn special garb. Malcolm's description of the Parsi minority in the Persian city of Yezd indicates that until the 1880s the community at large forced the Parsis to twist their turbans instead of folding them, denied them various colors, and prohibited rings, umbrellas, and other items.[31] As one outcaste occupational grouping, prostitutes have been subject to various clothing restrictions: in late medieval London they were prohibited from wearing certain silks, furs, and, at one time, wools.[32] Or they have gone about many feudal cities unveiled, being set apart from respectable women.

The outcaste's status is an inherited one; his chances of entering the mainstream of feudal society are slight, less than those of a commoner. The lower class, along with the elite, depreciates intermarriage with outcastes.

The universality of outcastes in culturally diverse preindustrial civilized societies must be explained. Several factors come into play. One is that the technology, being sufficient to support only a small, literate elite and a few skilled workmen, demands unremitting physical labor for the performance of most tasks. In this situation, slavery—historically more a part of the urban than of the rural scene[33]—has provided rulers with a readily disciplined labor force to carry out, at the minimal cost of keeping these workers alive, large-scale construction projects like public buildings, roads, irrigation canals, etc.

Moreover, to sustain its power and authority (the nature of which is detailed in later chapters), the upper class seeks to ostracize persons who pose a threat to the status quo. It is because elements of the society—including the elite—require the performance of certain despised, or "defiling," activities that some persons are permitted to pursue these, all the while removed beyond the pale of respectability. The result: the upper class "has its cake and eats it too." As an instance, stern religious injunctions in Hindu and Buddhist cities against the taking of life are in effect; notwithstanding, if leather goods are desired, animals must be slaughtered— thus the outcaste leather workers. And all non-industrial cities harbor prostitutes; but as long as these are socially isolated they do not disrupt the normal male-female relations or the family system: hence their clients can "sin" respectably.

More potent threats to the power and authority structure, and the supporting value system, are the merchants and entertainers of various sorts. We consider these briefly. Businessmen, or merchants, fall into the lower class or the outcaste groups. Every city tends to have some in the latter category, often large numbers of them. Why does the businessman occupy such a lowly status? One reason is that he is thrown into contact with a wide variety of social groups within the community and, if he is a traveling merchant, with outsiders as well: as such he is a potential disseminator of new and heretical ideas. And rubbing elbows with people from all walks of life in itself has a denigrating effect upon his position. Over and beyond this, success in the business world rests upon manipulation, speculation, and "expertness," rather than upon tradition and the appeal to absolutes (viz., the possession of "correct" family ties or knowledge of the sacred literature). Nevertheless, these essential mercantile activities must be performed.

Everywhere, entertainers—actors, dancers, singers, magicians, story-tellers—are outcastes, ostracized by respectable members of the feudal city. Not infrequently they are foreigners as well; as an instance, many of the entertainers in Afghanistan have been Hindus. Like the merchants, entertainers mingle with people from all walks of life and are deemed potential purveyors of ideas that threaten the authority structure. Almost as disturbing to the upper class is the entertainer's repertoire, which is usually a distorted form of the revered literature. Combine this with the entertainer's depiction of the roles of disreputable urbanites like criminals and prostitutes, and we sense that his isolation is a must if people are to be prevented from emulating and being corrupted by the denigrated elements. The unstable nature of the entertainer's income and, often, the impermanence of his residence simply reinforce his lowly status.

Inherent in industrialization are processes that steadily eliminate the various outcaste roles. The highly arduous and defiling tasks, formerly the lot of outcastes, are more and more being performed by machines. In the industrial order even the most humble must acquire a modicum of education, and the industrial system provides the means for such. And the formerly outcaste businessmen have had to have their status elevated if the industrial city is to function and prosper. So too, mass communication, the lowering of class barriers, and added leisure—essential ingredients or products of industrialization—have all served to project the entertainer into the limelight. In many industrializing societies entertainers have risen to the point that they are the chief "carriers" of the new nationalism for the mass populace. Consequently in Mexico in and about the 1940s the late screen idol, the "charro" Jorge Negrete, became the personification of Mexicanism itself.

Social Mobility

The rigidity of the feudal city's class system, compared with that in industrial centers, is attested to by both the lower incidence of mobility and the populace's mute acceptance of the status quo. The continuance of elite families in positions of favor over many generations is one index of this strain toward immobility. The poor—and those in feudal orders are dismally so by industrial standards—have little motivation to better their position. Overwhelmingly concerned with the immediate task of staying alive, they lack

knowledge of how to get ahead—i.e., where mobility is possible—and are imbued with a value system that rationalizes
and justifies the incontrovertibility of their lot; they see fate
as the prime determinant of one's life chances. Success or
failure is attributed much more to luck than to one's own
abilities or inadequacies.

Recognize we do variations among feudal societies in the
values pertaining to mobility and class rigidity. Undoubtedly,
the egalitarian orientation of the traditional Muslim center,
as compared to the Hindu city, has induced in the former
somewhat greater vertical and horizontal mobility. Yet because of the staticism of the feudal technology, and the resultant fixity of the occupational structure, little social mobility
could occur, even where values exist encouraging it.

Traditional China is oft cited as a case for high social
mobility in preindustrial civilized societies. Many writers view
its examination system for filling bureaucratic posts, for example, as a major vehicle for upward mobility, although,
we, like Chang,[34] see the examinations as having been primarily mechanisms for socializing persons into the value
orientations of the ruling group. Although preindustrial China
admittedly was far from a perfectly static order, recent writers
like Ping-ti Ho[35] exaggerate the degree of mobility therein,
especially that from the "commoner" group into the "ruling"
stratum. One of the several reasons for this[36] is that Ho has
defined as one segment of the "commoner" group those holders
of a higher degree who did not fill an official post—individuals
whom other scholars categorize as of the "lower gentry" or
"local elite." On the whole these persons clearly were much
farther up the social scale than the vast bulk of the peasants
and urbanites; after all, these lower gentry had extensive
formal education, no mean feat in preindustrial China, where
stark poverty was the order of the day—a fact Ho and others
tend to ignore. Moreover, it might be argued, though some
would dispute this, that most families capable of providing
their children with an education sufficient to pass advanced

examinations perhaps had some literate members (even though no degree-holders) and were well above the average economically—in all, closer to the elite than to the commoner group. Ho unwittingly seems to be dealing primarily with circulation within, not movement into, the elite.

Actually, those who assume high mobility in traditional China have not resolved the inconsistency between this notion and the admittedly strong stress given to kinship solidarity. Marsh, comparing the upward movement into the occupational elites for Ch'ing China and for twentieth-century industrial America, finds that the amount of such mobility varied inversely with the degree of kinship solidarity, the latter being much higher in traditional China. He concludes that upward social mobility has been far greater in the industrial setting.[37]

But again, some social mobility does occur in preindustrial cities. Downward movement, for at least segments of the elite, and perhaps upward mobility for others, results where a kingdom or empire experiences military defeat. So too, internal schisms among the elite serve to lower the status of some persons in this group. Alderson[38] observes that the Ottoman Empire, during certain periods, lacked any institutionalized patterns of succession; quite frequently brothers would kill one another off in an effort to seize the throne, the families and adherents of the victims undoubtedly experiencing some diminution of class position.

A possibly self-contradictory arrangement stimulates a degree of downward mobility for some. Land ownership is often a prime source of the elite's income, but simultaneously the elite maintains large extended families in order to staff the key positions in the societal bureaucracies so essential to this stratum's authority. But after a time landed property can not be accumulated rapidly enough to meet the needs of the proliferating kinship unit. Consequently the extended family begins to disintegrate, usually with downward mobility for some of its members.

Some vertical mobility occurs where the elite does not reproduce itself, or if elements are wiped out in the natural disasters that periodically sweep over the land (although the elite generally fares better than the lower class during such crises). Then too, we find lower-class families, generally those in the upper ranks of the commoner group, sacrificing all to push one member ahead; the chosen one, if successful, will do his utmost to elevate the rest of the family along with him.[39]

Contradictory functional requirements inducing upward mobility, and concomitantly some downward movement, involve the need of the upper class, if it is to be set apart and revered, to encourage its emulation by the humble folk, but emulation of necessity means that those below will attempt to be like those above, in effect encouraging some blurring of class distinctions. If only for this reason, every society evinces some class fluidity.

Contradictory functional requirements, and the associated contradictory structures, are most evident as a factor in upward mobility where the elite must ostracize the businessman because of the latter's threat to the former's authority; yet mercantile activity is essential to the operation of the city and the sustenance of the elite. Thus the field of commerce, though scorned, still offers some lower-class persons the possibility of amassing large sums of money, a resource the elite must have to pursue some of its goals. As a result the successful merchant, particularly one not in the outcaste category, can purchase the right to fill key governmental posts, landed property, or other trappings of eliteness. Or he may hire specialists to construct genealogies for him, achieving thereby the highly valued criterion of upper-class family ties. Businessmen gain a measure of respectability also by using their monetary gains to underwrite various intellectual activities.

We have been discussing mobility as between the lower and upper classes. A word about the movement into and out of the outcaste category. Although there is some upward mobility out of the outcaste group, tenuous evidence suggests that it is much more difficult to evade this status than it is to ascend from a lower class to an elite position. Conversely, dropping into the outcaste rank appears to be rather easy. For example, a child of poor parents may be sold into slavery, the entertainment world, or prostitution, or a lower-class woman who has lost her family ties may enter prostitution in order to eke out a livelihood, thereupon assuming a status from which there is little hope of escape.

To recapitulate: although preindustrial-urban systems definitely discourage and restrict social mobility, some assuredly occurs. Yet even where movement of individuals is considerable, personal attributes sharply set preindustrial urbanites off from one another, giving the actor an impression of fixity and marked distance between classes. And the basic form of the class structure remains largely unchanged through time.

Contrariwise, the industrial milieu witnesses the incessant creation of new occupations and the destruction of older ones, necessitating continual revamping of the status hierarchy. Certainly the functional demand for a servile stratum is rapidly diminished as the more arduous and menial tasks are taken over by machines, a trend that bids fair to continue with the heyday of automation nearly at hand. And mass communication, besides opening up new channels of mobility, eliminates the wide chasms that make an outcaste group possible. Associated with the high degree of horizontal and vertical mobility are a loosening of kinship ties and a decline in the utility of personal attributes as status-markers. As a result the class ordering is fuzzy and most difficult to pin down.

Nowadays much is made of the industrialite's strong drive to enhance his status. Unbelievably, some sociologists interpret this as indicative of increasing rigidity in the class system. But remember that the common man in the feudal city meekly accepts his lot. It is a highly fluid class system that opens up to persons new horizons of expectation, new worlds to conquer. And lest we forget, industrial man has come to enjoy a standard of living that exceeds the wildest imaginings of the most highly privileged in the older preindustrial orders.

NOTES TO CHAPTER V

1. Our framework with respect to social class is an adaptation of that in Talcott Parsons, *Essays in Sociological Theory* (Glencoe: Free Press, 1949), pp. 171-72.
2. Oscar Lewis, *Life in a Mexican Village: Tepoztlán Restudied* (Urbana: University of Illinois Press, 1951).
3. G. Morris Carstairs, *The Twice-Born* (London: Hogarth Press, 1957), especially pp. 19-22.
4. Morris Opler and Rudra Datt Singh, "The Division of Labor in an Indian Village," in Carleton S. Coon (ed.), *A Reader in General Anthropology* (New York: Henry Holt, 1948), pp. 464-96.
5. Ashish Bose, "The First Census of Free India," *Modern Review*, XCV (February, 1954), 114.
6. Raphael Patai, *The Kingdom of Jordan* (Princeton: Princeton University Press, 1958), p. 213.
7. Olga Lang, *Chinese Family and Society* (New Haven: Yale University Press, 1946), p. 69; Hsiao-tung Fei, "Peasantry and Gentry: An Interpretation of Chinese Social Structure and its Changes," *American Journal of Sociology*, LII (July, 1946), 7; Morton H. Fried, *Fabric of Chinese Society* (New York: Frederick A. Praeger, 1953), pp. 22-25.
8. A. Giry and A. Réville, *Emancipation of the Medieval Towns,* trans. and ed. F. G. Bates and P. E. Titsworth (New York: Henry Holt, 1907); J. Lestocquoy, *Les Villes de Flandre et d'Italie* (Paris: Presses Universitaires de France, 1952), pp. 20-24, 184; R. J. Mitchell and M. D. R. Leys, *A History of London Life* (London: Longmans, Green, 1958), pp. 162, 175, *passim.*
9. Henri Pirenne, *Medieval Cities,* trans. F. H. Halsey (Princeton: Princeton University Press, 1925).
10. Anon., "The Privileges of the Capital," *Korea Review,* III (May, 1903), 193-203; cf. Percival Spear, *Twilight of the Mughuls* (Cambridge: Cambridge University Press, 1951), p. 82.
11. E.g., see Chung-li Chang, *The Chinese Gentry* (Seattle: University of Washington Press, 1955), p. 52.
12. Karl A. Wittfogel, *Oriental Despotism* (New Haven: Yale University Press, 1957).
13. For a discussion of the difficulties of defining what is a "surplus," see Marvin Harris, "The Economy Has No Surplus?" *American Anthropologist,* LXI (April, 1959), 185-99.
14. The essence of this controversy is presented in Derk Bodde, *China's Cultural Tradition* (New York: Rinehart, 1957), pp. 58ff.

15. Ping-ti Ho, "The Salt Merchants of Yang-Chou: A Study of Commercial Capitalism in Eighteenth-Century China," *Harvard Journal of Asiatic Studies,* XVII (June, 1954), 130-68.

16. Justus Doolittle, *Social Life of the Chinese,* ed. Paxton Hood (London: Sampson Low, 1868), pp. 237-38; Der Ling, *Kowtow* (New York: Dodd, Mead, 1929), p. 54.

17. Tsung-lien Shen and Shen-chi Liu, *Tibet and the Tibetans* (Stanford: Stanford University Press, 1953), p. 121.

18. Charles Bell, *The People of Tibet* (Oxford: Clarendon Press, 1928), p. 256. Cf. Shen and Liu, *op. cit.,* p. 128.

19. A good discussion of this phenomenon in Persian cities can be found in S. G. W. Benjamin, *Persia and the Persians* (London: John Murray, 1887), pp. 101-2.

20. Cornelius Osgood, *The Koreans and Their Culture* (New York: Ronald Press, 1951), pp. 137-39.

21. Carroll Camden, *The Elizabethan Woman* (New York: Elsevier Press, 1952), pp. 235-36. For a good statement on China see: Chang, *op. cit.,* pp. 33-34.

22. Der Ling, *op. cit.,* pp. 53-54. Cf. Chester Holcombe, *The Real Chinaman* (New York: Dodd, Mead, 1895), p. 230.

23. Pierre Ponafidine, *Life in the Moslem East,* trans. Emma C. Ponafidine (New York: Dodd, Mead, 1911), p. 412.

24. E.g., Hide Shohara, "Honorific Expressions of Personal Attributes in Spoken Japanese," *Occasional Papers* (Center for Japanese Studies; Ann Arbor: University of Michigan Press, 1952), pp. 30-34; Eleanor Harz Jorden, *The Syntax of Modern Colloquial Japanese* (Language Dissertation No. 52; Baltimore: Linguistic Society of America, 1955); George W. Gilmore, *Korea from its Capital* (Philadelphia: Presbyterian Board of Publication, 1892), pp. 59-64; Horace Grant Underwood, *An Introduction to the Korean Spoken Language* (Yokohama: Kelly and Walsh, 1890); Fernand Mossé, "La formation des langues communes en germanique: le cas du Norvégien," *Journal of World History,* IV (1957), 187-88; Ernst Pulgram, *The Tongues of Italy* (Cambridge: Harvard University Press, 1958), pp. 360ff., *passim.*

25. Pulgram, *op. cit.,* p. 345.

26. Often the dialect of the elite in the capital city is taken as the standard for the total society. Thus the Peking Mandarin has been the high status dialect in China.

27. Andrée F. Sjoberg, "The Phonology of a Telugu Dialect" (unpublished Ph.D. dissertation, University of Texas, 1957).

28. T. Lobsang Rampa, *The Third Eye* (London: Secker and Warburg, 1956), p. 18. Cf. F. Spencer Chapman, *Lhasa: The Holy City* (London: Chatto and Windus, 1938), p. 239.

29. E.g., John D. Donoghue, "An Eta Community in Japan: The Social Persistence of Outcaste Groups," *American Anthropologist,* LIX (December, 1957), 1000-17; Donald N. Wilber (ed.), *Afghanistan* (New Haven: Human Relations Area Files, 1956), pp. 325-28; Chapman, *op. cit.,* pp. 167-68; Herbert Passin, "Untouchability in the Far East," *Monumenta Nipponica,* XI (October, 1955), 27-47.

30. Franz H. Michael and George E. Taylor, *The Far East in the Modern World* (New York: Henry Holt, 1956), p. 33.

31. Napier Malcolm, *Five Years in a Persian Town* (New York: E. P. Dutton, 1905), pp. 45-46.

32. E.g., Henry B. Wheatley, *The Story of London* (rev. ed.; London: J. M. Dent and Sons, 1930), pp. 44-45.

33. E.g., Chester G. Starr, "An Overdose of Slavery," *Journal of Economic History,* XVIII (March, 1958), 17-32.

34. E.g., Chang, *op. cit., passim.*

35. Ping-ti Ho, "Aspects of Social Mobility in China, 1368-1911," *Comparative Studies in Society and History,* I (June, 1959), 330-59.

36. Also, the very fact that Ho's so-called "commoners" left records concerning their family histories suggests many were from an upper educated group. Many other methodological and theoretical weaknesses in Ho's work could be enumerated.

37. Robert Mortimer Marsh, *Mandarin and Executive: Elite Mobility in Chinese and American Societies* (Ann Arbor: University Microfilms, 1959), p. 245, *passim.*

38. A. D. Alderson, *The Structure of the Ottoman Dynasty* (Oxford: Clarendon Press, 1956), p. 5, *passim.* For analogous patterns in other societies where schisms within the elite seemingly foster mobility, see, e.g., Howard S. Levy, *Harem Favorites of an Illustrious Celestial* (Taichung, Taiwan: Chung-T'ai Printing Co., 1958).

39. E.g., Hsiao-tung Fei, *China's Gentry* (Chicago: University of Chicago Press, 1953), pp. 31-32. Cf. Bernard Barber, *Social Stratification* (New York: Harcourt, Brace, 1957), pp. 361ff.

CHAPTER VI

MARRIAGE AND
THE FAMILY

IT IS now possible to move on from the subject of social class (but never too far away, for it pervades the entire preindustrial-urban social structure). As will become apparent in this chapter, the latter's marriage and family patterns are closely correlated with the class system. But this is not the only issue we explore. Data on the preindustrial city negate a number of the widely accepted propositions of sociologists concerning the marriage and family patterns that supposedly accompany the rise and development of cities.

Marriage

In the preindustrial city every normal person is expected to marry. There is little provision for, or tolerance of, the unmarried adult; except when he is part of a special group, e.g., a religious order, he plays no socially "acceptable" role in the social order. Apart from widows whose remarriage in societies like traditional India has been censured by the ideal norms, an unmarried woman is an anomaly with no voice in the affairs of the family. But then, even single men do not reach "adult" status until they marry.

Although the data are scant, we can assume from a variety of evidence that most preindustrial urbanites have married young. This results in large degree from the high premium placed upon family life in the preindustrial center, every effort being made to sustain the familial system. To this end young married people, particularly among the elite, are supported by the kinship system—e.g., they are usually absorbed into the ménage of the husband's parents. And lower-class children's need to go to work at a tender age thrusts them rather quickly into an adult role and the married state. This early matrimony, of course, obviates any "youth culture"—such a conspicuous part of the industrial-urban scene, where the rapid social change brings about a hiatus in the outlook of contiguous generations.

The lack of a "youth culture" is linked to the general denial to young people of the privilege of forming their own decisions, most strikingly attested to by parents' customary arrangement of their children's marriages. Young people, girls more so than boys, have little if any say in the matter. Although this norm is most rigidly adhered to by the elite, it is an ideal pattern for many lower-class and outcaste families as well.

Why should marriage in preindustrial cities be essentially an arrangement between families, not a union of "free" individuals? First and foremost, a family's reputation and class position in the community and the society are functionally associated with the kinds of marriage partners its members can secure for their children—most notably sons, for in most preindustrial cities a man's wife ideally becomes part of his father's household. In the final analysis, parental control over the marriage process stabilizes the feudal city's class system.

Parents' strivings to arrange their children's marriages is reflected in some milieu in the betrothal of offspring at an early age, sometimes before birth. Nor have child-marriages, of daughters especially, been uncommon, in cities of Central Asia, the Near East, India, China, Japan, and parts of Europe such as medieval Florence.[1] In this situation the couple, though married, do not cohabit and perhaps do not see each other until both have reached puberty.

As suggested above, the elite most closely adhere to the ideal norms, not just because they have the means to carry them out but because contracting advantageous marriages and perpetuating the family line is a must if its privileged station is to be maintained. How are marriages within this group arranged? Usually a boy's parents, or occasionally other relatives, select a spouse for him through the medium of a "go-between."[2] Recourse to an intermediary, no less when this is a relative, reduces the possibility of interpersonal friction or loss of face. Remember, with marriage a family affair, the prestige and status of the entire kin group are at stake. An intermediary makes inquiries concerning the availability of certain girls, their desirable and undesirable qualities, the amount of dowry the girl's parents can provide, and so forth. Preliminary soundings of this nature are intended to avert embarrassment for all concerned. Withdrawal of one party after the negotiations are well underway would engender ill will and bitterness between families, perhaps transcending many generations. Especially, if the boy's family rejects the girl after preliminary agreements are reached and this becomes widely known, her chances for an advantageous marriage will be sharply reduced and her family's status undermined.

Determining which girls are available and suitable for the boy is obviously the go-between's first task. Usually the family has some candidates in mind before it formally takes up the search. But this does not mean that the boy and girl know each other. Often they do not. While this is most likely where selections are made from outside the community, in large preindustrial-like cities to this day engaged couples from the same city may not be acquainted. For example, a student from an Indian urban center informed me that he did not see his wife until after the wedding ceremonies, although they lived in the same community and had been engaged for three years. After all, in some cultures the separation of the sexes within the elite reaches marked proportions: boys and girls do not play together after the age of six or eight or there-abouts, and girls are closely guarded after puberty, being rarely seen by men, who are potential threats to their virtue. Ruralites, on the contrary, at least where community exogamy does not prevail, are more likely to be acquainted with their prospective spouses. The small size of the rural community, combined with the more flexible division of labor between the sexes as contrasted with that in the urban upper class, throw young people into more frequent contact; one's future mate is usually not an unknown quantity. Because of the freedom it gives the sexes, the urban lower class resembles the peasantry more closely than it does the elite.

For certain cultural settings, the aforementioned generalizations require modification. In Islam the ideal arrangement is marriage with one's father's brother's daughter, and where this is carried out among the urban elite, the boy obviously knows his future wife; in some instances the cousins have grown up in the same household. Nevertheless, Le Tourneau contends that in the large feudal Muslim city of Fez, numerous young men never saw their brides until the wedding.[3]

But let us retreat a moment and consider the qualities upper-class parents seek in marriage partners for their children. These can be highly restrictive. The family status or social background of a potential mate are all-important. Marriages are not to transcend class lines, although in actual practice this occurs on a limited scale. Further restrictions appear in specific cultures: in India caste lines should not be crossed; in China persons with the same family name ideally should not marry.

Similarity of social background between the boy and girl is sought to minimize the possibility of friction, especially in the upper class, where marriage often entails the introduction of a new member into the boy's household. A young wife who lacks understanding of the norms governing so many of the family action-patterns would indeed be a disruptive force in a large extended household. And because she will be expected to make all the necessary adjustments in marriage for the sake of harmony, a girl is trained from early childhood for her exacting roles of wife, mother, and daughter-in-law. (The need for adaptability on the part of a bride entering her husband's household is one reason for child-marriages.) Culinary and household arts form a vital part of her instruction (in the upper class, to oversee the servants in their work), but more than this she is inculcated in the desired personality traits of a wife, or indeed of any respectable woman in the traditional city: she must be modest, docile, dutiful, and agreeable—in all, a paragon of virtue.[4]

Not infrequently, marriage within the elite is contracted for political advantage, in line with the principle that it is chiefly for the benefit of the family rather than for the pleasure of individuals. Political gain through strategic matches has been common among the nobility in many traditional societies, including medieval Europe, with survivals to the present, and it persists in traditional Middle Eastern cities. Matrimonial alliances between the offspring of heads of state obviously cement political bonds. In a sense children of the ruling stratum are pawns of their families as these maneuver for political power and social position, on either the community or the societal level. Marriages may also be contracted for more direct economic gain—to establish or to further commercial ties. Through matrimonial alliances families can develop monopolies or combine their capital and thus achieve economic goals otherwise not possible. In this regard, the parallel-cousin type of mating in Islamic cities is a device for keeping property within the family circle, and is a means for eliminating a dowry.

Let it be recalled that in the industrial city—though social background is unquestionably a determining factor in mate selection—parents have relinquished much of their control over the marriage process; they may set limits to the range of potential mates, but rarely do they make the specific selection for their children.

Turning back to the non-industrial milieu, although family status ranks paramount in the selection of a spouse, other considerations such as good health are deemed vital in most cities. The advertisements for marriage partners in the large urban newspapers in India are apt to stress this even today. Such is understandable where so many persons live on the margins of existence. Even for the privileged group in pre-industrial cities, morbidity and mortality rates are exceedingly high; only the hardy survive. Poor health hampers a girl's chances for marriage, inasmuch as a wife's primary duty is the bearing and rearing of children; so too, a man in ill health would not be a good provider and thus is a poor marriage risk.

Chastity is another universally desired trait in wives, although the stress placed upon it varies from culture to culture. The prestige of the entire family can be lowered by any waywardness on the part of its women; its respectability is measured largely by the conduct of its female members. A girl's virginity even has some economic worth; without it the family may find it difficult to arrange an advantageous marriage for her, or at the very least they have to provide her with a larger dowry than would otherwise be the case. Consequently the family takes elaborate precautions to ensure the girl's inviolability. In some traditional Muslim cities a girl whose reputation were adversely affected might be killed by her own father or brothers. Intense preoccupation with female chastity persists among high-status urban families in the Middle East and India and in the more traditional parts of southern Europe and Latin America. Such a norm is attainable only where women lack "freedom" within the community and where parents retain control over the marriage process. The ideal patterns, once again, generally can be fulfilled only by the urban upper class.

Unlike respectable women, men are permitted, and often expected, to engage in sexual activity before marriage (and afterwards in extra-marital affairs). For this purpose every preindustrial city has its prostitutes. Man's greater sexual license is condoned on the grounds that he is inherently different biologically, morally, and socially from women and requires more outlets for his stronger sex drives. Although industrial cities may also display a double standard regarding premarital sexual behavior, it is by no means as marked.

Finally, physical attractiveness in a prospective spouse, especially a wife, is a consideration, but one that is de-emphasized in preindustrial-urban communities. Beauty and a "winning personality" as crucial determinants in the choice of a bride are almost unique to industrial centers. In the feudal city a homely girl from a high-status family, trained in the household arts and having an agreeable personality, good health, and an unsullied reputation, is still considered a good marriage risk. After all, a husband can resort to concubines or mistresses. Only lower-class or outcaste women, such as entertainers, can use their beauty as a means of social climbing into, say, a favored concubine position;[5] contrastingly, in the industrial city, beauty is a more respectable mechanism for upward mobility.

Before proceeding further, we must examine in some detail the role of "romantic love" in the marriage process. Romantic or personal attachment as a factor in the choice of mates has been rare indeed in preindustrial cities. All too many writers imbedded in the American scene are wont to correlate the growth of romantic love with urban development per se. In so doing, they overlook cities of the preindustrial type, the social norms of which militate against "dating" or any other companionship based primarily upon personal attraction between young men and women. It is functionally impossible for romantic love to blossom when parents arrange marriages for their offspring and when young people may not be acquainted prior to their wedding. This is not to deny that affection between husband and wife may develop after marriage, but strong emotional attachment is unlikely within the context of the traditional extended family which acts in so many ways to inhibit it.

Only in recent decades has the romantic love concept taken root in cities in industrializing societies—e.g., Japan or those in Latin America—and then it affects only a small segment of the urban scene. Dore[6] comments upon the difficulties young people in a mid-twentieth-century Tokyo ward are experiencing as new marriage patterns are imposed upon the old. Love marriage is among many the ideal, though as yet no institutionalized system of courtship exists for attaining this new goal; the result is feelings of guilt and frustration.

But, you ask, are not libraries replete with literary works depicting love affairs (mostly unrequited) in preindustrial cities? Most assuredly, though such incidents, where they occur, have been external to the structural arrangements of marriage and the family. Deep emotional attachment between thc sexes has rarely been permitted to lead to marriage in the traditional city. Romantic love has been quite commonplace between a man and a courtesan or concubine. Writers who have argued for the relatively high status and freedom of women in cities of ancient Greece fail to realize that the women who were the companions, intellectual or otherwise, of the philosophers and men of affairs almost invariably were courtesans, "respectable" women being very much restricted in their associations with men and in their opportunities for formal intellectual attainment.[7] The geisha in traditional Japan, the nautch, or professional dancers, of Indian cities, among others, have all cultivated the arts of entertainment and of stimulating conversation, enabling them to cater to men in their own inimitable fashion. Ofttimes, romantic attachments have grown out of these relationships, and the girl might achieve the status of a concubine or a mistress—though rarely that of a full-fledged spouse. Obviously, the elite alone possesses the means to support these women versed in special skills.

The strict seclusion of respectable women of the elite has fostered homosexuality among upper-class males in a number of preindustrial cities. In ancient Greece and various Middle Eastern cities, romantic attachments between a man and a youth were considered quite acceptable.[8]

A specific and somewhat aberrant phenomenon, limited in time and space, is the "courtly love" complex that sprang up in parts of Europe in the late Middle Ages.[9] Here troubadours, supported mainly by the nobility, came to establish platonic, sometimes more intimate, relations with upper-class women, often married ones. But the goal of this courtly love was not marriage. For one thing, most of the troubadours, certainly those who made this a career, were of much lower station in life than the elite and, therefore, not acceptable as husbands for women of noble birth. The argument that romantic love patterns in industrial cities of the Western world originated in these medieval forms is a dubious one at best: the two phenomena diverge in so many respects and have served different functions.

Observe also that the romantic love themes in the Arthurian romances or the *Arabian Nights* or other literature of pre-industrial-urbanized areas do not reflect the actual norms in marriage. Nor do the highly sentimental love songs so typical of, say, Spanish and Latin American popular music, for romantic love as a basis for marriage is only recently emergent in urban centers in the societies in question.

As to why romantic love in the preindustrial city is confined to temporary, or at most semi-permanent, attachments external to the family system, it is clear that it poses a threat to the solidarity of the kinship system with its ties of mutual obligation and with its ideal of the individual as subordinate to the good of the whole. Romantic love is, of all things, an expression of individualism, and as such it is at variance with the maintenance of a well-integrated extended kinship unit.

What havoc could be wreaked by the introduction into an extended family of a bride chosen simply on the basis of her beauty and personality or a man's intense emotional involvement with her!

Then too, romantic love can be a significant part of marriage (and family life) only where the eligible women are liberated from the harness of parental dominance and can exercise freedom of choice. It is no accident that in highly industrialized societies where women have acquired economic and social independence romantic love is for large numbers of young people a necessary condition for marriage. Moreover, in industrial-urban communities the conjugal unit is often the sole organizational apparatus through which "emotional fulfilment" for the individual can be achieved. For reasons of emotional security, persons seek mates who are compatible in terms of personality. But choice on this basis is of necessity highly subjective; it can be effected only by an individual, not by his parents, although the latter seek to limit their children's range of choice. It can be readily observed, moreover, that in this situation the family is no longer the final determinant of a person's social status; the freedom of choice involved in selecting a mate tends to make the class structure more fluid, and vice versa.

Sociologists have observed that in the industrial-urban center romantic love helps to allay some of the frictions and misunderstandings that inevitably arise after marriage, inasmuch as couples so often enter this state with very divergent social backgrounds and values. The romantic aura that surrounds the marriage serves as an emotional bond while other grounds for mutual understanding are being established.

The ideal family in the preindustrial city allows no such place for romantic love; especially among the elite, husbands and wives seek emotional support not so much from one another as from members of the broader kinship system, or in the case of men, in temporary liaisons with outsiders.

Having completed this diversionary excursion into the realm of romantic love, we return to our summary of the steps leading to marriage. Discussed already are the criteria for selecting potential mates. Now assume that the parents of a boy, or of a girl, have through a go-between decided upon a possible spouse for their offspring. In most instances children do not contravene the decisions of their parents, but where they do object strongly to a particular marriage partner, they may exercise some veto power, though generally only boys do this. But still other pressing matters are to be considered.

Within numerous preindustrial cities, cutting across divergent cultures, magical rites are used to decide whether the union is an auspicious one. In Indian cities to this day horoscopes are read to determine the suitability of a marriage, and marriage advertisements in Indian newspapers like the Madras *Hindu* contain numerous references to this practice. It was apparently much more widespread in feudal societies in the past. If the horoscopes of the couple are deemed incompatible, marriage is impossible, and the families must renew their efforts to secure a spouse for their offspring. A favorable horoscope reading assures all parties concerned that the marriage will be successful.

A dowry and/or bride-price, varying according to the cultural situation, is passed in numerous feudal cities. The amount is often indicative of the relative statuses of the two families—e.g., if the girl is marrying upward her family may have to provide a larger dowry for her than if she is marrying down. The dowry or bride-price may take the form of money, household goods, or other property. Although it is in a sense a nest-egg for the couple and, in some cultural settings, insurance for the wife (in Islamic cities a woman's bride-price must be returned to her if her husband divorces her), it is more important, especially among the elite, as a symbol to seal the marriage contract.

These hurdles having been successfully cleared, preparations for the elaborate marriage ceremony can get underway. In this most significant rite of passage the upper class indulges in highly splendacious affairs, and persons in other strata, in their attempt to emulate the elite, are apt to "squander" their meager earnings and sink deeply in debt to provide as elaborate a wedding as possible for their children,[10] for now, of all times, the family finds itself in the public eye with its social position at stake. Among the elite the nuptials may last for several days; sometimes a week of music, dancing, and much feasting and gaiety accompany the proceedings to which a staggering number of guests may be invited.[11] (Generally only after the partying is over do the bride and groom meet in private.)

The lavish display of wealth only deepens the aura surrounding the elite in feudal cities. Such conspicuous consumption does not usually excite envy or resentment on the part of the lower class and outcastes, but rather it evokes admiration and awe. Generally the lower strata accept their lot in life, seeing no alternative to the status quo; only a breakdown of the traditional social structure, and the consequent broadening of the ordinary man's horizons, incites them to question the monopoly of wealth and power enjoyed by the upper stratum.

Aside from heightening the individual's or family's status, the vast expenditure of time, energy, and financial resources on marriage ceremonies permits an assembling of the broad kin group, including relatives in far-flung communities, thereby reinforcing its "collective representations," to borrow a term from Durkheim.

Furthermore, in those preindustrial cities where marriage is a sacrament—in medieval Europe and in India—the rites reinforce the ties between the familial and the religious organizations. And in all feudal cities these ceremonies advertise to the community, and at times to the broader society, that the bride and groom have undergone a shift in status.

The Extended Family

Upon completion of the marriage vows the couple comes to function within a family whose structure is surprisingly similar throughout the non-industrial-urban world. Typically the bride becomes part of her husband's family and, particularly among the upper class, moves into his parents' household. So firmly entrenched is this pattern that the traditional elite in China did not give a daughter a family name, noting her in the genealogical registers only by number, for upon marriage she would be absorbed into her husband's family and her name recorded in the latter's genealogy.[12] Deviations from the norm of patrilocal residence are met with among the lower-class urbanites and peasantry, and special violations occasionally appear: as among the Uzbeks of Kabul,[13] where a man may take up residence in his wife's parents' household if, for instance, his own parents are deceased. Moreover, as we mention further on, survivals of older matrilocal forms from the preliterate era are to be found in some communities in Southeast Asia.

In its ideal form, the feudal city's extended family includes a man and his wife (or wives), their unmarried children, married sons, and the latter's wives and children, and perhaps other relatives such as widowed daughters or sisters of the family head, as well as numerous servants. The most spectacular households have been those of royalty—in urban Siam, Central Asia, India, China, and the Near East—sheltering dozens of wives and concubines and several score, in some cases over a hundred, children. Servants have been superabundant. So too, the households of others of the elite have been imposing: Wong[14] describes her childhood home in a Chinese city as having included 51 persons. Twenty-seven of these were relatives, extending over four generations, 17 were slave girls, and seven were hired servants. The families of each of her brothers had separate apartments or quarters, but many of the family activities were carried out in common, and above all the household was a joint economic enterprise. Tsai's[15] home in Peking was even larger, embracing not only her parents, her eight brothers and their wives and children —each family lodged in a separate apartment with its servants —but also eight unmarried brothers and sisters, each with two special servants, and about 20 cousins, some of them with their own wives, children, and servants. Besides these, there were other servants dwelling in the household—cooks, bearers, gardeners, some of them with their own assistants. Obviously such a tremendous household could never be sustained by any but an upper-class urban family with considerable economic and political power.

In Indian cities, the "joint families" of the elite have often included over a hundred members, a formidable system indeed into which to introduce a shy, young bride who is expected to fit herself into it with a minimum of friction. So too, we have evidence for very large households among the upper class in Middle Eastern cities.[16]

The conjugal, or nuclear, family as a separate social unit, the prevailing form in industrial cities, is not the typical upper-class form for any preindustrial city for which the writer has adequate data. Even in traditional societies that are being strongly affected by industrialization, the large extended family system, grouped into a single household, persists and remains strong; the Indian social scene illustrates just this.

Rural families and those of the urban lower-class and outcaste groups are much less able to maintain large households, and, consequently, close family ties, though they seek to do so wherever possible. The peasants' land holdings are too small to support a large family unit, with the result that many of the sons must seek occupational opportunities elsewhere. Likewise the commoners and outcastes in urban centers must pursue a livelihood where the opportunity presents itself. At best they can maintain a "limited" extended family system consisting, for example, of one or two elders, usually grandparents, one married son and his wife and children. This is the sociologist's *famille souche,* characteristic of both the urban lower class and the small peasant villages.

Challenge we must the popular assumption among sociologists that large extended family units, sharing large households, are products of the rural milieu. Fei,[17] as a result of his study of rural villages in China, saw the "limited" extended family as the common pattern in rural areas and the "true" extended family, the members of which reside under a single "roof," as an urban trait, though the latter is obviously most achievable by the upper class. Dube[18] drew similar conclusions for India on the basis of his field work in a rural community in what is now Andhra Pradesh.

In the villages of Andhra-desa, particularly Telangana, it is impossible to find a family in which all nuclear families of three generations share a common house. Among the higher castes of Hindus such large joint families are still met with in the small towns and cities, but they are not often seen in the villages.

Dube's statement is confirmed by statistical data for at least part of India that point up the persistence of a definitely feudal pattern.[19]

The more closely one approaches the preindustrial city, the more common is the large household—flourishing best among the elite—and the more deeply one penetrates the rural countryside, the less likely is this feature to be encountered. Herein resides one of the most striking differences between rural and urban communities in preindustrial civilized orders, one that supports as well the argument of the previous chapter that the elite is pre-eminently urban, not rural.

Besides the strategic functions of socialization and procreation, the extended family, particularly that embraced by a single household, is an effective security agency. The preindustrial world produces only a limited surplus of food, goods, and services, and its inhabitants stand helpless before pestilence and the unleashed forces of nature like floods or earthquakes. Life hangs by a slender thread. In the absence of any real public welfare programs, the family is the prime security agency. The extended family, where it can be achieved, is a much more effective mechanism for mutual aid than is the simple conjugal unit. Whereas the incapacity of one or two breadwinners can be disastrous to the small nuclear unit, the extended organization, wherein economic co-operation is the rule, can more readily adjust to adversity, for if illness or unemployment strikes a member, the others can support him and his wife and children until the crisis has passed. The large extended family fills many of the functions that in industrial cities are assumed primarily by governmental welfare agencies.

The lower class and outcastes—with the exception of a few wealthy outcaste merchants—are economically unable to maintain large households. Although relatives do seek, wherever possible, to assist one another, the bonds among a number of small family units of either the conjugal or the *famille souche* type are never as resilient as those within a large congregation of family members residing in a single "household." In the latter situation, one's obligations are more immediately visible, and the pressures to proffer mutual aid are more insistent. The elite not only maintain large households, but their families are interlinked to a degree not attainable by the poor. The former are socially more stable and have access to media of communication that provide contacts beyond community boundaries.

Some of the poor may even find themselves isolated from any family unit, driven to begging or scavenging as a means of eking out a bare subsistence or, more probably, a slow death through starvation and disease. A woman isolated from her kinship system is readily reduced to prostitution, and children, most often girls, orphaned or from poor families, are not infrequently sold to buyers who turn them into servants, entertainers, or prostitutes—as in traditional China and Japan.

In addition to its welfare role, the extended family performs strategic economic and political functions. Often it is only the maintenance of the extended family that keeps property, especially landholdings, intact; this in turn unquestionably promotes the extended family's survival. Moreover, the elite strives to place members of the kinship unit in key political, educational, and religious posts in the community and society, thereby ensuring the continuance of the extended organization. In smaller non-industrial cities, one or a few families dominate the whole community, demonstrated, for instance, in the community of Gaziantep, Turkey.[20] The pre-eminence of a handful of families is made possible by the norm that stresses the selection of personnel for various occupations on particularistic, primarily kinship, grounds, and this personnel is expected to utilize their posts to enhance the economic and political power of the family.

Another function of the extended family is sustaining ties with the past, which in turn reinforces its status. Authority in the feudal order being legitimized by appeal to tradition, families justify their claim to present superiority in terms of their former eminence. A favorite device—in cities in cultures as divergent as China, India, Turkey, and medieval Europe—for achieving this end has been constructing and maintaining genealogies.[21] Chinese farmers who were able to amass some wealth sought to assume a higher status by moving to nearby towns and cities, and there they had specialists construct genealogies for them. Italian parvenus of the last century purchased titles and genealogies from impoverished noblemen, or had fictitious ones created, to justify or rationalize their presumption to a higher status.[22]

The literate elite enjoy a distinct advantage over the illiterate commoners in the matter of genealogies, for the recording of family histories is far more effective through writing than through an oral tradition. And the possession of written records advertises the family's link with a literary heritage. Honsinger[23] mentions a Chinese urban family whose genealogy covered 70 generations. Once in a generation the records were revised and reprinted and sent to all members of the kin group. Who among the urban poor or the rural peasantry could achieve such remarkable continuity through time? Few, if any.

Genealogies also reinforce the family's authority by providing it with a sense of identity and cohesion. Not surprisingly, elite families in some cities stage elaborate ceremonies involving the periodic display and revision of the genealogical books. Through this means the historical and present state of the kin group are brought to the attention of the younger members of the household.

We have emphasized the tremendous import of the extended family in feudal cities, noting that the large household unit is an urban phenomenon. However, as industrial-urbanization becomes firmly entrenched, the large extended household is no longer the ideal toward which people strive. The conjugal family system now becomes the accepted, and often the preferred, norm. Although deviations from the conjugal system are present in all industrial cities because of various contradictory requirements, a fluid, flexible, small family unit is necessarily the dominant form in a social order characterized by extensive social and spatial mobility. Individuals by shifting their occupational and class positions or by engaging in spatial mobility tear asunder integrated or extended family units. Then too, the government in industrial societies provides welfare services that were once largely the province of the family, the extended kinship unit losing thereby much of its raison d'être.

A special configuration in industrializing societies confuses many writers. The *famille souche,* exhibited mainly by the lower class in feudal orders, tends to survive in the rural areas, and, more to the point, so do the feudal upper-class ideals of an extended family that at one time were primarily urban. The explanation for this seems to be that with the higher living standards made possible by industrialization, ruralites can maintain larger households than they could under the feudal regime. And because industrialization first affects the city, the ruralites are the last to relinquish the older feudal values and norms. Sociologists studying partially industrialized feudal orders in Europe, or elsewhere, can understand present rural-urban divergencies only if they fully grasp those of the past.

Family Roles

The feudal family, most typically in the urban upper class, is a rather strict hierarchy, with rigid ranking according to age and sex. We begin with an analysis of husband-wife relationships, with special emphasis upon the role of women, seen in the context of the familial organization. Next parent-child relationships are treated, followed by a consideration of the structural arrangements that obtain among siblings.

Women are unquestionably subordinate to men. The preindustrial city is a "man's world"; a woman's social and legal rights are startlingly few. In childhood she is dependent upon her father, after marriage upon her husband, and in widowhood upon her sons. The men are the family's representatives in the external world; their primary duty is to support the women, children, and the aged and infirm in the family. Throughout feudal cities in India, China, Japan, the Middle East, ancient Greece, and medieval Europe this structural arrangement has prevailed.[24] In essence a woman's lot in life is determined first by the kind of family she is born into, and then by the family she enters through marriage.

A definite hierarchy obtains between husband and wife. In numerous preindustrial cities their differing statuses are reflected in the linguistic forms each employs, including special honorific terms of address, grammatical constructions, and, occasionally, phonemic patterns. In Japan the husband addresses his wife by linguistic forms that are indicative of her inferior status, whereas the wife utilizes those conveying respect. In various languages of India, like Gujarati or Hindi, a traditional term for one's husband is _svāmī_ signifying "lord," or "master." Figuratively, the husband is a "god" who requires unswerving obedience.

Around the world in traditional Middle Eastern, Chinese, Indian, and Korean cities, upper-class spouses seldom converse with one another in public, even in the presence of family members, and when they must do so they employ formal terms of address. Very frequently, husband and wife refrain from using each other's given names. Employing teknonymy, the wife refers to her husband as "the father of . . ." (usually the name of their eldest son follows), and she in turn is called "the mother of . . ."[25] Other members of the community also refer to the husband and wife in these terms.

As with the class system, the linguistic forms reflect and reinforce the formal and highly institutionalized patterns of relationship between spouses, minimizing both personal interaction and social conflict and ensuring highly segregated roles. Where discord does arise, the husband possesses the legitimate means for resolving it, usually in his favor.

Concerning the duties of the wife, she is expected to serve her husband, to be at his beck and call and to anticipate his every need. An ideal norm in, for example, Japanese and Korean cities has been for a wife (or servants under her command) to help her husband dress and undress. A Korean girl from Seoul informed me that her mother carefully sets out the father's clothes so that when he dresses in the morning all the necessary items are in readiness for him. Writings on India—even in the modern, more highly industrialized and westernized urban communities—indicate analogous patterns. Wives, or the servants they oversee, wait on their husbands hand and foot.

Let us examine more closely the wife's role in preindustrial cities as it is differentiated from that of her husband. In the early period of marriage the young bride makes numerous adjustments. In many cities, she leaves the home of her child-hood and enters a strange household, where she is under her mother-in-law's thumb. Her agreeableness is put to the acid test, for she occupies a most disadvantaged position vis-à-vis the unmarried daughters in the family, whom, naturally, their mother favors. To add to her tribulations, the husband is likely to side with his mother and sisters against his wife in cases of domestic infelicity. Nor does it profit the young bride to complain to her own parents. Though sympathetic, they exhort her to accept her fate: divorce would be far worse.

The wife's first step toward increased social status in her husband's family is giving birth to a child, preferably a son. Having contributed to the continuance of her husband's family tree, she is no longer considered an interloper by her hus-band's parents and siblings. And she attains greater signifi-cance in her husband's eyes and has a much better chance of staving off divorce or the imposition of other wives or concubines. Now too, she can identify emotionally with her children.

Because of the rigid division of labor between husband and wife, most transparent among the urban elite, women can consider certain realms of activity as definitely their own and from this derive satisfaction. Women do wield authority with-in the home: but for them, the household would not function. A Sanskrit saying in India, *Grhinīrahitam grham, vanasa-mānam* (Without the housewife, a house is like a jungle), puts it well. Women are responsible for the care and training of children and numerous household tasks—including cook-ing—though in the upper class their duties involve directing servants in many of these activities. In many urban homes in India, parts of medieval Europe, China, the Middle East, the kitchen is the woman's realm, and men are rarely per-mitted access to it. This sharp division of labor and the func-tional segregation of women in the family shield them from the arbitrary whims of the males.

Because she has been taught from childhood never to

question her role, a woman experiences considerable emotional security and encounters few problems once she has established herself through the bearing of children. Her sons and their families, where possible, reside in the same household, and until her death or very old age she continues to play a vital role in the extended family system. It is now her turn to dominate her daughters-in-law and their children, as well as the servants. In the event of the death of the family head, his widow not infrequently becomes at least the nominal leader of the household. Even if a son, usually the eldest, takes over formally, the old mother is still a symbol that keeps the extended family together and, as such, wields considerable power and influence.

Although a woman is in time able to achieve fairly high status within the household, this does not carry over into the community context. She has few rights in matters of property ownership or contracts and performs no real function in the political, economic, and educational spheres of the city and society—even in the religious realm she plays a definitely subordinate role. Any independent action on the part of an upper-class woman threatens the status of the entire kinship unit. Wage-earning by the wife is considered a slur upon the capabilities of the husband.

Sociologists have viewed women as the carriers of status in social systems, an observation that is best dramatized in the world of the preindustrial city elite. Here, women, utilizing elaborate dress, make-up, coiffures, and/or display of jewelry, reflect, indeed advertise to other women of the elite, the family's socio-economic position, their own exemption from physical labor, and their ability to spend long hours in self-adornment. Furthermore, loading women down with jewelry and ornate clothing (or the special cultural phenomenon of foot-binding in traditional China, where high-born ladies could barely hobble around and often had to be carried by servants), dramatizes womens' role in contrast to mens' and serves as a rationalization for restricting their activities, for such an obvious display of wealth and debility makes them easy prey for thieves and subject to other kinds of aggression.[26]

Within the upper class, women's seclusion in the community setting can reach extreme proportions. Most women in traditional Muslim cities don a face veil, and often a head covering as well, when venturing outside the house. Those in urban centers in Afghanistan to this day wear a shroud-like garment that envelops them from head to toe. A strip of gauze across the eyes enables the wearer to see where she is going, but permits no one to view her features. Only marginal women like prostitutes, or occasionally lower-class working women on the order of shopkeepers, have gone about unveiled.[27] A recent study of Rowanduz, a town in northern Iraq, suggests that the ordinarily unveiled peasant woman who neglected to put on a face veil when entering the community was placed by the local citizenry in the same category as the prostitute.[28]

In the home itself, urban upper-class Muslim women have been set apart.[29] Only the closest male relatives ever see another man's wife or his adolescent daughters unveiled. Male visitors to the home are entertained in a special section reserved for male guests, while the women retreat to their own quarter, the harem. To insure the isolation of women, doorways, for example, may be constructed so that guests passing through the halls can not look into the women's sector. While these feudal patterns are evanescing in modernizing Muslim cities as upper-class women gain educational and employment opportunities, they exhibit surprising tenacity in the face of new social forces.

Though no other culture quite approaches the Islamic in the cloistering of women, some segregation is the norm in preindustrial cities. Those in Europe were no exception. During the Middle Ages, ladies of high birth frequently wore face veils in public, and most respectable women at least covered their heads with a cloth. Ideally, in Elizabethan England women left the confines of the house only on special occasions.[30] Similarly in traditional Chinese, Japanese, and Indian cities.[31] An intriguing pattern in Seoul, Korea, at about the turn of the present century is described below:[32]

> Although most of the lady's life was spent in seclusion in the house over which she ruled as mistress, she sometimes left her restricted domain to visit family friends. She would not walk on the street in daylight to do this but took a sedan chair from courtyard to courtyard, the bearers retiring while she made her entrance and exit from the conveyance. . . . .
>
> At night, . . . ladies walked through the streets under the most extraordinary circumstances, as the thoroughfares of the whole city were turned over to them alone, except for blind men and officials. This situation came about after dark when the fire beacons converging on the capital brought the evening message that the kingdom was secure and peaceful. Word being conveyed to the palace, the royal band played appropriate music, the great bell was rung, and the guards closed the gates of the city. . . . Until one in the morning, women were free to walk abroad, and any man found on the streets apart from those mentioned above as specially exempt was subject, if caught by the patrols, to imprisonment and severe flogging. The women carried paper lanterns as they strolled, but in even so little light they protected their faces with their silk jackets.

Concerning the foregoing generalizations, some readers may wonder about societies like Thailand, Burma, and Tibet, for these have been singled out by writers as exceptions to the rule regarding the repression of women in feudal orders. Yet almost invariably the contrast is made not with industrial orders but with surrounding societies—most notably, traditional India and China—and from this perspective, women in cities of Southeast Asia and Tibet seem to have enjoyed greater freedom. One explanation for this may be that in Southeast Asia and Tibet, the feudal order was superimposed upon a preliterate base characterized by matrilineal descent and matrilocal residence (and in the case of Tibet, polyandry), and moreover that this overlay of preindustrial forms occurred rather late in history and has had a relatively short period in which to obliterate the older way of life. Even so, higher-status urban women in these societies have been much restricted to the home—consider the women of the upper class in Southeast Asian cities or in Lhasa.[33] Certainly these societies are much more like feudal orders than industrial-urban systems.

Thus far we have said little about urban lower-class and rural women. Although they stand in awe of the upper class and seek to emulate them, the realities of their existence preclude their adherence to many of the ideal norms that the elite are able to sustain. Many urban lower-class and outcaste women are forced to some kind of gainful employment from time to time to keep the family going. If a woman loses her husband she can not always depend upon relatives for support—they are also struggling to make ends meet—and thus must make her own way in the community. But it is in the peasant countryside that these phenomena are more markedly apparent. Peasant women universally work in the fields alongside their husbands. And in so doing they gain a degree of prestige and status relative to the men in the family not possible for urban women, notably those in the elite. Although urban lower-class and outcaste women, like those in the villages, lack many economic and political rights and function within a well-defined patriarchal system, they do enjoy a measure of freedom never attained by those in the upper ranks. How can women be cloistered when the whole family is crowded into a one- or two-room shanty? If seclusion of women is to be carried out, a large house is required with entirely separate living quarters and recreational areas. All of this necessitates additional servants, more clothes for the women, and special conveyances when they travel—patterns that the urban poor and peasant families could never hope to achieve.

We emphasize again the divergencies in the position of women within the family in rural and in urban areas, the broadest gap lying between the elite and the peasantry, but prevailing to a degree between the urban lower class and the ruralites as well. Bacon commented upon the greater degree of freedom of women in rural areas in Japan at the turn of the present century, and at about the same time Gilmore was observing this pattern in Korea and Wilson in Iran. Its persistence well into the twentieth century has been noted by Wong and others for China, Wilber for Afghanistan, and Kennedy for Pakistan.[34] More specifically, one writer observed that in contradistinction to the women of the feudal city of Yarkand, in Chinese Turkestan (Sinkiang), peasant women of the surrounding countryside dressed much as did the men, dramatizing the lesser degree of sex differentiation in the rural areas.[35] Sociologists who contend that the urban milieu in and of itself induces higher status and increased freedom for women are unaware of the vast body of literature on preindustrial cities that refutes their ethnocentric generalizations.

Unlike the humbler classes, the feudal urban elite alone have the resources to cloister their women, and, concomitantly, restricting the latter's contacts with ordinary persons helps to sustain the family's respectability and privileged status. As a further consequence of their seclusion from the mainstream of life, upper-class wives are thoroughly inculcated in the values of perpetuating the family, which in turn ensures the continuance of the kinship unit.

With industrialization and its attendant high degree of social and spatial mobility, not only does the extended family splinter but, most revolutionary of all, woman's role and status change dramatically. Educational and economic opportunities, once considered illusionary, now become a reality, and in conformance with the disintegration of sharp status distinctions within the total society, those between men and women begin to fade as well. And women's participation in community activities becomes an accepted norm.

As to the status and role of the husband in the ideal feudal family, much less needs to be said. He functions first and foremost as protector and provider for his wife (or wives) and children, and perhaps other relatives, and if he is the eldest male in the household he serves as spokesman for the entire group in its relations with the community at large. Theoretically, he wields considerable authority within the home, although in actuality the rather strict division of labor according to sex sets limits upon his effective degree of power. Nevertheless, the outward signs of his superiority are ever present. In many preindustrial cities the husband eats before his wife does, walks ahead of her on the street (if indeed she appears with him in public at all), is not accountable to her for his actions, and so on. In line with the segregation of the sexes, especially among the elite, he passes much of his leisure time in the company of other males, usually of his own class, and to a degree with women of marginal, non-respectable status.

In a large number of feudal orders a husband can divorce his wife on a wide variety of grounds, including barrenness on her part, and with relative ease. Those in Muslim cities have had merely to say "I divorce thee" and it is a *fait accompli*. For men, remarriage is a simple matter; it is rarely so for the divorced wife. In many feudal societies he can introduce other wives or concubines into the household without the consent of the first wife. (Little or no ceremonial activity marks these auxiliary unions.) Although the first wife tends to dominate over the others, if she has not borne children, especially sons, her status will soon be undermined by those who do.

We must not assume that the wide separation of roles of husband and wife, or more generally of men and women, is entirely conducive to harmony. Although the clear-cut definition of functions does much to reduce friction, strains and an absence of mutual trust and understanding are nonetheless apt to result. Women are apt to fear men, and men view women in a startlingly ambivalent manner. On the one hand, women are the fount of all that is pure and good: the long-suffering mother may take on a "goddess-like" quality. But paradoxically, women in general, even a young wife, are

considered inherently "evil" and even capable of undermining a man's virility if given the chance. In some Indian cities
wives are popularly thought to be sexually insatiable. Practically everywhere in traditional urban milieux—in China,
India, medieval Europe, Latin America, and the Middle East
—women are adjudged by men to be deficient in intellectual
qualifications, to be flighty, insincere, irresponsible, treacher-
ous, to be physically weak, and what is more, to lack the
will to resist temptation—all deemed sufficient reasons for
denying them a significant role in community and societal
affairs.[36]

Actually the pivotal relationship in the preindustrial city
family is that between parents and children. The husband-
wife axis is subordinate to it and its functions decidedly limited. Not unexpectedly, children are highly desired. The
prestige and status of both husband and wife are enhanced
with the birth of each new child, especially a son. This,
coupled with the lack of effective birth control methods, means
that families, irrespective of their economic means, have as
many as possible.

As indicated earlier, the advent of a child greatly amel-
iorates a wife's position in the extended family, not only with
her husband but with her in-laws. And through her children
she acquires added emotional security, with the result that
she is likely to identify with them throughout her lifetime.

A man, too, gains prestige in the family and community
when he becomes a father, especially one with sons. Generally, descent is reckoned through the male line, so that the
family's continuance through time is dependent upon the
production of sons. More, a man ensures his future welfare
through perpetuation of the family, no small consideration
in a social system that contains so few agencies for the care
of the aged, the sick, and the destitute.

So strong are the motivations for having offspring that
special structural arrangements, varying among cultures, have
evolved to ensure the continuance of the family in the event

of the wife's "sterility"; the blame for the failure to bear children is adjudged to be hers, not the husband's. Mentioned already is the latter's recourse in many feudal cities to plural marriage or to concubines; besides adding to his sensual pleasures these are means of continuing the family tree. Adoption of children, especially boys, is another widely employed technique for ensuring an heir. In Japan, parents who lack a son may adopt the husband of a daughter and so perpetuate the family line. All of these arrangements, of course, are most accessible to the elite—support of additional wives or children being a costly venture—and accounts in part for the larger families in this stratum.

But the data also indicate that parents in the urban upper class have more offspring who reach adulthood than do the lower strata. It is not that the birth rates of the upper and lower classes differ significantly; the crucial differential seems to be the mortality rate—both for infants and for older children. Upper-class persons, in control of the economic surplus, enjoy a higher standard of living and, concomitantly, a longer life-span than the rest of the populace. And we might expect this, given the nature of the feudal social order.

Studies by Gist on the Indian cities of Bangalore and Mysore and by Dandekar and Dandekar on Poona lend credibility to our view, though none of these writers perceives the implications of his findings.[37] Too, Chen's[38] survey of population in the Kunming region of China suggests that upper-class parents have more surviving children than those in the lower socio-economic strata. It appears, then, that differential mortality rates in feudal cities mean more living children in the upper class than in the lower, whereas in industrial cities the upper strata, by availing themselves of the birth control devices created by the advancing technology, have, generally speaking, fewer children than lower-status groups.

The social forms revolving about childbirth can profitably be contrasted with industrial-urban patterns. The roles of father and mother in the feudal city diverge greatly, for the whole matter of birth is largely a woman's affair; men are almost totally excluded. The mother is usually attended by a midwife and female relative, almost never by a male doctor. Although the family announces the birth of a child, particularly a son, with considerable rejoicing, an upper-class father rarely discusses with his male acquaintances the impending birth or the arrival of a child, just as he rarely mentions his wife to outsiders and considers it bad form if someone asks about her.

The preindustrial city—certainly its upper class—lacks any patterns resembling *couvade*. This phenomenon, displayed in many preliterate orders, involves the father-to-be's abstinence from various activities and certain foods; in some cases he has well-defined duties to perform during the birth process and even takes to his bed for days, sometimes weeks, to "recover his strength" after the birth. His portraying the role of the mother is thought to facilitate the birth process and to provide protection for the child from a host of malevolent forces. And in industrial-urban communities we find strong identification of husbands with expectant wives. A recent study suggests that some husbands in American society may actually undergo "labor pains."[39] Be that as it may, without question husbands in many industrial-urban communities come to perform a wide range of tasks associated with preparation for birth and care of the mother and child. This is a reflection of the lack of a rigid division of labor between men and women as well as the absence of a supporting extended family to give aid and comfort to the wife. With respect to husband-wife relationships at parturition, the industrial city and society may be considered to resemble more closely the folk order than the feudal system.

Something might be said about the upbringing of children in the traditional city. They are shown unrestrained attention and affection, the only point in the life-cycle (except at death) when an individual is the focus of strong emotions. For as he becomes a little older he is no longer the center of attention but must adjust to the needs and desires of the family as a whole. Elders are to be respected and obeyed. In some societies, upper-class children bow when greeting or taking leave of their parents, and everywhere in feudal cities terms of address reinforce the status system between elders and children. Compare this with industrial cities, where children seem to wield considerable influence and remain the prime focus of familial activity until they reach adulthood; through both childhood and adolescence they possess a degree of influence over parents and other adults almost unheard of in the preindustrial city, except in very rare instances where a given personality may overcome the definition of the situation.

The mother in the traditional urban milieu is the chief disciplinarian while the children are young—though in the extended family the mother-in-law does not hesitate to take charge. The father, during the infancy of his children, leaves most of the training to the mother, but as the sons grow older, they more and more come under the influence of the father. Generally the mother is more indulgent than the father and on occasion acts as intermediary between father and child. She is the source of love and reassurance for her children and lavishes affection upon them. The father on the other hand is apt to be highly authoritarian, demanding complete obedience and imposing harsh discipline when this is not forthcoming. Considerable formality and social distance typify the father-child relationship. Sons, even married ones, remain under the father's authority as long as they live, more readily achieved among the elite, where sons continue to live in the parental home. Fathers will go so far as to query their married sons as to their friends, activities, and whereabouts. A father, of course, may relinquish his authority and power in old age, when enfeebled, but he is at all times to be accorded great respect.

Childhood in the preindustrial city is marked by various rites of passage, though these vary considerably across cultures in their specific make-up.[40] All preindustrial cities evince one or more of the following, or variations thereof: a naming ceremony, special rites involving godparents (these serve to reinforce kinship bonds with more distant relatives and often to solidify ties among unrelated families), a circumcision ceremony, observances that mark the child's formal introduction to the religious organization, and ceremonies indicating passage into adulthood. Childhood in the highly industrialized city is characterized by less rigidly defined steps toward the adulthood role.

With respect to sibling relationships in the feudal city, these reflect a definite hierarchy of roles on the basis of sex and age. Very young children of both sexes play together. But as early as the age of six or seven the activities of boys and girls become separated. The girls take on various household tasks, and the boys in the elite begin to attend school, while those in the lower class aid, where possible, their fathers at their place of work. It is at this stage of life that girls more and more come to be isolated from the outside world, and by the time of puberty their seclusion, among the elite, is almost complete.

Girls, as noted above, are considered to be inherently different from boys—socially, biologically, mentally, and emotionally—and are trained from an early age to be more docile and well-mannered than boys. Early it is impressed upon them that they are not quite as important as their brothers, just as the latter soon learn to assume a dominant role over their sisters. A brother exercises a certain amount of authority over his sister and in some cultures—e.g., Islam—can, according to traditional norms, kill her if she brings dishonor to the family. Nevertheless, brothers feel strong affection for their sisters and exercise jealous protectiveness concerning them. In a number of societies a brother is expected to take a special interest in the welfare of his sister's children.

Rapport between brothers is apt to be characterized by feelings of rivalry which, while the father or mother, or other elders, are alive, will be repressed, but after the elders are gone the brothers generally split up and set up separate households of their own. In almost all preindustrial cities the eldest son commands a degree of authority over his siblings and is accorded considerable respect. Often distinct terms are employed for older and younger brothers (and sisters and cousins), appellations that may be used throughout a lifetime. The Chinese go so far as to rank siblings in order of birth: relatives may be addressed as First Elder Brother, Seventh Younger Sister, Third Uncle, and so on.

The sharpest age-grading in the family is that between young people and their elders. Unlike the tendency in many industrial-urban communities to shunt elderly persons aside, these enjoy high status, prestige, and authority in feudal cities. As conveyers of the family's and the society's sacred values upon which the young are supposed to, and in the traditional milieu do, base their actions, old people are the fount of authority. They know how things have been done in the past and this is the guidepost for the present.

While the older males are definitely dominant, a woman, too, as she becomes older and takes on the role of mother and then mother-in-law, gains prestige and authority within the family. Moreover, in numerous preindustrial cities a woman after the age of forty is thought to be approaching "old age" (true where life expectancy is so low) and has become so "sexless" that she is permitted to come and go with greater freedom. This increasing age finds expression in dress: after marriage a woman wears more sober garb than before, her clothing takes on increasingly quieter hues after the age of thirty or so, until eventually her clothing makes her sexually hardly noticeable.[41] Women in many industrial cities appear to strive to maintain their sex appeal through dress to a much later age.

Concerning the final stage of the life-cycle—death itself —relatively few cross-cultural generalizations can be offered with confidence, the treatment of the dead in non-industrial cities varying markedly from one culture to the next. But one pattern seems to prevail throughout, exaggerated among the elite: the women of the household are expected to mourn relatives by displays of violent emotion—by weeping and wailing —and the wearing of somber apparel; the wife and daughter of the deceased may maintain official mourning for many months, sometimes years.[42] In an extreme form, widows are enjoined from remarrying, and not so long ago in Indian cities a woman might mount her husband's funeral pyre to join him in death, one expression of the wife's submergence of her individuality into that of her husband.

The Family and the Community

The family's interconnectedness with the economic, political, religious, and educational structures has been commented upon and will stand out more fully in the succeeding chapters.[43] For purposes of emphasis, we observe here that positions in all of these tend to be filled largely on the basis of kinship ties. In turn a family's links with these spheres of activity determine its class position. If an elite family were to loosen its grip upon a corner of the political apparatus, and through this part of the economic surplus, it could not continue for long in its privileged station. The strain toward monopoly of power reaches the point that in many communities one or two large extended families, or on the societal level a mere handful of widely ramified kin groups, hold the reins of government.

Moreover, the feudal city's family plays a far more prominent role in matters religious and educational than does its industrial counterpart. And it fulfils certain other functions that in the industrial city tend to be assumed by community organizations. One of the most obvious is providing recreation for women (and children). Extensive leisure, of course, is limited to the elite, whose servants and other attendants free them from the endless toil that the common man endures. Though the men find diversion to some extent in the community, respectable women generally confine their leisure-time activities to the home. To be sure, in special situations women may engage in community-wide festivals or attend the theatre. But more often, entertainers are hired and brought to the home. Actually these diversions are all secondary to the visiting, gossiping, and partying that is the daily routine for women of the elite. Industrialization sharply transforms these patterns, turning recreation over to non-family agencies —e.g., mass communication media and community-wide or societal organizations.

NOTES TO CHAPTER VI

1. E.g., Walter B. Scaife, *Florentine Life During the Renaissance* (Baltimore: Johns Hopkins Press, 1893), p. 94; Francis L. K. Hsu, *Under the Ancestors' Shadow* (New York: Columbia University Press, 1948), p. 88; Roger Le Tourneau, *Fès: Avant le Protectorat* (Casablanca: Société Marocaine de Librairie et d'Édition, 1949), p. 505; Brinda, Maharani of Kapurthala, *Maharani: The Story of an Indian Princess* (New York: Henry Holt, 1954), p. 1.

2. Le Tourneau, *op. cit.*, p. 527. Le Tourneau remarks upon a guild of go-betweens in Fez; George C. Vaillant, *The Aztecs of Mexico* (Harmondsworth: Penguin Books, 1956), pp. 117-18; Justus Doolittle, *Social Life of the Chinese,* ed. Paxton Hood (London: Sampson Low, 1868), pp. 45ff.; Horace Miner, *The Primitive City of Timbuctoo* (Princeton: Princeton University Press, 1953), pp. 182ff.

3. Le Tourneau, *op. cit.*, pp. 520-21.

4. E.g., consider data on women in contemporary Indian cities. Margaret Cormack, *The Hindu Woman* (New York: Teachers College, Columbia University, 1953).

5. E.g., C. Snouck Hurgronje, *Mekka in the Latter Part of the Nineteenth Century,* trans. J. H. Monahan (Leyden: E. J. Brill, 1931), pp. 106ff.

6. R. P. Dore, *City Life in Japan* (Berkeley: University of California Press, 1958), p. 170.

7. H. D. F. Kitto, *The Greeks* (Harmondsworth: Penguin Books, 1951), p. 220.

8. *Ibid.*

9. E.g., Jacques Lafitte-Houssat, *Troubadours et Cours d'Amour* (Paris: Presses Universitaires de France, 1950); Herbert Moller, "The Social

Causation of the Courtly Love Complex," *Comparative Studies in Society and History,* I (January, 1959), 137-63.

10. E.g., Hurgronje, *op. cit.,* pp. 143-44.

11. Le Tourneau, *op. cit.,* pp. 518ff.; Hsu, *op. cit.,* pp. 93ff.; Doolittle, *op. cit.,* pp. 45-68.

12. Su-ling Wong and Earl Herbert Cressy, *Daughter of Confucius* (New York: Farrar, Straus and Young, 1952), pp. 85-87.

13. Babur Çağatay and Andrée F. Sjoberg, "Notes on the Uzbek Culture of Central Asia," *Texas Journal of Science,* VII (March, 1955), 85; for China see Hsu, *op. cit.,* p. 99. Among both the Chinese and the Uzbeks, however, this practice has been much depreciated.

14. Wong and Cressy, *op. cit.,* pp. 10-11, 88.

15. Christiana Tsai, *Queen of the Dark Chamber* (Chicago: Moody Press, 1953), pp. 27-29. Also see Pu-wei Yang Chao, *Autobiography of a Chinese Woman* (New York: John Day, 1947), p. 9.

16. A description of the enormous household of one of the leading families in Jordan by a member of it is in the author's possession.

17. Hsiao-tung Fei, "Peasantry and Gentry: An Interpretation of Chinese Social Structure and its Changes," *American Journal of Sociology,* LII (July, 1946), 4-5. Supporting observations can be found in Maurice Freedman, *Lineage Organization in Southeastern China* (London: Athlone Press, 1958), p. 28.

18. S. C. Dube, *Indian Village* (Ithaca: Cornell University Press, 1955), p. 133.

19. K. M. Kapadia, "Rural Family Patterns: A Study of Urban-Rural Relations," *Sociological Bulletin,* V (September, 1956), 111-26.

20. Ernest Landauer, "Aspects of Culture and Society in Modern South Central Turkey" (unpublished M.A. thesis, University of California, Berkeley, 1956).

21. E.g., Hsu, *op. cit.,* pp. 229ff.; Wolfram Eberhard, "Change in Leading Families in Southern Turkey," *Anthropos,* XLIX (1954), 992-1003; Khanikoff, *Bokhara: Its Amir and its People,* trans. Clement A. De Bode (London: James Madden, 1845), pp. 234-35.

22. Francis L. K. Hsu, "The Myth of Chinese Family Size," *American Journal of Sociology,* XLVIII (March, 1943), 559-60. Luigi Villari, *Italian Life in Town and Country* (New York: G. P. Putnam, 1902), pp. 29-30.

23. Welthy Honsinger, *Beyond the Moon Gate* (New York: Abingdon Press, 1924), pp. 92-93.

24. Cormack, *op. cit.;* T. G. Tucker, *Life in Ancient Athens* (Chautauqua: New York: Chautauqua Press, 1917); Doolittle, *op. cit.;* Le Tourneau, *op. cit.*

25. Çağatay and Sjoberg, *op. cit.,* p. 86; Cornelius Osgood, *The Koreans and Their Culture* (New York: Ronald Press, 1951), p. 51; Hsu, *Under the Ancestors' Shadow, op. cit.,* p. 60. Teknonymy has also been widely used in upper-class families in Indian cities, a pattern cutting across divergent linguistic groups.

26. A good discussion of this for one cultural setting can be found in Mary Jean Kennedy, "Panjabi Urban Society," in Stanley Moran (ed.), *Pakistan: Society and Culture* (New Haven: Human Relations Area Files, 1957), pp. 81-103.

27. E.g., Edward W. Lane, *The Manners and Customs of the Modern*

Egyptians (5th ed.; New York: E. P. Dutton, Everyman's Library, 1923), p. 195, *passim.*

28. William M. Masters, "Rowanduz: A Kurdish Administrative and Mercantile Center" (unpublished Ph.D. dissertation, University of Michigan, 1954), p. 83.

29. Lane, *op. cit., passim;* Hurgronje, *op. cit.,* pp. 83-84.

30. Carroll Camden, *The Elizabethan Woman* (New York: Elsevier Press, 1952), p. 125. Cf. William D. Howells, *Venetian Life* (rev. ed.; Boston: Houghton Mifflin, 1907), pp. 337ff.

31. E.g., Doolittle, *op. cit.,* p. 68, *passim;* Alice M. Bacon, *Japanese Girls and Women* (rev. ed.; Boston: Houghton Mifflin, 1902), *passim.*

32. Osgood, *op. cit.,* pp. 145-46.

33. E.g., Tsung-lien Shen and Shen-chi Liu, *Tibet and the Tibetans* (Stanford: Stanford University Press, 1953), pp. 143-44; Vibul Thamavit and Robert Golden, "The Family in Thailand," *Marriage and Family Living,* XVI (November, 1954), 382; Virginia Thompson, *Thailand: The New Siam* (New York: Macmillan, 1941), Chapter XIX.

34. Bacon, *op. cit.,* p. 231; George W. Gilmore, *Korea from its Capital* (Philadelphia: Presbyterian Board of Publication, 1892), p. 97; S. G. Wilson, *Persian Life and Customs* (New York: Fleming H. Revell, 1896), p. 256; Wong and Cressy, *op. cit.,* p. 52; Donald N. Wilber (ed.), *Afghanistan* (New Haven: Human Relations Area Files, 1956), p. 347; Kennedy, *op. cit.* Rural-urban differences in the life-ways of women are dramatized most sharply in the Middle East—generally, urban women have been veiled, rural women have not.

35. H. E. Bellew, *Kashmir and Kashghar* (London: Trubner, 1875), pp. 129-223.

36. E.g., G. Morris Carstairs, *The Twice-Born* (London: Hogarth Press, 1957); Wong and Cressy, *op. cit.,* pp. 102-7; Hurgronje, *op. cit.,* p. 144; Wilson, *op. cit.,* p. 266; Lafitte-Houssat, *op. cit.;* Camden, *op. cit.,* Chapter I.

37. Noel P. Gist, "Caste Differentials in South India," *American Sociological Review,* XIX (April, 1954), 132; V. M. Dandekar and Kumudini Dandekar, *Survey of Fertility and Mortality in Poona District* (Poona: Gokhale Institute of Politics and Economics, 1953), Chapter IV; N. V. Sovani, *The Social Survey of Kolhapur City,* pt. 1, *Population and Fertility* (Poona: Gokhale Institute of Politics and Economics, 1948).

38. Ta Chen, "Population in Modern China," *American Journal of Sociology,* LII, Part 2 (July, 1946), 31.

39. "Expectant Fathers," *Time,* LXVI (August 8, 1955), 42-43.

40. Doolittle, *op. cit.,* pp. 92-101; Le Tourneau, *op. cit.;* Miner, *op. cit.;* P. Thomas, *Hindu Religion, Customs, and Manners* (2d ed. rev.; Bombay: D. B. Taraporevala Sons, 195-), pp. 87ff.

41. E.g., Jukichi Inouye, *Home Life in Tokyo* (2d ed.; Tokyo: Tokyo Printing Co., 1911), pp. 105-6; Osgood, *op. cit.,* p. 114.

42. Hurgronje, *op. cit.,* pp. 144-49; Doolittle, *op. cit.,* pp. 70ff.; Osgood, *op. cit.,* p. 147; Wong and Cressy, *op. cit.,* pp. 149-54.

43. For a discussion of the dangers of a familistic interpretation even of traditional Chinese society, see Morton H. Fried, *Fabric of Chinese Society* (New York: Frederick A. Praeger, 1953).

CHAPTER VII

ECONOMIC STRUCTURE

THE feudal city's class structure is not only intercon-
nected with the familial organization, discussed earlier, but
both are interwoven with the economy—evidence, once again,
of the interrelatedness among the component elements of the
total social structure.

Despite the current preoccupation of social scientists in a
variety of disciplines with so-called "underdeveloped" countries, cross-cultural analyses of the economic structure of preindustrial cities are woefully deficient, most of the attention
being directed to the traditional peasantry.[1] The present chapter attempts to fill in, to some extent, this lacuna in the literature. The feudal past must be understood if the many changes
now underway in cities over the world are to be appreciated.

Below we examine the over-all nature of economic activity
in preindustrial cities (with special attention to the values relating to business activity and work in general), the guild
system, and the salient features of industry, commerce, and
services. The chapter concludes with an analysis of prices and
wages, the extent of standardization of economic activity,
and credit and capital formation, with emphasis upon the
divergencies from the industrial-urban system.

General Orientation Toward Economic Activity

We noted previously the low status of persons engaged in commercial or industrial ventures. Typically these are either commoners or outcastes. Here we elaborate somewhat more fully upon the generally depreciated role of the merchant, and then discuss the negative values attached to manual work, the effect of which is to denigrate the status of those who engage in commercial, manufacturing, and service occupations.

Simply because a few merchants have penetrated the privileged elite in medieval Europe, traditional Japan and China, and other societies is not prima facie evidence that most businessmen enjoy a favored position. Far from it. Many are unequivocally lower class and a goodly number are of outcaste, ethnic minority groups.

The humble status of the typical merchant results in part from his preoccupation with money-making and other mundane pursuits that run counter to the religious-philosophical value system of the dominant group, one that in almost every feudal society, relative to the industrial type, emphasizes "other-worldliness" and censures any attempt to manipulate or to revise the natural order of things. The hiatus between businessmen and the elite is further widened by the fact that the authority of the political-religious-educational leaders derives from tradition and from absolutes (the divine right of rulers is an instance of the latter), rationalized in the sacred writings, whereas the occasional merchant can through skill and manipulation, i.e., through profit-making and money lending for interest, accumulate wealth and thereby gain power and authority without appealing to tradition or absolutes. Obviously, this is a threat to the privileged group.

The chief basis of this threat is that the elite requires wealth to survive as such. True enough, it seeks to achieve this through landholding or taxation or tribute, sources of income that are integrated into the authority structure. Still, these may not provide the upper class with sufficient funds to live in the "grand manner." And because no city can function without commerce, a few of the more fortunate merchants are able to use business enterprise as a vehicle for achieving wealth. Through it they can wield influence over the ruling group or purchase certain symbols of eliteness—say landholdings or education and governmental posts for their children. Interestingly, the ultimate dependence of the upper class upon commerce to satisfy its "needs" and its desire for added financial resources act to nullify its efforts at exclusiveness and open the way for a privileged status for a few merchants. Nevertheless, in the end, only "respectable" merchants, not those in outcaste ethnic groups, actually enter the upper stratum; the marginal businessmen must be content with amassing wealth and with indirect manipulation of the ruling elements.

It is not only the machinations of the merchant element that cause them to be scorned; the liberality of their social contacts has much the same effect. The merchant comes into face-to-face contact with lower-status groups throughout the society. Or he may have extensive dealings with foreigners. The result is the same. He is continually suspect because of these associations, being in a position to transmit to the rest of the social order values that may endanger the authority of the elite. Too, the upper class everywhere, to preserve its aura of superiority, maintains social distance between itself and the mass populace. Concomitantly, anyone who associates with the lower-status groups is considered one of them. The nobility in earlier Japan would not deign to talk about money or handle it;[2] no doubt this was one means of removing themselves from identification with lower-status elements, including merchants.

Significantly, the wealthy merchant who acquires prestige and entrée into the upper class seeks to insulate himself from the common man. One method is delegating all negotiation in the market place to brokers and middlemen.[3] In this fashion the upper-class merchant is spared from direct contacts with the lower class and outcastes.

Further, the devaluation of manual labor by the elite, found in cities in all feudal societies—in China, India, the Middle East, medieval Europe, and so on—serves to diminish the status not only of merchants but of all manner of occupational groups. A distinguishing characteristic of the lower class and outcaste groups is the need to engage in work that dirties the hands and, more than this, in labor of an exhausting and menial sort. Life is a never-ending struggle to subsist: the ordinary man's travail ends but with death.

It is the upper class, supported as it is by a myriad of servants, that is exempt from manual labor. It reinforces its own superiority by depreciating non-intellectual activity as degrading, beneath the dignity of men of learning and authority. Conversely, leisure, literary pursuits, and conspicuous consumption are all glorified. A prominent status-marker of the elite is maintaining one's womenfolk in a life of indolence, depending upon servants to perform the menial tasks about the household.

Everywhere the elite use various symbolic indicators to dissociate themselves from manual work. In Lhasa and Bokhara, cities in quite divergent cultural settings, the elite have worn long sleeves extending considerably below the fingers, dramatizing the exclusion of manual work from their lifeways. A similar pattern obtained in Korea where, in fact, the commoners were forbidden to wear long, flowing sleeves. Besides covering their hands with long sleeves the elite in China let their fingernails grow several inches long, emblematic of their negation of "ugly" work habits.[4] In contrast today, the Communists, seeking to industrialize China, are bent upon uprooting this deeply ingrained ideology; one scientist-traveler[5] reports that Chinese "intellectuals" perform daily exercises to purge themselves of the older views and demonstrate to the populace that physical work is prestigeful; and students regularly engage in arduous physical labor, an unthinkable pursuit for this group only a few decades ago.

The lauding of leisure and the scorning of manual labor influence the very economic routine of the feudal city. If no work is immediately at hand, the craftsman or merchant is unlikely to look for more. Consequently, the small trader in the market refuses to sell all of his goods if it is still early in the day, for if he did he would be without an excuse to continue chatting with others. Rarely does he utilize his spare time aggressively to acquire additional stock to sell and thereby augment his income. Nor does the craftsman make an effort to speed up his work or labor overtime to get out promised orders. Initiative and enterprise are not as highly esteemed as leisure. It is the pattern also for the work schedule to be interrupted frequently by festivals.[6] The common man works hard for the little he earns; yet his efforts are ineffectively utilized, relative to the norm in industrial cities. The devaluation of work and efficiency in preindustrial civilized societies, in part attributable to the assumption that man can not with impunity tamper with the natural and/or divine order, accounts in many respects for the failure to expand the economic base.

The devaluation of work is a problem that faces every feudal society that is now seeking to industrialize. Some leaders in India are currently preaching the "gospel of the dirty hand."[7] They are publicly castigating university students and graduates for their unwillingness to undertake manual labor of any kind despite the plethora of applicants for the very limited number of office jobs. Even persons trained in the applied sciences—engineering, geology, and the like—eschew fieldwork and seek desk jobs, all out of keeping with the demands of an industrializing order.

Given these facts, it is easier to appreciate Weber's[8] contention that the concept of "work" took on a special character in the Western world after the rise of Protestantism. Earlier a symbol of low status, work became a virtue in and of itself.

It was now accepted that man could, through work, change the natural order of things. As such, this new perspective was a major impetus to the Industrial Revolution. In light of this, the current picture in industrial societies is a source of surprise. Today in the United States and other highly industrial orders, the common man continues to strive for a shorter work week; but he is faced with a new problem—how to use his leisure time effectively, and, along with this, how to maintain a purpose in life. On the other hand, the managerial and professional groups, engaging in high-status occupational pursuits, seem to be enjoying less and less respite from their labors. The result, if present trends continue, will be a reversal of the patterns that have obtained in preindustrial cities, where the elite enjoys extensive leisure and the lower class is forced to toil more or less unremittingly.

Let us proceed to an analysis of the formal organization of economic activity in the preindustrial city.

Guilds

The most obvious aspect of the preindustrial city's economic organization is its guild system, one that pervades manufacturing, trade, and services, even marginal forms of economic activity like begging and thievery. Guilds are peculiar to towns and cities, not to the villages; only in the former are full-time specialists to be found in appreciable numbers. The few craftsmen and merchants that grace the rural scene usually combine their special functions with part-time farming, and, given the absence of competition among occupational groups in any real sense, they do not organize into economic associations.

Theoretically, a guild includes those persons who are members of a particular occupation or a highly specialized branch of an occupation. In actual practice not everyone who is gainfully employed is affiliated with a guild. In some cities slaves have been excluded from the guild system, as are farmers on the urban fringe. Working women are far less likely than men to belong to guilds. And the governmental, educational, and religious bureaucracies are not so organized. Nevertheless the overwhelming number of craftsmen, merchants, and persons in service occupations are organized along guild lines.

Consider some of the occupational groups organized into guilds in one city, Peking, in the 1920s.[9] Among them were the awning-makers (Cloth Tent Guild), carpenters (Sacred Lu Pan Society), cloth pasters (Cloth Filling Guild Association), shoe fasteners (Sewers of Boots and Shoes Guild, or Double Thread Guild), silk thread-makers (Silk Thread Guild), tinkers (Clever Stove Guild), clock stores (The Clock Watch Commercial Guild Association), hat stores (Hat Guild), leather stores (Five Sages Hide and Skins Guild), second-hand clothes stores (Metropolitan Old Clothes Guild Association), vegetable merchants (Green or Fresh Vegetable Guild), actors (Pear Garden Public Welfare Association), barbers (Beautify the Face Guild), story-tellers (Story Tellers Discussion and Study Association), and waiters (Tea Guild).

A rather wide range of occupations form into guilds in other preindustrial cities as well. Japanese cities have had their money-changers', diviners', and wrestlers' guilds, Katmandu (Nepal) its porters' guilds. Among the panoply of guilds in Fez were those of couriers and musicians.[10] Gibb and Bowen write concerning traditional Muslim cities (and their comments would hold for preindustrial cities in other areas as well):[11]

> Indeed, even the pursuit of disreputable and criminal callings was organized in the same way; so there were guilds of beggars, prostitutes, pickpockets, thieves, and other evil-doers. The criminal guilds had of course no *Kâhyâs* recognized by the authorities, though they paid taxes to the police, and some of them proudly acknowledged patron "saints."

Some preindustrial cities may have lacked guilds, or their

equivalents, but they have been few. We know that early cities of the past—in Babylonia, Assyria, and ancient Greece—had them, as well as Rome and Meso-American cities like Tenochtitlan.[12] Guilds existed in the early Hindu cities, although in more recent centuries the castes and sub-castes—many of which are organized along occupational lines—have assumed numerous functions of guilds (as well as others not ordinarily performed by these): thus we see potters' castes, genealogists' castes, leather-workers' castes, beggars' castes, and many more in traditional Indian cities.[13] Then too, everywhere ethnic groups whose activity has been limited to a particular occupation, whether organized into guilds or not, have, like the castes, performed guild-like functions.

What are some of the generalizable patterns with respect to guilds that seem to recur in feudal cities irrespective of time and space?

The craft and service guilds, and most merchant guilds, are local entities that seldom transcend community boundaries. However, some commercial guilds, those concerned with interurban trade, extend across a number of communities to embrace businessmen dealing in specific products.

Within the city the various guilds are localized into specific quarters or along certain streets. This sets apart the members of one guild from those of others, as well as from the rest of the community, reinforcing the esprit de corps of each guild.

Guilds also maintain their esprit de corps through a formal internal organization. Such has been described for Peking, Constantinople and other Islamic cities, medieval cities of western Europe, etc.[14] The roster of offices ranges from the simple to the elaborate. The Guild of the Blind in Peking, consisting mainly of street singers, had a wide variety of officials: judge, sheriff, counselor, inspector, reporter, chief of police, timekeeper, and others. Below the leading functionaries in the typical guild is a hierarchy of members, usually divided into masters, workers or journeymen, and apprentices, in descending order of rank.

We have been talking about guilds as if they all enjoy comparable status in a community. This is far from the case. Usually the guilds within a city are arranged informally into a hierarchy that is generally co-ordinate with the gradations of social status within the lower class and existing between the latter and the outcastes. Leather-workers' guilds, for example, are almost everywhere at the bottom of the social scale.

With respect to the functions of guilds, one of the most salient is to maintain a monopoly over a particular economic activity within a community. This has been documented for such medieval European cities as Liège, and in Peking the head of the porters', or carriers', guild frankly observed that the chief aim of his association was to prevent outsiders from carrying goods.[15] The right to pursue almost any occupation concerned with manufacturing or trade, or even services, is possible only through membership in the guild that controls it. Monopolistic practices have existed even in cities where a guild may have no "legal" standing; here it exerts controls through informal social pressure, based upon long-standing custom and full acceptance by the community.[16]

The extent of monopoly achieved by guilds has been a source of controversy, particularly among medieval European historians. Some economic historians, caught up in the "romantic" tradition, glorify the medieval order and the supposed lack of competition among the guilds; they see only harmony and integration. But Hirshler[17] contends that competition among guilds—for instance, among those making various kinds of cloth—did indeed exist in medieval cities in Europe. Granted. Nevertheless, here and in other parts of the world there have been strong tendencies toward closure, and in some urban centers almost complete monopoly has been achieved by the guilds. This control has had several consequences. The attempt to introduce new manufacturing techniques, especially those developed by outsiders, is most often suppressed. And it has meant that the recruitment of personnel into many occupations has been the province solely of the guilds.

This selection of personnel into an occupation is, then, a second function of the guilds. Guild membership is a prerequisite to the practice of any occupation, and among the qualifications for membership, kinship ranks paramount. We have already mentioned the primacy of kinship ties in numerous spheres of activity in the preindustrial city. It is the ideal and usual pattern for a son to follow in the footsteps of his father.[18] Guilds usually set up a preference rating—first sons, then nephews and other close relatives, and finally more distant relatives and close friends. But sometimes even the near relatives can not be absorbed into the guild, for the occupational ranks can not swell unduly without harm to the existing membership. And the members themselves have so many children that not all can be accommodated as apprentices.

These recruitment patterns are carried over in many formerly feudal cities that present the outward appearance of "modernization" in high degree. In Beirut today, as an instance, one who wants to hire an office boy does not put an ad in the paper but informs the head clerk of the opening. When all of the head clerk's relatives, not just in the city but often also in outlying villages, have refused the job, the second clerk's relatives have their chance at the position, and so on to the other employees in the office.[19]

Entrance into an occupation thus rests upon who one is (particularistic criteria) rather than what one can do (universalistic criteria). Obviously, even in the preindustrial city particularism is not carried to an extreme; mentally or physically defective persons are excluded from various occupations. Nevertheless, particularism is the norm, and such is feasible in an economic system that is so little dependent upon specialized knowledge. Almost anyone can learn to perform a particular task. In the industrial-urban order, where specialized, highly technical skills are essential in many manu-

facturing, service, or commercial ventures, emphasis upon
universalistic criteria in the selection of personnel is vital to
the continuance of the economic system.

A third function of the guilds consists in training personnel
for an occupation. The craft guilds, and to an extent the
merchant and service ones, provide a formal system of apprenticeship, after which the individual rises through a series
of positions leading ultimately to that of master, or its equivalent. This pattern is well known for the cities of medieval
Europe, but it is often not recognized that it occurs in most
other preindustrial cities as well.

Often the son or other close male relative of a guild member
starts as an apprentice at an early age. In Fez, tailors' apprentices were customarily seven or eight years of age or even
less. In some of the Peking guilds until a few decades ago boys
started as apprentices between the ages 10 and 15. Apprentices do menial tasks about the shop for a number of years,
but rarely are they given any recompense except their food
and lodging and the informal training they acquire through
observation and practice. Their position is a very low one,
akin to that of a servant, although often tempered by a pa-
ternal attitude on the part of their superiors—a relationship
system typical of so many areas of activity in the city. In the
craft guild, after a person becomes a full-fledged worker he
attempts to perfect his techniques under the watchful eye of
the master until eventually he attains the skill, the prestige,
and the power to become a master craftsman himself. The
steps in the ascendancy seem to be less marked in some of
the merchant and service guilds and in certain marginal pursuits like begging. Nevertheless, the humble beggars must
acquaint themselves with the numerous rules governing the
practice of their "occupation," and their guilds normally have
low-status neophytes who must defer to the senior members.

This leads to the fourth function of the guilds: regulating
the activities of the members with respect to the occupation
in question. It is usual for craft guilds to set relatively rigid

standards for workmanship and to seek to control the size of the output. The guilds sometimes stipulate minimum prices for goods and services rendered. While such regulation by the guilds guarantees a higher quality of goods and services than would otherwise be the case, it is also a conservative force inhibiting innovation.

The officers of the guild seek to settle arguments among guild members, to eliminate competition among them, and to arbitrate disputes between the guildsmen and outsiders. Guild members are expected to show a keen interest in their work and to uphold the honor of the guild in their personal lives. Often the guild has a "court" of special officers—including an "executioner" in the Guild of the Blind in Peking—to deal with erring members. Punishment may take the form of fines, physical torture, or expulsion from the guild, which last abrogates one's right to practice the occupation in question.

A fifth function of the guilds is political. The guild serves to protect its body of workers against excessive strictures upon economic activity emanating from the governmental bureaucracy (and even the religious apparatus). For not uncommonly the government exacts tribute from artisans, merchants, and purveyors of personal services and has special functionaries to regulate activities within the market place.[20] Through organized resistance the guild can to a degree reduce the harsh effects of taxation and control. On the other hand, in late medieval Europe, as an instance, the merchant guilds became rather potent special interest groups in their own right, influencing and in some cases determining local governmental policy.

A sixth function of the guilds is strictly economic. The merchant organizations may assist members in establishing shops, or the craft guilds may pool their resources to enable members to purchase the raw materials or services they require in their work. Capital formation, exceedingly difficult for the individual, is then possible for the group.

A seventh function, intimately related to the economic, is

concerned with members' welfare. In traditional China, for example, merchant guilds dealing in intercity trade would set up guild halls in other cities. Merchants traveling to a strange city were protected in what was often an environment hostile to "foreigners." But much more than this, the guild serves as a social security agency on the local level, ranking next to the family as a haven for the worker in time of crisis. The government's role in public welfare is usually minimal. In literate preindustrial, i.e. feudal, societies with their low level of subsistence and high morbidity and mortality rates—where the illness or death of a breadwinner can be disastrous to a lower-class family—the guild can be a vital welfare agency. Among other things, it assures its members of a proper burial and lends assistance to widows and children of the deceased, if destitute. And the guild may supply funds to members for important ceremonial occasions—e.g., for the marriage of a son or daughter. In Fez, certain guilds even assumed responsibility for debts contracted by any of their body. A few medieval European guilds had their own hospitals. And occasionally we find guilds in feudal orders assuming responsibility for public projects and dispensing aid to the poor who may be in no way connected with the organization.

Eight, the guilds perform significant ceremonial functions. Often they have shrines within the guild hall and at times separate temples, mosques, or other special religious edifices of their own. Generally each guild has a patron saint or god or supposed guild founder whom they worship. In Peking "merchants trading with paints for painting the outside of houses say that the paints all belong to gods, Mei Hsien . . . and Ko Hsien. . . . The makers of jade objects say that their god (Ch'ang Ch'un Chen-jen . . .) taught them their technique."[21] This characteristic is widespread—from ancient Babylonia, where Nintukalamma was god of the metalworkers, to medieval Liège, where the millers had St. Germain as patron and the bakers had Notre-Dame de Grivegnée as their protectress, to other medieval European cities, where

St. Éloi was patron of the goldsmiths, St. Crispin patron of the shoemakers, and so on, to Fez, where Sidi Ya'qūb has been patron of the tanners, Sidi 'Ali Bou Ghaleb, patron of the potters.[22]

The work schedule of the guildsman is interrupted periodically by festivals. Annual, semi-annual, or more frequent ceremonial activity honoring the guild's patron saint has been the rule. Banquets, religious rites, and/or processions through the streets accompanied by much pageantry, music, dancing, and general merriment are the order of the day. According to a description published in 1875 of the beggars' guild of Canton,[23] incense was burned twice daily before the image of the tutelary god of the guild and before the ancestral altar containing tablets bearing the names of departed guild members. Each guild member carried a talisman on his person at all times and used the guild's secret password upon demand. Activities of this kind, though varying among cultures, cement social ties and reinforce the guild's collective representations. Moreover, the festivals frequently serve to integrate the guildsmen into a community, for non-guild members at times join in the processions, just as the guild takes part in many of the city-wide festivities.

The reader will readily discern resemblances between the various functions of the guilds and those performed by the labor unions, business associations, and professional organizations of industrial-urban orders. But striking differences appear as well. Considerations of kinship only mildly affect the recruitment of personnel into occupations in the industrial city. The mobility and rapid change in the industrial world, combined with the notion of universalism—i.e., judging each man according to his training and ability—often run counter to the bonds of kinship. Then too, the occupational associations are usually interurban in nature, while preindustrial guilds are local entities that rarely, with the exception of a few merchant guilds—primarily those dealing in export-import trade—develop extra-community ties. Difficulties of transportation and communication in preindustrial orders prevent extensive contacts among cities and therefore among the guilds themselves; on the other hand, industrialization has overcome these hurdles. Now many industrial communities comprise groups, notably scientists, whose very functioning is dependent upon national and international contacts, forcing these persons to a "world view" in the performance of their tasks.

Manufacturing

Manufacturing in the feudal society, overwhelmingly dependent upon animate sources of energy, is of the handicraft type. While some inanimate sources of energy have been employed in the later preindustrial cities—as in windmills or water wheels—these provide only a small fraction of the power required to sustain production in the city. Instead, human beings or animals lift water, turn grinding mills and potters' wheels, transport goods or people (as do rickshaw pullers, for instance); human energy alone, unaided by animal power, performs a multitude of tasks in production. Thus, of the numerous occupations in Fez at about the turn of the present century, only the millers made use of water power, only the oil-makers animal power, in the performance of their tasks. All other industries relied upon human effort.[24] In a situation such as this, typical of preindustrial cities over the world, large construction projects can be realized only through the combined efforts of an enormous number of human beings. How divergent is the industrial city, where machines perform the work of hundreds, yea thousands, of men!

Nonetheless, during the time-span between the world's first cities and the most recent preindustrial centers of Asia and Africa, some technological devices—levers, wheels, pulleys, hammers, etc.—were created to multiply the effects of the muscle power of the craftsman. The very existence of the city, with its concentration of diverse crafts, stimulated innovation. But none of the advances in the feudal world was as revolutionary as the momentous shift to dependence upon inanimate providers of energy.

Manufacturing in the preindustrial city is a small-scale undertaking, confined usually to the homes of craftsmen or small shops in the market place. A few "large" workshops have existed in preindustrial centers, but even these have rarely enclosed more than a few score of workers. The generally small size of the productive unit reflects the simple technology, one that sets barriers to capital formation and prohibits the development of a mass market for goods: purchases are made in small quantities and often for one's immediate, daily needs. And unlike the industrial technology that requires a rational utilization of its complex machinery, preindustrial processing techniques have little need for the concentration of many workers in one spot.

Specialization in production occurs in product, not in process. The craftsman, instead of concentrating upon a particular step in the fashioning of an item, performs all or most of the steps from beginning to end. Starting with the raw materials, he shapes a cup, tray, or whatever, and ends by decorating it himself. These tasks, furthermore, are performed under one roof. Specialization in product is often carried to the point that the craftsman devotes his full time to producing items made from a particular raw material; thus we have goldsmiths, coppersmiths, silversmiths, silk weavers, wool weavers, and so on, each with their own guild.

Besides fabricating an item from start to finish, the craftsman, sometimes his guild, purchases the raw materials from which he fashions his wares; moreover, he functions as a merchant in the marketing of the finished product, devoting part of his workshop to the sale and display of his handiwork. Master craftsmen often make goods to order, especially luxury items. Gadgil[25] observed the persistence of this practice in the Indian city of Poona as late as the 1940s, despite the pressures toward modernization.

For which groups are manufactured items destined? Primarily they are intended for consumption by urbanites. Although some of the city's products are conveyed to the countryside by traveling merchants, these constitute but a small fraction of the total urban manufactures. Contrariwise, the feudal city receives far more from the rural hinterland, subsisting largely on the fruits of the peasant's labor—the "surplus" food and raw materials he produces and the taxes or tribute he renders.

Many of the goods dispensed throughout the city—say, clothing or household utensils—are destined for use by all classes, though they vary in style and quality according as they are meant for the upper or lower strata, with their wide disparities in purchasing power. Luxury goods like jewelry and tapestries are fashioned mainly to cater to the tastes and demands of the upper class. Indeed the royal courts in most feudal orders, as in traditional India, have had their own artisans. The elite alone can afford certain items; in turn "conspicuous consumption" sets it apart as a "superior" stratum. Writers who glorify the medieval world in Europe or Asia—notably the fine objets d'art produced by its craftsmen, requiring years of tedious labor—are actually venerating articles destined for the pleasure of the upper class and the enhancement of its status. In the feudal city, little effort is made to determine the desires and needs of the mass populace or to fashion articles designed to attract more of them as consumers. Their purchasing power is so negligible and the producer's problems of acquiring capital so formidable that a mass market is out of the question in the preindustrial city.

Although production is confined mainly to small workshops, we must not overlook another type of "industry," the construction of large-scale private or public works, some of which survive today as symbols of the former glory of preindustrial civilized societies. Governmental bureaucracies have utilized slave labor or other kinds of forced labor (corvée) on a grand scale to erect city walls, aqueducts, irrigation works, canals, or roads between cities. Theocratic governments like those in Sumer, Pharaonic Egypt, or Meso-America have exacted labor from the populace for the raising of temples and tombs, among other works. Some large-scale projects, in both earlier and later preindustrial centers, required hundreds, even thousands, of men for their construction, a labor extending over years, sometimes decades.

Religious organizations in feudal societies demand toil from their adherents as well so as to concentrate sufficient energy-resources to erect some of the awe-inspiring edifices that dominate the skyline in the cities. According to Gernet,[26] the corvée exacted from the peasantry and other lower-class persons by Buddhist leaders in fifth-century China, for the construction of monasteries, was so excessive that numerous farmers could not raise crops and so had to sell family members into bondage to obtain money for food.

Although the use of forced labor on a massive scale persists in many industrializing societies, the very need for this diminishes with advanced mechanization. Even laborers, to run the machines, must be literate persons with specialized training. No ignorant slave can drive and service a caterpillar tractor or steam-shovel.

Trade

Trading activities engage the energies of more persons than perhaps any other form of economic activity, for the city's manufactured goods, and agricultural and other produce introduced from the hinterland, must be distributed to the urbanites. As indicated earlier, the craftsman himself frequently markets the results of his handiwork at the site of manufacture, which may be his home or a special market.

Furthermore, he may sell directly to the consumer or on a wholesale basis to retail merchants. In any event, the distinction between artisan and merchant is often a fuzzy one in actual practice.

But many persons do confine their activities to buying and selling and organize into guilds according to the commodity or class of commodities in which they deal. Merchants in the city may obtain their stock from farmers or the agents of large landowners, from local craftsmen, or from still other merchants who specialize in importing goods from the rural areas or distant cities or beyond the society's borders. And there are middlemen who specialize in selling at auctions, one of the few occasions where goods are sold in large quantities within a city.

The large merchant may have his own brokers or agents, middlemen who serve a vital economic function and also enhance his status by removing him from direct negotiation with lower-class and outcaste persons. Unlike the vast body of small shopkeepers, the large export-import merchants are apt to deal in a wide range of items, a pattern that has long prevailed in feudal cities. According to one report,[27] almost 300 kinds of "spices" (a term that includes seasonings, perfumes, dyestuffs, and medicinals) were imported into European cities in the early fourteenth century from Asia and Africa. Among these were cultivated cardamoms, cinnabar, castor, camphor, caraway, native (India) ginger, wrinkled (black) ginger, Baghdad indigo, cinnamon flowers, mustard, pine nuts, and tamarind. This trade, we reiterate, is primarily for the sake of the elite, who alone possess the resources to support such efforts.

Although intercity trade, relative to that within cities, supports and requires a more complex organization, the basic principles of its operation are much the same. Once again we see an orientation toward particularism. Vreeland[28] suggests that interurban commerce in Iran is carried out largely between merchants who are friends or relatives, marriage ties being used to cement business relationships among cities, thereby ensuring a steady flow of goods.

Most retail merchants in the city function on a small scale with little stock and a minimum of overhead. Many ply their trade in booths or minuscule shops that they rent in the market place, while not a few, particularly vendors, simply spread a mat on the ground in the market and set out their goods thereon. Merchants generally deal in one, or at the most a few, products and these in relatively small amounts, given their restricted market and the barriers to capital formation. Not infrequently, a number of merchants selling the same product will be located side by side.

The retailer makes little effort to gain customers through any attractive display of his wares. Advertising is literally non-existent. And the shopkeeper rarely selects the assortment and quantity of items in his stock with an eye to consumer demand. Nor is there any grading of produce. The merchant is not customer-oriented, nor could he be in this community devoid of mass communication facilities; the small merchant has merely the vaguest notion of the supply of and demand for specific goods in the city.

The merchant's lack of knowledge of the market is one reason that he keeps only a small supply of goods on hand. This trend is accentuated by the facts that he usually possesses inadequate storage facilities and his customers, who like him exist from hand to mouth, purchase minute quantities of food and other items on a daily basis. If the merchant deals in perishable goods, he must dispose of any excess stock at a loss, refrigeration facilities being absent. A paradoxical result, from the industrial-urban perspective, is that it may actually cost more to buy in quantity, rather than less, if indeed one can purchase goods in large amounts at all. Ordinarily the merchant who has storage space for non-perishable commodities, for example, will attempt to obtain the highest price possible for each item, even if it means a negligible turnover.

Besides the merchants with fixed stations, itinerant vendors travel about the city hawking their wares—water, milk, and foodstuffs being their specialties, although others offer goods and services of all sorts. A study of the peddlers in Peking a few decades ago reveals a startling variety within just one city.[29] Among them were: glutinous rice cake peddlers, pomegranate blossom peddlers, turnip and radish peddlers, sesame oil peddlers, thread peddlers, paper pattern peddlers, melon seed peddlers, gate god peddlers, reed horn peddlers, "moon cake" peddlers, jew's harp peddlers, and charcoal peddlers. Many wore distinctive dress and most had special calls by which they could be recognized by the residents of the locale through which they wandered. A few blew Buddhist temple horns, others struck a kettle with a stick, and still others emitted a loud shriek or sang a special tune. Although, obviously, the particular complex of peddlers that graced the Chinese cityscape is not duplicated in other cultures, this structural arrangement is common throughout the preindustrial-urban world.

The existence of ambulatory merchants is in part a reflection of the familial organization of the preindustrial city, specifically the restriction of "respectable" womenfolk to the home. Ideally only a servant goes to the local market to purchase food and other provisions for the family. Or occasionally the men of the family do the marketing. But when the itinerant peddler comes to the house, the women have an opportunity to examine his goods and to make purchases themselves.

Peddlers, who make their rounds of the city at roughly periodic intervals (they generally have specific territories staked out by their guilds), eliminate some of the inconveniences of shopping for families of all classes, especially if one must travel a considerable distance, utilizing very inefficient transportation media, to obtain a particular product. Of course, in the final analysis, it is not alone for the convenience of the customer that ambulatory vendors exist. Merchants of this type can survive with a modicum of capital. They pay no rent, and the outlay for the merchandise they sell or the services they render is pitifully small.

Services and Other Economic Activities

As a consequence of the low-level technology, the categories of personnel engaged in service occupations in the feudal city are relatively few. Those who serve all classes of the urban populace include barbers, magicians, sweepers, scavengers, washermen, and prostitutes. Peking, like numerous centers, has had its ambulatory entertainers—"the trained mice men," "the trained monkey men," and so on—for most segments of the population.[30]

Nonetheless, most of the purveyors of personal services cater to the needs and desires of the upper class. Teachers and most household servants are among the persons oriented to this group. As to the latter, the elite's devaluation of work, above all manual labor, makes a host of menials mandatory. Cooks, sweepers, carriers, drivers, nursemaids, valets are all indispensable to the effective functioning of the household.

The society's supreme ruler has the most extensive entourage of servants. He also subsidizes the work of poets, dancers, painters, sculptors, or musicians by making them retainers of the court. He is supported in this effort by others of the elite who serve as patrons of the arts. In traditional Siam almost every artist of merit was attached to some member of the upper class, particularly the royal court.[31] Everywhere—in feudal China, Japan, India, medieval Europe—artists of various kinds concentrate in the cities, overwhelmingly in the capital. They lend an air of sophistication to urban living.

Still another form of economic activity—though non-productive in nature—demands attention. This is begging. (Economists might not consider begging an economic activity, but we must do so.) Mendicants from religious orders are prominent in many a preindustrial city. Yet these account for but a small percentage of the persons who eke out a living by seeking alms. Most are from the army of the destitute and the handicapped, and children automatically follow their parents into this "profession," entering it at an early age.

Beggars, in line with other occupational groups, tend to organize into guilds. Here a rigid set of rules governs their activities. Often these define the territory allotted each member and the kinds of tactics to be employed. And a degree of mutual aid obtains within the guild; so, for example, each person might be assured a "decent" burial.

In the non-industrial city, beggars are known to make such a nuisance of themselves that shopowners or others toss them a few coins at regular intervals just to get rid of them. Or some alms-seekers mutilate themselves to increase their "take." An American doctor who practiced in Chungking, China, a few decades ago records that when he attempted to rid a beggar of his sores, the latter resisted on the grounds that his deformities were essential to his occupation.[32] The omnipresence of beggars in most preindustrial cities, along with the thieves and prostitutes, reflects the utter poverty of much of the urban populace and the difficulties of earning a livelihood through productive effort.

The chief categories of the economic organization now considered, we can explore some special features of it that contrast dramatically with those in highly industrialized cities.

The Price System

The price system cuts across the aforementioned areas of economic activity—industry, commerce, and services.

A few fixed prices are discernible, more in interurban than in intracity trade. And the guilds occasionally set prices for their products, though usually this is merely an amount below which its members may not sell their wares or services. Nevertheless, for most goods and services a specific price is universally arrived at through haggling, or higgling, between buyer and seller.[33]

In the haggling process the seller sizes up the customer by his dress and mannerisms to determine whether the latter has any notion of the "real value" of the article in question and what he is probably able to pay. The seller then states a price considerably higher than what he expects to receive. The buyer in turn offers an amount considerably less than what he expects to pay. Gradually each party raises or lowers the figure, as the case may be, until a meeting point is reached.

In the process the verbal duel may wax violent. Usually the customer belittles the item in question and tries to evince little interest in purchasing it, while the seller uses counterarguments to persuade the customer to buy it at the asking price. Occasionally friends, even strangers, will join in, interposing remarks as to the probable worth of the article. Not only does the skill of the participants enter into the final figure, but the relationship of the buyer to the seller is a decisive factor. Friends are likely to obtain goods at favored prices.

Why individual bargaining should be the usual mode of establishing prices in preindustrial civilized orders has been little analyzed by economists. May we offer some probable explanations? Haggling typically occurs in transactions between a single buyer and a single seller, or where organized groups of buyers and sellers dicker collectively (e.g., corporations and labor unions in some industrial societies). In industrial societies, characterized by mass markets, there is widespread recourse to fixed prices. Haggling is excessively time consuming and hardly effectual where a seller must handle large numbers of customers, i.e., where he makes his appeal to a mass market. The need for fixed prices is all the more compelling in industrial cities where the sellers of merchandise, as in a large department store, are not the owners of the goods and have no real knowledge of what is a fair price. Chaos would surely ensue if each clerk were given

free rein to determine, with the help of the buyer, the final
price of an item.

The prevalence of haggling in non-industrial cities can also
be attributed in large degree to incomplete knowledge on the
part of buyer and seller concerning the market. Actually, the
fluctuations in supply and demand during a single day can
be dramatic. Only when a customer shops for an item does
he form an idea of the kind and amount of goods in supply,
and only when the merchant deals with a customer and the
haggling process gets underway does he gain awareness of
the current demand for an article in the city. The reader must
bear in mind that in the feudal city we are describing there are
no mass communication media—no newspapers, radio, television—to inform buyers and sellers as to the market situation. The slow dissemination of information via word-of-
mouth may provide both customer and seller with some notion as to the supply-and-demand situation, but such data are
far from reliable, for by the time the information is received,
conditions may have changed again; add to this the rumors
that flow about the preindustrial city's market place, intensifying the existing instability.[34]

Haggling results also from the usual absence of a fixed
set of weights and measures within the city and the modicum
of standardization of goods and services—in the case of manufactured articles each one is slightly different from the other,
forcing customers to judge the value of most items individu-
ally. Gadgil remarks concerning certain commodities in Poona
in the 1930s:[35]

> The entire absence of grading and standardisation of qualities
> makes it impossible to compare prices from week to week either in
> the same market or as between different markets; and in the absence
> of careful grading, the range of variation in prices, given for a single
> fruit, is so large as to make it very difficult to discover regular trends.

This absence of any basic comparability among goods and
services drives both buyer and seller to haggling as a method
of establishing prices, and from this viewpoint it might be

considered a rational procedure, though not from the perspective of industrial man.

The bargaining process has some marked social functions as well. Lane has described with acumen the selling process in nineteenth-century Cairo.[36]

When a person would make any but a trifling purchase, having found the article that exactly suits him, he generally makes up his mind for a long altercation: he mounts upon the maṣṭabah of the shop, seats himself at his ease, fills and lights his pipe, and then the contest of words commences, and lasts often half an hour or even more. Sometimes the shopkeeper, or the customer, interrupts the bargaining by introducing some irrelevant topic of conversation, as if the one had determined to abate his demand no further, or the other to bid no higher: then again the haggling is continued.

Patterns of this kind prevail in preindustrial cities in divergent cultural contexts.

The popularity of haggling stems in part from the inattention to time as a scarce commodity. People are rarely in a hurry to accomplish their daily tasks. Bargaining constitutes a diversion for both buyer and seller. Ideally, each comes away from a transaction with the feeling that he has outwitted the other. Certainly the merchant assumes no responsibility for bilking a customer by passing off inferior merchandise as of high quality, nor can the customer complain, for these are the rules of the game.

Returning to the price system per se. Besides fluctuating as a result of bargaining, prices oscillate because of the considerable variability in supply and demand in the feudal order, especially where farm produce is concerned. The government exerts almost no controls over what and how much the farmer produces. Certainly the rural villagers have little knowledge of consumer demands in the city. The farmer, moreover, brings his produce to the urban centers at irregular intervals and in varying amounts. Add to this his subjection to the forces of nature. Flood or drought leading to poor crops in one sector of the society can have devastating effects upon the cities nearby. The poor communication and transportation make it well-nigh impossible, or at best extremely costly, for the city to import food from more distant regions.[37] Evidence from traditional India suggests that while famine wreaked havoc in one part of the subcontinent, surrounding areas often were little affected. The local nature of the market and the poor distribution facilities preclude supply movements to devastated areas, assuming that the situation is even known to other parts of the society.

Political instability contributes to the erratic nature of the market. Foreign or intrasocial conflicts have periodically reduced farmers in the countryside to ruin or have cut off supplies to the city, causing prices to skyrocket.

Moreover, inadequacies in storage facilities and the complete absence of such a technological device as refrigeration mean continual fluctuations, both diurnal and seasonal, in the supply of many commodities. And the wide price variations within a single day are functionally related to the nature of the technological base. In the early morning the seller of perishable items attempts to obtain relatively high prices for them, but as the day wears on into late afternoon he is faced with the alternative of selling his goods for whatever he can get or allowing them to spoil. The haggling process, as noted earlier, must and does take this into account. By way of contrast, we find that the technological advances of the industrial city tend here to stabilize the supply of many products.

In this discussion of prices it must be borne in mind that not all commercial transactions are realized in terms of money. Barter of goods and services is widespread. In the earliest preindustrial cities, before the invention of metallic coins, it probably was the rule. As to feudal societies of more recent vintage, barter is common between urbanites and farmers who come to the city to purchase goods, for the latter have access to little currency.[38]

Payment in kind is usual for certain kinds of services rendered. Household servants and apprentices in the guilds, sometimes full-fledged workers, are customarily reimbursed in this fashion. Fried records this practice for a Chinese city as late as the 1940s,[39] and it has been mentioned for many others as well. In many preindustrial cities school teachers have been paid partially or totally in kind,[40] and the ranks of the clergy are frequently supported by offerings in the form of food and clothing. The persistence of these patterns, alongside the recourse to coined money, can be attributed to the low standard of living of so much of the citizenry as well as to the relative paucity—compared to conditions in industrial cities—of currency in circulation. And a good part of the existing currency tends to be corralled by the privileged few.

Non-standardization of Economic Activity

The typical market place—the shop fronts or stalls flush with the street, wares spread on the ground almost under the feet of passers-by, the crowds of shoppers and vendors milling about, and animals everywhere adding to the noisy confusion—is in a sense a reflection of the state of the economic organization. Formal, purposive planning in the economic realm by either the business community or the local government is sparse. From the standpoint of the industrial-urban system at least, little "rationalization" of economic activity can be said to exist, hardly surprising, given the low prestige accorded commercial ventures.

Considerable laxity and "irrationality" appear, first of all, in the expenditure of time and effort. Merchants and handicraft workers generally do not adhere to any fixed schedule. Shopkeepers open and close their shops as they see fit. They may open one morning at nine, the next at ten, and so on. The lunch hour is likely to be longer on some days than others. Ambulatory merchants, likewise, are apt to keep rather irregular schedules. To a degree these patterns are an expression of the fact that performing one's tasks in a leisurely manner and chatting with one's neighbors and friends are highly valued pursuits. Indeed, because much business is carried out on a highly personal plane, it becomes mandatory for the businessman to maintain friendly relations with customers, and vice versa—quite disparate from the impersonality of shopping patterns in industrial cities.

Economic life in the urban community is characterized also by minimal synchronization of effort, particularly with respect to work schedules. In the industrial milieu the irregular work habits of one group could upset whole enterprises. And with the emergence of highly specialized experts, the functional interrelationships among occupational groups or subgroups within these become increasingly complex. The tie between segmentation of function and social interdependence needs to be more carefully examined. In general, sociologists fail to realize that division of labor can take several forms. As indicated above, minute division of labor obtains among vendors in the feudal city, but this does not closely integrate shopkeepers, peddlers, and so on. It is only when division of labor involves highly specialized knowledge—when a few men become indispensable to the others—as in a highly industrialized city, that strong interdependencies and "organic solidarity" can be achieved.

The non-standardized work habits of the preindustrial city are further correlated with the view that time is not a scarce commodity, something to be utilized to the fullest. The prodigality with which time is expended is functionally related to the simple technology. Precise means of time-measurement are simply not available. Preindustrial urbanites, even if they wanted to, could not adhere to fixed schedules. Students of underdeveloped countries tend to assume that the peasantry alone encounters difficulties in adjusting to the fixed routine of the industrial community; they fail to recognize that inherent in the preindustrial city's structure is a devaluation of regularity, uniformity, and speed in the performance of ordinary, mundane tasks. The preindustrialite views industrial man as in a sense a slave to the machine.

Marketing in non-industrial cities is likewise characterized by little standardization in goods and services, in weights and measures, and in the monetary system. It is true that the guilds have attempted, not always successfully, to regulate the type and quality of manufactures; however, they are for the most part local entities whose jurisdiction does not extend beyond the city. Admittedly, marketing practices are not fully standardized in the industrial city, but the latter is well ahead of the preindustrial community in this respect.

For many commodities, grading, sorting, and processing are uncommon. Certainly there is almost no branding of products by the producer. Foodstuffs, in particular, are left unsorted by producers, wholesalers, and retailers. The farmer or merchant simply dumps various types and qualities of fruit into a single container and presents them thus for sale. And fruit frequently arrives in the city in either an overripe or an immature condition, a reflection of the poor timing in the marketing process. In turn, rotting fruit, being mixed in with that of better quality, naturally accelerate spoilage of the whole. From the viewpoint of the feudal city's merchant, sorting and grading are unfeasible in the absence of a mass market; nevertheless, this historical pattern acts to impede the development of efficient marketing practices in present-day traditional societies.

Purposive adulteration of goods is common; with caveat emptor the rule in the preindustrial city, the customer must be ever on guard to avoid being defrauded. The dangers of purchasing large lots of produce or ordering goods sight unseen are obvious. Adulteration of agricultural products is so rife in Teheran that large-scale buyers automatically assume adulteration has occurred and offer consistently low prices by way of self-protection.[41] In Pakistani cities today gravel is mixed in with rice, and milk diluted with water. Like practices were widespread in European cities until a few centuries ago and persist still in urban communities in Latin America. According to a recent study, the Marwari,[42] a merchant caste in India, have long indulged in this practice but feel that now, with the advent of a mass market, adulteration is no longer economically profitable. In the industrial city, where customers are better informed and have more rights, adulteration is much reduced. And in some highly industrialized societies profit rests upon a vast turnover of goods at a small margin of gain, accomplishable only if the quality of products is standardized.

Perhaps the sector of least standardization is weights and measures. Contemporaneously within a single city—in parts of traditional China, India, the Middle East, or medieval Europe—a variety of systems of weights and measures have been employed. Each guild may set its own standards, and different commodities are sold by merchants according to varying systems of measurement. Not that attempts have not been made to impose a degree of uniformity, but these efforts have been largely ineffective.

As illustrative of intracommunity variability in weights, a traveler to Kabul at the turn of the present century observed that the shopkeepers dispensing grains and liquids—here sold by weight rather than measure—resorted to ordinary stones of varying sizes for determining weights. True standards were non-existent (indeed, the technological state obviated standardization, were this a goal). Weights, then, differed from shop to shop, encouraging cheating by merchants.[43]

Measures are apt to be imprecise indeed. In Fez the official gauges of length for certain artisanal groups have varied according to the individual: e.g., one unit of measure is the length from the elbow to the tip of the middle finger, another the space to which a man can extend his arms sideways. Besides these "official" measures a craftsman may employ a personal gauge such as the flaps of his shirt. In Bokhara one measure involved the distance from the tip of the nose to the forefinger when the arm is extended; in Lhasa it was standard practice to measure the length of small items against the joints of the forefinger or the breadth of the fingers when held together.[44]

Correlated with the intracommunity divergencies in weights and measures is the latter's strong variability among communities—in Middle Eastern societies, medieval Europe, and so on. In China:[45]

The unit measure of capacity is the *tou,* or peck. In Nanking for rice it contains 558.3 cubic inches. In Shanghai for rice 728.6, but for beans only 655.4 cubic inches. In Ningpo a *tou* of rice measures 565 cubic inches, but in Swatow 768.8. . . .

The linear unit is the *ch'ih,* or foot, which is divided into ten *ts'un,* or inches. The foot is fixed by treaty at 14.1 inches English, but in common practice its length depends upon locality and upon the calling. In Shantung, in the city of Linch'ingchou, a foot in brick-work is 11.15 inches, in land measure 12.2 inches, and in measuring cloth it is 23.75 inches. In the neighboring city of Tsinan the land measure is a foot of 14.55 inches and the cloth measure one of 21.4 inches. In Nanking the tailor's foot is 13.75 inches, while the carpenter's is 12.5 inches.

Currency, too, is little standardized in the feudal milieu, despite the sporadic attempts of governments, as in China, to achieve uniformity in the monetary units employed. Not only do the size and weight of coins of a particular denomination frequently vary within a city, but disparate systems of currency may be in circulation at the same time. The marketing process is made much more complex and dishonesty encouraged thereby. Ignorance on the part of the common man concerning the rates of exchange among these currencies makes him easy prey for money changers, necessary functionaries in this situation.

Empirical evidence for intracommunity variations in currency exists across cultures and through historical epochs: in ancient Greece, medieval Europe, and Middle Eastern societies, and it has been documented in considerable detail for traditional Chinese cities by Morse and others.[46]

The paucity of standardization within and among cities is functionally related to the social and technological order: to the dearth of communication, to the fact that the market in one community is not linked to that in others, to the pattern whereby each guild (as an autonomous body) sets its own standards, and to the highly personalized nature of the marketing arrangement.

At the same time, the non-standardized systems of currency, of weights and measures, and of quality contribute to much duplication of effort in the economy, low output in industry, and poor integration of the component aspects of the marketing process. It is a cause for wonder that as much trade is accomplished as it is.

Credit and Capital Formation

We turn briefly to an analysis of credit and capital formation. Credit is not easily obtainable in preindustrial cities. Particularly in medieval Europe and the Muslim world have religious norms, strongly enforced by the elite, discouraged the lending of money for interest. Some merchants have been able to contravene these injunctions through certain sub rosa practices. Or outcaste groups—e.g., Jews, Christians, and Hindus in otherwise Muslim cities—have become specialists in money lending.

The extension of credit is not a highly organized activity. Much of it is realized on a small scale by individuals. Banks exist in some non-industrial centers—as in ancient Greece, medieval Europe, and traditional China. But by and large these have played a minor role in furthering economic enterprise. Even in the important commercial city of Fez, true banking did not develop until about 1890, when the Jews were largely responsible for its introduction.[47]

Why should credit—the basis of so much of the industrial-urban economy—be so poorly developed in preindustrial cities? We have stressed the elite's negative valuation of usury, the latter being a threat to the authority structure. In addition, extending credit to the common man is a risky venture. Most persons lack any form of collateral; the impoverished urbanite has little more than a hovel and the shirt on his back to call his own. Besides, a host of unforeseen disasters can befall any debtor; morbidity and mortality rates are high, and the possibility of property destruction through the vagaries of nature—flood, storms, insects, etc.—is ever present. Credit is, consequently, extended to the ordinary man at exorbitant interest rates (relative to those in industrial cities). Then at best he receives short-term loans, for a few weeks or months.

Pertinent data point to steep interest rates in non-industrial cities everywhere. Those in China are no exception. For nineteenth-century Korea, Dallet observed that 30 per cent interest (presumably per annum) was considered ridiculously low. In cities of Iran today rates of 25 to 35 per cent or slightly more are usual, while in the late nineteenth century, according to Wilson, interest varied from between 12-18 per cent to as high as 48-120 per cent. Interest on loans in the medieval Italian city of Prato ranged between 20 and 40 per cent.[48] These are all rates charged by money lenders, pawnbrokers, and similar functionaries.

Admittedly, expedients of various kinds do develop to circumvent the difficulties of obtaining credit and the excessive interest charged. Korean and Chinese cities have had their loan associations set up by circles of friends who pool their resources to ensure each person of funds in times of emergency.[49] The religious ban on usury in Muslim Middle Eastern cities has led to a system whereby a trader-money lender buys from a person seeking cash, goods at bargain rates for future delivery and pays part of the price immediately; then months later, when delivery is made, the money lender pays the balance and, as intended, resells the goods for considerably more than he paid for them—the difference forming his "interest."

In the end, with the limited credit facilities available, the kinship system plays a conspicuous role in capital formation.

A large extended kinship unit, by pooling its resources, may raise an appreciable amount of capital to enable some of its members to finance business ventures or to carry out special construction projects. Here again the extended family reinforces the socio-economic position of the haves as opposed to the have-nots.

True, the guilds have acted as reservoirs of capital for their members as well. However, the amount of capital that can be amassed by the typical artisan guild is far from impressive, though some do better than others in this respect. Undeniably, the paucity of capital available to manufacturing enterprises or merchants or persons dispensing services accounts in large degree for the failure of preindustrial urbanites to undertake new ventures or expand existing ones.

The government, through its power of taxation and appropriation of labor, can accumulate capital to realize some large-scale activities. Yet, as a "passive" organization (discussed in the ensuing chapter), it undertakes a minimum of public works.

Ultimately, it is the simple technological base that makes enterprise on a grand scale well-nigh impossible. The slowness of technological innovation limits capital formation, technology itself being one of the most potent forms of capital available. Conversely the dearth of capital, combined with the considerable underemployment, cheap labor, etc., hinder technological advance, a vicious circle broken by the advent of industrialism. The industrial system amasses capital with relative ease, in turn fostering technological advance. Witness the vast expenditure of funds today in the attempt to conquer outer space—with resultant discoveries and innovations that will have an incalculable impact upon the urban social structure. An advancing technology demands ever more experts, with consequent increase in the complexity of the economic organization that directs it.

Gone forever are the days of small-scale production and an uncontrolled economy. For good or for ill, it is conscious

direction of the economy—by private or governmental bureaucracies—that leads to purposive efforts to create added
capital, often through the medium of fostering scientific advancement—the backbone of modern industrialization. And
a built-in value of modern science is the ideology of manipulating the "universe" for man's own advantage.

NOTES TO CHAPTER VII

1. For an exception to the rule, see Morton R. Solomon, "The Structure
of the Market in Underdeveloped Economies," in Lyle W. Shannon (ed.),
Underdeveloped Areas (New York: Harper and Bros., 1957), pp. 131-40.

2. Matsuyo Takizawa, *The Penetration of Money Economy in Japan*
(New York: Columbia University Press, 1927), p. 35.

3. E.g., Justus Doolittle, *Social Life of the Chinese*, ed. Paxton Hood
(London: Sampson Low, 1868), pp. 451-52; Roger Le Tourneau, *Fès:
Avant le Protectorat* (Casablanca: Société Marocaine de Librairie et d'Édi-
tion, 1949), pp. 377-78.

4. Heinrich Harrer, "My Life in Forbidden Lhasa," *National Geographic
Magazine,* CVIII (July, 1955), 26-27; O. Olufsen, *The Emir of Bokhara
and His Country* (London: William Heinemann, 1911), p. 470; Cornelius
Osgood, *The Koreans and Their Culture* (New York: Ronald Press, 1951),
p. 232; Welthy Honsinger, *Beyond the Moon Gate* (New York: Abingdon
Press, 1924), p. 27.

5. J. Tuzo Wilson, "Red China's Hidden Capital of Science," *Saturday
Review,* XLI (November 8, 1958), 47-56.

6. E.g., Le Tourneau, *op. cit.,* p. 363; Georges Renard, *Guilds in the
Middle Ages* (London: G. Bell, 1918), p. 15.

7. K. M. Munshi, *The Gospel of the Dirty Hand* (Delhi: Government
of India, 1952).

8. Max Weber, *The Protestant Ethic and the Spirit of Capitalism,* trans.
Talcott Parsons (New York: Charles Scribner's Sons, 1950).

9. J. S. Burgess, *The Guilds of Peking* (New York: Columbia University
Press, 1928), pp. 109-18.

10. E.g., George Sansom, *Japan: A Short Cultural History* (rev. ed.;
New York: D. Appleton-Century, 1943), pp. 37-42; Jukichi Inouye, *Sketches
of Tokyo Life* (Yokohama: Torando, 1895), pp. 38ff.; Herbert Tichy,
"Leben in Nepal," *Westermanns Monatshefte,* XCIX (November, 1958),
68; Le Tourneau, *op. cit.,* pp. 406, 560.

11. H. A. R. Gibb and Harold Bowen, *Islamic Society and the West,* I,
Part I (London: Oxford University Press, published under the auspices of
the Royal Institute of International Affairs, 1950), 290.

12. E.g., I. Mendelsohn, "Gilds in Babylonia and Assyria," *Journal of
the American Oriental Society,* LX (March, 1940), 68-72; Fr. Bernardino

218   *Economic Structure*

de Sahagún, *Historia General de las Cosas de Nueva España,* ed. Angel María Garibay K., III (México, D. F.: Editorial Porrua, 1956), Book 9.

13. D. R. Gadgil, *Poona: A Socio-Economic Survey,* Part II (Poona: Gokhale Institute of Politics and Economics, 1952). Gadgil points up the continuance of traditional patterns as well as recent deviations from them.

14. Burgess, *op. cit.,* p. 104; Charles White, *Three Years in Constantinople,* I (London: Henry Colburn, 1845), 202; Gibb and Bowen, *op. cit.,* p. 284; Renard, *op. cit.,* p. 29.

15. Burgess, *op. cit.,* p. 88; René van Santbergen, *Les Bons Métiers* (Liège: Université de Liège, 1949), pp. 260ff.

16. E.g., C. Snouck Hurgronje, *Mekka in the Latter Part of the Nineteenth Century,* trans. J. H. Monahan (Leyden: E. J. Brill, 1931), pp. 27-28.

17. Eric E. Hirshler, "Medieval Economic Competition," *Journal of Economic History,* XIV (Winter, 1954), 52-58.

18. E.g., T'ai-ch'u Liao, "The Apprentices in Chengtu During and After the War," *Yenching Journal of Social Studies,* IV (August, 1948), 90-106; Le Tourneau, *op. cit.,* pp. 297, 360-61; Horace Miner, *The Primitive City of Timbuctoo* (Princeton: Princeton University Press, 1953), p. 52.

19. Sydney Nettleton Fisher (ed.), *Social Forces in the Middle East* (Ithaca: Cornell University Press, 1955), p. 89.

20. Gibb and Bowen, *op. cit.,* p. 288; A. N. Kuropatkin, *Kashgaria* (Calcutta: Thacker, Spink, 1882), p. 45; Daniel L. Gifford, "Korean Guilds and Other Associations," *Korean Repository,* II (February, 1895), 43.

21. Niida Noboru, "The Industrial and Commercial Guilds of Peking and Religion and Fellowcountrymanship as Elements of their Coherence," *Folklore Studies,* IX (1950), 182.

22. E.g., van Santbergen, *op. cit.,* p. 349; Renard, *op. cit.,* p. 44; Le Tourneau, *op. cit.,* p. 304; cf. Francesc Curet, *La Vida a la Llar* (Barcelona: Dalmau i Jover, 1952), p. 263.

23. John H. Gray, *Walks in the City of Canton* (Hongkong: De Souza, 1875), pp. 259-60.

24. Le Tourneau, *op. cit.,* p. 357.

25. D. R. Gadgil, *Poona: A Socio-Economic Survey,* Part I (Poona: Gokhale Institute of Politics and Economics, 1945), p. 140.

26. Jacques Gernet, *Les Aspects Économiques du Bouddhisme dans la Société Chinoise du Ve au Xe Siècle* (Saigon: École Française d'Extrême-Orient, 1956), p. 13.

27. Robert S. Lopez and Irving W. Raymond, *Medieval Trade in the Mediterranean World* (New York: Columbia University Press, 1955), pp. 108-14. Cf. J. C. van Leur, *Indonesian Trade and Society* (The Hague: W. van Hoeve, 1955).

28. E.g., Herbert H. Vreeland (ed.), *Iran* (New Haven: Human Relations Area Files, 1957).

29. Samuel Victor Constant, *Calls, Sounds, and Merchandise of the Peking Street Peddlers* (Peking: The Camel Bell, 1936).

30. *Ibid.*

31. Walter F. Vella, *Siam Under Rama III* (Locust Valley, N. Y.: J. J. Augustin, 1957), Chapter IV.

32. George C. Basil, *Test Tubes and Dragon Scales* (Chicago: John C. Winston, 1940), pp. 257-60. Cf. R. Mukerjee, "Causes of Beggary," *Indian Journal of Social Work,* IV (June, 1943), 23-28.

33. In some large preindustrial cities—Fez, Cairo, Poona, Kabul—goods in large lots may be disposed of at auctions. Here there is competitive bidding among a number of buyers for a quantity of merchandise.

34. Vreeland, *op. cit.*, p. 216.

35. D. R. Gadgil and V. R. Gadgil, *A Survey of Marketing of Fruit in Poona* (Poona: Gokhale Institute of Politics and Economics, 1933), p. 36. Cf. Abdel Aziz el Sherbini and Ahmed Fouad Sherif, "Marketing Problems in an Underdeveloped Country—Egypt," *L'Égypte Contemporaine*, XLVII (July, 1956), 48-50.

36. Edward W. Lane, *The Manners and Customs of the Modern Egyptians* (5th ed.; New York: E. P. Dutton, Everyman's Library, 1923), p. 324.

37. Miner, *op. cit.*, p. 48.

38. E.g., C. P. Fitzgerald, *The Tower of Five Glories* (London: Cresset Press, 1941), p. 58.

39. Morton H. Fried, *Fabric of Chinese Society* (New York: Frederick A. Praeger, 1953), p. 165; Cf. Liao, *op. cit.*, p. 97; Renard, *op. cit.*, p. 10.

40. E.g., Yan Phou Lee, *When I Was a Boy in China* (Boston: Lothrop, Lee and Shepard, 1887), p. 52; Le Tourneau, *op. cit.*, p. 538; Khanikoff, *Bokhara: Its Amir and its People*, trans. Clement A. De Bode (London: James Madden, 1845), p. 275.

41. Herman S. Hettinger, "Marketing in Persia," *Journal of Marketing*, XV (January, 1951), 292.

42. Harry A. Millman, "The Marwari: A Study of a Group of the Trading Castes of India" (unpublished M.A. thesis, University of California, Berkeley, 1954), p. 70.

43. Frank A. Martin, *Under the Absolute Amir* (London: Harper and Bros., 1907), pp. 145, 245.

44. Le Tourneau, *op. cit.*, pp. 276-77; Khanikoff, *op. cit.*, p. 146; Austine Waddell, *Lhasa and its Mysteries* (New York: E. P. Dutton, 1906), p. 354.

45. Edward T. Williams, *China, Yesterday and Today* (5th ed.; New York: Thomas Y. Crowell, 1932), p. 192. Cf. Nicola A. Ziadeh, *Urban Life in Syria* (Beirut: American Press, 1953), pp. 141-44; Lopez and Raymond, *op. cit.*, p. 152.

46. E.g., Hosea Ballou Morse, *The Trade and Administration of China* (New York: Longmans, Green, 1913), Chapter V. Cf. Lopez and Raymond, *op. cit.*, p. 13; Ziadeh, *op. cit.*, pp. 143-44.

47. Le Tourneau, *op. cit.*, pp. 289-90.

48. Charles Dallet, *Traditional Korea* (New Haven: Human Relations Area Files, 1954), p. 180; Hettinger, *op. cit.*, p. 291; S. G. Wilson, *Persian Life and Customs* (New York: Fleming H. Revell, 1896), p. 283; Iris Origo, *The Merchant of Prato* (London: Jonathan Cape, 1957), p. 150.

49. Doolittle, *op. cit.*, pp. 458-59; Gifford, *op. cit.*

CHAPTER VIII

POLITICAL STRUCTURE

CENTRAL to the stratification system that pervades all aspects of the feudal city's social structure—the family, the economy, religion, education, and so on—is the pre-eminence of the political organization. The time has come to probe more deeply into the operation of the governmental apparatus, the bases of its authority, and the specific functions it performs.

Control of the Governmental Structure

We reiterate: the feudal, or preindustrial civilized, order is dominated by a small, privileged upper stratum. The latter commands the key institutions of the society. Its higher echelons are most often located in the capital, the lower ranks residing in the smaller cities, usually the provincial capitals.

At the apex of the ruling stratum is the sovereign, the supreme ruler. He of all personages basks in comfort, splendor, and luxury—i.e., relative to the society's poor—though his mode of existence does not approach in physical comforts that of many an industrial-urbanite. The best the feudal society has to offer, plus what luxuries can be imported from

without, are the sovereign's. Serving at times as both temporal
and spiritual head, his power and authority can be overwhelming. So the Dalai Lama, supreme ruler of traditional
Tibet, was to his subjects a reincarnation of Buddha, and
each pharaoh in ancient Egypt was a manifestation of a deity.

Seldom, however, does a person rule single-handedly: the
sovereign is assisted by his ministers and advisers. Alongside
the governmental bureaucracy's leading officials are the heads
of the religious and educational organizations, who wield
much power and authority in societal affairs. Subordinate to
these topmost leaders in the capital are a series of officials
ranging downward through the leaders in the provinces to
those in charge of local community affairs.

The governmental functionaries at the pinnacle of the society are very commonly drawn from large extended families
whose exercise of community and societal power persists
over many generations. Such kin groups, large and small,
have ruled the destinies of most feudal societies from the beginning of history. Their claim to power is translated into
authority through appeal to divine right and tradition. What
appear at first sight to be exceptions, closer inspection reveals
to be not far from the rule. Though the Dalai Lama, god-king
of traditional Tibet, was regularly drawn from the commoner
group, he was isolated at a tender age from ordinary society
and passed a lifetime enfolded in the wings of a small, hereditary nobility, comprising, until recently, about 200 families.[1]

The number of ruling families in most feudal societies is
small. Yet members of these occupy virtually all the strategic
seats of control in the social order, especially in the smaller
feudal societies. This pattern is reinforced by the sizeable
progeny of many of the elite: kings have had dozens of children. These and other close relatives fill the main bureaucratic posts, thereby providing the ruler with a loyal administrative staff in the capital as well as in the provincial centers.
Actually the ruling clique is generally smaller than the total

upper class, and it is the most privileged segment of this stratum because of its control of the top echelons of the educational, religious, and governmental organizations.

Although advantageous kinship ties are usually necessary if power and authority is to be attained, we occasionally find wealth, or sheer force alone, propelling a person to the summit of the social pyramid. Even then the individual must buttress his new-found gains by building up "correct" kinship ties, say through marriage, for in the end his children can sustain themselves in positions of power only through an influential kinship apparatus.

So today Afghanistan continues under the rule of a very few large families whose power and authority pervades the total society. The number of families in Iran who dominate the political structure on the societal level, and by implication the local scene as well, is perhaps between 200 and 1,000.[2] Societal dominance by a handful of kinship groups is a recurrent theme throughout the histories of European, Middle Eastern, and Indian societies.[3]

As implied above, not a few local communities are dominated by one, or at best a few, families. These local family units, however, must be linked to some regional or societal power structure if they are to survive. One means of accomplishing this is intermarriage with elite families in other cities. The desired result will be various branches of a kinship unit distributed in a number of communities over the society.

Landauer's[4] study of the traditional twentieth-century Turkish community of Gaziantep illustrates this world-wide phenomenon. He discusses the Göğüş family's historic pre-eminence in the community, which it has achieved through its strong representation in the city's religious, educational, and governmental bureaucracies and its shunning of commercial pursuits (although recently some movement into the latter sphere by other elite families has occurred). Moreover, the Göğüş family has branches in other cities; and through these links the family's power and authority extends across community boundaries; conversely these extra-community ties have apparently helped to cement its authority in Gaziantep.

Our argument is not intended to embrace any form of familistic determinism, for non-kin forces are also operative in preindustrial cities and societies.[5] Nevertheless, because the bonds of kinship tend to be more binding than any others in the feudal setting, it is normal for the dominant group to utilize these to the fullest, thereby ensuring a faithful cadre of supporters throughout the social order.

Before the awesome supremacy of the ruling clique, the lot of the humbler strata, from the viewpoint of industrial man, is unenviable indeed. The commoner, faced with what seem to be arbitrary decisions on the part of the elite, "is not to reason why, but to do or die." The dominant element, the educated, "cultured" body, stands in dramatic contrast to the illiterate mass populace, who cringe before their superiors and have little or no awareness of what is transpiring in the social system. Yet, harsh though the existence of the lower class and outcastes may be, mass insurrection against the governing stratum is relatively rare in most preindustrial civilized societies. Internal dissensions within the upper class and attack by power groups from without are much more potent threats to those at the apex of the social pyramid.

The characteristic inertia of the common man, whether in the village or in the city—a result of his lack of knowledge of the machinations of the political functionaries—explains some of the attitudes and values of the populace in societies now endeavoring to shift from a preindustrial to an industrial base. Public opinion pollsters, imbued with the democratic ideals of Western social science, are slowly coming to realize that often the common man has no opinion on prevailing political practices. The notion that the ordinary person is capable of making meaningful judgments on societal issues is unheard of in the feudal order. Public opinion, at least as defined by the pollsters in industrial orders, does not exist. It is a commonplace, no less in the cities than in the countryside, for the humbler strata to accept the opinions and the decisions of their superiors, who think for them and act for them. When questioned, persons may flatly refuse to express themselves on controversial subjects, and of course women of all classes are not supposed to think independently. The interviewer is likely to be referred to local leaders or to husbands who will speak for them. Opinions in preindustrial civilized societies are largely a matter of joint decisions by elders and well-established leaders.

How different is the industrial order, where persons play multiple roles and view questions from different angles, forming in the process unique judgments. The mass populace here gains self-awareness and knowledge, through education, of alternative modes of acting. Industrial-urbanization is a necessary, if not sufficient, condition for these developments.

Legitimization of the Elite's Rule

Just how do a few upper-class families manage to sustain their privileged position, their essentially autocratic rule, and their obliviousness to the needs and desires of the common man? That the elite is the sole determiner of what is right and good for a city or a society must somehow be rationalized and justified if the lower class and outcaste groups are to accept the status quo and the society is to continue essentially unchanged through time.

Weber[6] is one of the few scholars to have examined in detail the bases of authority in a social order, and particularly the means by which power is transmuted into authority. His work serves as a convenient take-off point for our analysis. We must, however, voice our opposition to the contention that authority is institutionalized power, that power is non-institutionalized dominion. According to this conception, authority exists when people accept a particular group's right to control their life chances; power simply means dominance without popular concurrence. But mere non-acceptance of one's rulers does not mean that the latter's power is non-institutionalized. For without institutionalization—i.e., regularization of activity—power could not be exercised in the first instance. Power is indeed institutionalized and legitimized from the standpoint of the wielders. Authority exists where the ruled accept the hegemony of their rulers, where control is institutionalized from the viewpoint of the ruled as well as of the rulers.

Just how is the power of the ruling group transformed into authority? The answer to this question lays bare the very marrow of the preindustrial city's social structure. Weber argued for priority of charisma, traditionalism, and legal-rational factors as the bases of authority. But his formulations demand revision.

Charisma, first of all, is hardly sufficient in and of itself to sustain the authority of a ruling group over long periods. For in the final analysis it depends upon other mechanisms for its effectiveness, e.g., a charismatic leader will appeal to tradition or, in industrial societies, to the consent of the people to justify his "calling." Granted that during brief periods in some preindustrial civilized orders, particularly in the cities, charisma has been sufficient to justify political and religious authority, it hardly merits equal billing with other, more fundamental mechanisms. And as an emotional element it can not be sustained for long without the support of more basic rationalizations.

We contend that apart from the emotive element of charisma, there exist four principal modes of rationalizing and justifying the suzerainty of one body of persons over all others: 1) the appeal to absolutes, 2) the appeal to tradition, 3) the appeal to experts, and 4) the appeal to the governed. The first two are paramount in literate preindustrial societies and their cities: the last two dominate the industrial-urban scene.

The appeal to absolutes is, in essence, a claim to legitimization by forces independent of human action. Thus the rule of the sovereign and the existing normative structure are justified on the grounds that they are in conformance with the will of God, or the gods, and/or "natural law." Such a state of affairs is held to have existed from the beginning of time and can not be modified; indeed the average man in the traditional city or the peasant community can conceive of no other situation.

The "divine right" of kings in traditional European societies was, then, an appeal to absolutes. And the principle is no less applicable to ancient Sumer, Egypt, Meso-America, and parts of the Middle East down to modern times. The emperors of Japan through the ages were considered descendants of a deity, as were those of traditional China. Similarly, the Dalai Lama in Tibet was selected with the assistance of the supernatural as revealed in oracles, for, as noted, he has been deemed a reincarnation of Buddha.

The right to rule is not based upon personal competence or the consent of the governed. Even a sovereign who is mentally or physically incompetent can remain a symbol of authority, while his advisors make the critical decisions, a not-uncommon occurrence in feudal orders.

A corollary of the principle of divine right is the belief that a particular person is inherently superior not because of any specific skills he acquires but because he is born into a family, itself of "divine origin" or enjoying divine sanction. This ideology of biological superiority sets rulers apart as inviolable beings whose actions are not to be questioned or countermanded.

On the other hand, divine law itself, in calling for "fairness," "justice," or similar obligations, sets limits to a ruler's despotic powers over his subjects. Elites usually have some form of the concept, noblesse oblige, paternalistic though this may be, but this principle, of course, does not extend to outsiders.

Apart from belief in divine right, the appeal to absolutes in feudal cities may take the form of adherence to "natural law." We do not contend that natural law as conceived, say, in traditional China was identical to that in medieval Europe, but the concepts are strikingly similar in form and function.[7] The notion of natural law is generally interwoven with that of divine right. But even where it is not, the physical and social worlds are still viewed as unvarying entities. The educated, as we observe later on, do not seek to manipulate, revise, or control the physical world. And the legal and moral structure is deemed non-rescindible. Tampering with the social order is not permitted to any but the highest powers in the land.

The appeal to natural or divine law as fundamentally immutable justifies the status quo and rationalizes the authority of the overlords. Wherever the notion of absolutes prevails, the common man lacks any ideological justification for personal interest in the management of societal or community affairs. Nor can he take action to modify the status quo. Only through attachment to another set of absolutes, usually one external to the system, can he justify this kind of activity.

A second mode of legitimizing the position of the ruling group is through appeal to tradition, a practice closely interwoven with, and accessory to, the appeal to absolutes. Although the notion of tradition, unlike that of absolutes, implicitly recognizes the man-made nature of rules, the two share many features. Tradition, like divine and/or natural law, can and does justify a multitude of practices, above and beyond those pertaining strictly to political authority—to familial, educational, religious, and economic affairs as well.

The reasoning employed in arguments that refer to tradition runs something like this: The past actions of men are the safest guide to present and future conduct; if these were adequate in the past for sustaining the system, they should be good enough for the present. The established patterns being the right ones, the descendants of past rulers are those deemed best qualified to reign today, and the norms governing political and other actions are viewed as timeless.

A concomitant of the appeal to absolutes and tradition is the minimum of formal legislation realized. The laws that

shape men's behavior were formulated long ago, and new
situations that arise require little more than reinterpretation
of the existing laws by persons steeped in the traditional literature, an impossible pattern in a complex and ever-changing
industrial-urban order.

One by-product of the appeal to absolutes and tradition is
the fatalism that pervades the thinking of preindustrial civilized man—the humbler strata in particular. It follows that
it is useless to struggle against the inevitable; natural law
and tradition demand acquiescence from the man-on-the-
street, and the justification for drifting with time and tide is
fully provided for by the ideology. Contrariwise, in industrial-
urban orders absolutes and tradition are clearly subordinate
to other modes of translating power into authority: specifically, appeal to consent of the governed, and appeal to the
expert who possesses the technical knowledge necessary for
governing the industrial order. The rapid change character-
izing modern societies obviates justification of a ruler's authority, or of a legal structure, simply by recourse to absolutes
or tradition, for the very fluidity raises doubts concerning
the validity of absolutes and of tradition. Nonetheless, contradictory functional requirements are at work: even an industrial
city may require some absolutes and some tradition as a
supplement to its prime dependency upon the consent of the
governed and the appeal to experts.

Although Weber conceived of "legal-rational mechanisms"
as the media for transforming power into authority in "capitalistic" societies, we have broken this concept down into its
component parts—to wit: "appeal to the consent of the
governed," the ultimate basis of legal authority, and "appeal
to experts or to expertness," the latter being the foundation
of rational action par excellence. And unlike Weber, we move
beyond the culture-bound concept of "capitalism" to consideration of the industrial-urban society.

It is through reference to one or both of the aforestated
that the governing elements in industrial cities and societies

justify their rule. Although tradition and absolutes lurk in the background, their efficacy in legitimizing power must be regarded as slight. Leaders in industrial-urban societies look to the public for support, most notably in the election process. Dictators in industrializing societies feel compelled to stage "elections" so they can claim support by the populace. With the demise of the traditional modes of government, numerous societies have experienced upheaval in the very bases of rule and, concomitantly, the leaders find their positions subject to the consent of the governed, a concept foreign to the feudal society's rulers. Today the rulers in societies undergoing industrialization find that they must demonstrate that their policies and actions are for the common weal. Slowly but surely the common man is being catered to.

This tranformation is functionally related to industrialization. With the proliferation of mass education and the extension of communication facilities that only an industrializing order can provide, the public gains awareness of the political process and the activities of the governing groups.

Power in the industrial-urban milieu is also rationalized into authority by the appeal to experts. The latter typically are steeped in the knowledge and method of modern science, at once a product of and a stimulus to industrial-urbanization. These experts, especially scientists, through their command of specialized and technical know-how are considered to think and act in a rational manner and to reach responsible decisions. Today politicians and the heads of governmental bureaucracies in industrial-urban centers lean heavily upon economists, psychologists, engineers, physicists, and the like. In many instances the politicians become captives of the experts, who alone possess the knowledge to frame policies on a wide range of pressing technical matters, including, today, those relating to the atomic and hydrogen bombs and to the conquest of outer space. The functioning of the total society can be said to hinge upon the skill and judgment of such experts.

Experts of sorts—priests, astrologers, etc.—function in preindustrial cities and societies as well. Their role is such a salient one that the sovereign may refuse to formulate decisions before consulting these personages. The reliance of rulers upon the advice of astrologers continues in Burma today,[8] and the practice was widespread in feudal societies of the past—from Rome to China to India to the Near East to pre-Columbian America. But unlike the industrial-urban communities' experts, these persons base their thinking upon tradition and absolutes. They seek knowledge of the future through discernment of natural law or the divine will; generally they do not attempt to control the natural order in either its physical or its social aspects, as do experts in urban industrial centers. As an instance, the rational organization of the market place is outside the realm of the experts in the feudal city; yet it commands the attentions of so many in industrial cities.

It seems opportune to comment briefly here upon the role of the "intellectual"; in the process we may dispose of a number of misconceptions. In the traditional world we are describing, the intellectual, one kind of expert, is first and foremost a moralizer, an interpreter of the sacred literature that only he is thought to understand. But unlike the intellectual in many industrial cities, he does not criticize the status quo; it is his task merely to reinforce it. He is fully integrated into the social system and enjoys high prestige and authority, for, as a religious and/or educational leader, he is an expositor of the divine and a carrier of the sacred tradition upon which the social order has been built. The intellectuals, then, reinforce and rationalize the authority of the sovereign by lending credence to the validity of the latter's position, by arguing in terms of absolutes and tradition.

This is in line with Hoffer's[9] thesis that where intellectuals are in favor and enjoy a high degree of power, authoritarianism in government is the norm. Certainly this is true of the preindustrial city and its broader society. On the other hand, the advent of industrial-urbanization seems to provide the necessary conditions for diminution of the moralizing intellectual's power and authority. As the general populace is educated, people begin to think for themselves, and scientific experts must be relied upon to an increasing degree, at the expense of the traditional type of intellectual. Various Communist societies undergoing industrialization are encountering problems in keeping the moralizing intellectual integrated into the social system; a fundamental question is: How successful will they be, with increasing industrial-urbanization?

Conditions That Foster and Delimit the Elite's Power

We have considered the mechanisms by which the dominance of a small, select group in the preindustrial city and society is legitimized. It is now time to examine the factors that make this structure possible as well as those that act to inhibit the power and authority of the ruling stratum.

In earlier chapters we stressed the abysmal ignorance of the populace and the starkness of their existence, not just in the small villages, but in the city, the fountainhead of civilization. The rigidity of the stratification system sets up almost insuperable barriers to the diffusion of knowledge in this society that lacks any mass communication media. In particular, any blocking of the spread of "practical" knowledge inhibits progress in the technological sphere, and of course the simple technology demands little special training on the part of its wielders—a vicious circle indeed. Poverty, illiteracy, and the lack of specialized knowledge on the part of the lower class and outcaste groups all promote the power and authority of the ruling group. We discuss each of these factors in turn.

The bare subsistence level of much of the lower class can not be minimized as a variable that augments the elite's position. For where the primary concern of most persons is sheer survival, the horizons of expectation for these persons are narrow indeed. In their incessant preoccupation with survival, the poor have little time or inclination for seeking to change the system and so outwardly appear satisfied with, or at least resigned to, their lot, a situation reinforced by a value system that emphasizes the acceptance of one's fate.

Likewise, the illiteracy and general ignorance of the lower class and outcaste groups, combined with the dearth of communication facilities, enables a privileged few to seal themselves off socially from the common man to such an extent that they can not be held accountable for their actions. Few if any "legal" safeguards exist to protect the common man from exploitation. Yet an unlettered person can hardly question a system he does not understand. Once industrialization shatters the tranquility of the feudal order, the lower class experiences broadened economic opportunities, a smattering of education, and the impact of radios, movies, and other mass media that open up new horizons and point up other alternatives; they are bound to become somewhat restive.

Associated also with the widespread illiteracy in the pre-industrial city is the low degree of specialized knowledge among the lower strata. Except for a few skilled artisans and very specialized merchants, lower-class and outcaste persons are readily replaceable in their jobs by others of their rank. To substitute one worker for another is a simple matter when a weak mind and a strong back are the primary prerequisites for the task. Quite a contrasting picture is presented by the industrial city, whose entire superstructure rests upon the unique faculties of its specialists—upon skills acquired through long periods of training. Some individuals, ranging from machine-tool operators to theoretical physicists, become well-nigh indispensable. Consequently, modern dictators are themselves forced to cater to and seek the advice of persons of this stamp if the industrial order is to be maintained. Politicians, no matter how intelligent, find it patently impossible to encompass more than a fraction of the specialized knowledge necessary to operate such a system.

Although the feudal order both fosters and demands authoritarianism, countervailing tendencies are at work. Wittfogel[10] is perhaps the most extreme of those scholars who see traditional societies, most of which fall into our feudal category, as governed by a truly despotic ruling clique. Yet his thesis is subject to several criticisms. Conceding no despotic elite as having arisen in Western Europe, his work is an apologia for the West. Moreover, it is highly doubtful whether *absolute* despotism is functionally possible in any society, including a preindustrial civilized one. Implicitly, both Eisenstadt and Eberhard[11] have challenged Wittfogel's thesis on this score, arguing for limits in preindustrial cities and societies to the amount of absolute dominion a ruling group can exert.

For one thing, the artisan and merchant guilds serve to blunt the elite's authoritarianism, and to a degree the kinship system acts as a buffer between the individual and his government. Another brake upon the elite's dominance are the schisms that inhere within this group. Although we have stressed the cohesion that exists among members of the ruling body, reinforced by the interlocking kinship ties, divisive forces are ever at work. Some internal strains among the educational, religious, and governmental bureaucracies seem inevitable. Part of this arises from the fact that even in theocracies the "secular" and "sacred" activities never fully merge: so in Tibet the Dalai Lama was both spiritual and temporal head, yet below him within the bureaucracy were some officials concerned with religious matters, others with secular problems of government. The functions and goals of the sacred and the secular officials diverge sufficiently that contradictions are built into the system.

Personal rivalries within the elite further undermine its solidarity. Tibet long witnessed a rivalry between the Dalai Lama in Lhasa and the less potent Panchen Lama, centered in another city, potentially a contender for the spiritual leadership.[12] The divisive intrigues within the feudal society's ruling element, and among members of the royal court itself, have absorbed the attentions of many an historian of Europe or China. Nor did the Ottoman Empire, during much of its history, institutionalize the succession to the throne. The death of each sovereign occasioned struggles for power and authority among his heirs or other claimants to the throne, and among the diverse cliques that supported the various contenders.[13] Moreover, the lower ranks of the upper class, coveting the privileged position of those who formally command the governmental apparatus, seek to undermine or overturn the actual rulers.

In keeping with our notion of the presence of internal contradictions in all societies, some of the conditions that enhance the elite's position at times detract from it. The scanty communication facilities that permit the ruling elite to isolate itself from the general public also detract from the effectiveness of its control by enabling the lower class, or elements of the upper class who are at odds with the rulers, to evade some of the royal edicts. Until quite recently, the capital city of Lhasa could never keep in touch with all the goings-on toward the Tibetan frontiers, nor could Kabul be kept informed of what was transpiring in Andkhui or Mazar-i-Sharif, to say nothing of the activities of the nomadic ruralites.

By way of contrast, the giant strides in mass communication in the industrial-urban order sharply curtail the freedom of individuals, families, or other groups to flout the directives of those who govern, or to engage in deviant political behavior. It is becoming increasingly difficult for any industrial urbanite to elude the authorities. Moreover, mass propaganda, transmitted through modern communication media, induces conformity and homogeneity, particularly in the more authoritarianly led industrial societies. Yet the achievements in mass communication and education have sensitized the man-on-the-street to the intricacies of government and have encouraged him to demand more of his political leaders.

In addition to the aforementioned strictures upon the elite, the latter's own value system tends to orient it toward some concern with the plight of the disadvantaged. Paternalism is one such value. It may stem from religious tenets, as in Muslim cities and societies, where regular dispensation of alms to the poor is expected. Still, such values do little to curb the fundamental authoritarianism of the feudal urban social structure.

Rebuttal to Potential Criticisms

By now the reader is undoubtedly muttering to himself, "What about the emergence of democracy in Athens?" Did not the common man have an effective voice in the affairs of state? And are not some industrial cities and societies highly authoritarian?

Contrary to the impression created by writers who see the feudal world through romantically tinted lenses, the rulers in Athens and other Greek city-states did not grant the populace any substantial role in the governmental process. Early Athens was ruled by a king and a body of nobles, and even during the Classical age a small, select group held the reins of government, the ranks of the commoners being unlettered. It is generally admitted that the numerous slaves and metics —including foreign merchants many of whom, as in other pre-industrial cities, belonged to outcaste ethnic groups—were denied political rights, as were women as well. These elements constituted no mean proportion of the Athenian community. Persons who qualified as "citizens" actually formed a small minority, and the poor and illiterate among them, caught up in the incessant struggle for bread, could not conceivably have had the training or the leisure time to understand the functionings of government. This is not to imply that the Greek cities did not differ culturally from other preindustrial-urban communities in the area of government or that their so-called "democratic" ideology and assembly system did not help to lay the groundwork for the later emergence of democracy in the Western world. But all too many eminent writers, including historians like A. H. M. Jones, are misled by the ideal norms of Periclean Athens.[14] Their line of reasoning forces them to assume that democracy can glow in a social order dominated by mass ignorance and ruled by a small educated elite. Others, more realistic, take somewhat the stand we espouse,[15] mainly that although the Greek city was unique for its time, in its political structure it actually approximates the typical preindustrial city far more closely than it does the industrial-urban order. After all, authoritarianly oriented industrial orders evince a more pervasive democratic ideology than did the Greek city-states.

This leads us to a consideration of current dictatorships in industrial-urban societies. Although we offer no apologia for these, whether in industrializing or industrialized orders, they deviate markedly in form from the feudal oligarchy. The contemporary dictator is much more attuned to the "needs" and opinions of the citizenry than is the feudal despot, who tends to have little knowledge of or interest in his subjects and can readily flout their wishes. Illustrative of the modern dictator was Juan Perón of Argentina, much of whose following came from the urban populace, above all in Buenos Aires, the capital and largest city. Through government-sponsored labor and welfare organizations, Perón, and more conspicuously his wife Evita, made continual overtures to the "working class" to garner its support. Even Hitler, dictator as he was, found it advantageous to stage elections to legitimize his policies and programs and to use large-scale organizations to build up mass support for his regime. And the indications are that Khrushchev is not only staging elections in the Soviet Union but is making greater concessions to the populace than in the past.

Newspapermen like the Alsops, and Djilas[16] as well, have theorized that maturing industrial-urbanization in totalitarianly oriented societies will carry with it certain democratizing influences. According to this line of reasoning, dictators can function most effectively as feudal societies move to industrialize but must relinquish more and more of their power as full industrialization is neared. Looking back over the past century and a half, we do find a positive relationship between the advance of industrial-urbanization and of democracy, although we must recognize periodic relapses or deviations from this trend. A legitimate working hypothesis is that with the expansion of mass education and the upsurge of multitudinous specialists, a democratic government, embodying some institutionalized opposition, seems to be furthered. For one thing, experts in the industrial order are imbued with the scientific method, which stresses the negation of traditional idols and demands that attention be given to alternatives, and this tends to encourage the development of democracy. Even if democracy, as the West knows it, does not blossom, greater appeals to expertness and to the consent of the governed, in one form or another, seem in the offing. But "democratic" government does not necessarily mean peace and plenty: strains inhere in it, making any heaven on earth as real as a desert mirage.

Bureaucracy

We turn our attention from the ideological bases of authority to focus upon the nature of the political bureaucracy in the preindustrial city and its society. Just as our previous generalizations with respect to authority have implications beyond the political sphere, so too, most of those we make concerning the governmental bureaucracy should be applicable to, say, the religious and educational structures as well.

The term, bureaucracy, as we use it, refers to any complex hierarchically ordered organization with a long life-span. Though some scholars reserve the concept for structures that are unique to capitalist societies, or at most, to industrial-urban orders, others are increasingly assuming the existence of bureaucratic structures in feudal, or preindustrial civilized, societies.

Weber's[17] theoretical model of rational bureaucracy, though intended to refer only to Western capitalism, can be considered to encompass industrial-urban orders in general, and a number of writers, like myself, have adapted it to just this end. It is noteworthy that Weber constructed his typology of capitalistic bureaucracy in apposition to the structure in medieval Europe. Weber's critics, most of whom fail to understand his reference points, have censured him for what he did not set out to do. They are usually concerned with comparing the actual with the ideal in modern bureaucracies, which was not Weber's aim.

Weber saw modern bureaucracy as resting upon "legal-rational" authority; for us it derives its authority from the consent of the governed and the appeal to experts. Bureaucracies in industrial-urban societies, moreover, attach greater significance to the office than to the person who fills it. The occupant consequently is subject to numerous formal restrictions upon his activity. A set of abstract principles guides him in his handling of specific issues as they arise. This bureaucracy is characterized by a well-defined hierarchy of offices, with the chains of command and the rights and duties of each carefully defined. Positions tend to be filled according to universalistic rather than particularistic criteria, and advancement in the hierarchy is made on this basis. Ideally at least, personnel are selected according to their technical competence as determined through impersonal mechanisms —for instance examinations of various kinds. Of course, as always, contrary functional requirements are present, so that some degree of particularism, as manifested for example in the rise of cliques, is demanded by the system.

Employees in modern bureaucracies enjoy a measure of protection through tenure systems and the like. Remuneration is in terms of fixed salaries that are sufficiently adequate so that each office constitutes the primary occupation of the incumbent—i.e., it is a full-time career. The full implications of these generalizations are perceived when the industrial-urban bureaucracy is set off against its counterpart in the pre-industrial city.

The feudal bureaucracy derives its authority from the appeal to tradition and to absolutes. But over and beyond this, it differs from the industrial-urban type in the following ways: 1) For each office there is no clearly defined sphere of activity subject to impersonal rules. This means that the person is often more important than the "office" and that few generalized regulations exist to form the basis for most decisions; within broad limits the officeholder deals with each new situation according to his personal inclinations. 2) No universalistic criteria govern the appointment or promotion procedures. This is related to the fact that, except in rare instances, highly specialized, technical knowledge is not a requirement for a position in a preindustrial bureaucracy. 3) There is no system of tenure rights or fixed salaries, and a bureaucratic position is very often not a full-time task. It is common for personnel, particularly in the lower echelons, to supplement their income through other kinds of employment.[18]

What are the implications of these patterns? First, personal whims and self-aggrandizement loom large in the operation of the bureaucracy that functions within the preindustrial city context. The occupant of a post can make it his own personal province. But the general insecurity of position and indefiniteness as to rights and duties make one reluctant to reach decisions. If one has ties with prominent officials in the bureaucracy or is linked by kinship to key personages in the urban community or in the society, one is more likely to possess the freedom to act as he chooses and, especially, to use his position to promote the interests of his family and friends. It is indeed expected that a bureaucrat will render aid to persons close to him at the expense of the general public. We see this still in southern Europe, in many Latin

American countries, throughout the Middle East, and in India.[19]

Such "license" on the part of office-holders arises from the fact that the rights and duties of persons in the structure are ill-defined, and clear-cut channels of communication are lacking. Yet this does not mean that there is no rank ordering in the preindustrial city's bureaucracy. Far from it. In Tibet and traditional China or Korea the officials of the various strata in the governmental and religious bureaucracies have been clearly distinguishable by their dress.[20] The gradations, particularly among the upper echelons, are sometimes very fine. But again, these minute distinctions of rank reflect neither ordering on the basis of "competence" nor any well-arranged system of responsibility between one status-level and the next.

The vagueness of the rights and duties that attach to the various positions reflects the low level of technology—the dearth of technical specialists whose competence can be objectively evaluated and arranged into some hierarchical scheme. Because there are so few objective skills, one acquires a post and advances through the ranks by "knowing the right people," not just those within the bureaucratic apparatus but those out in the local community and the society at large. How can the preindustrial bureaucrat be objectively evaluated when the criteria for such are so amorphous? In part because of these conditions, buying one's way into a position is not uncommon in preindustrial cities and societies. Swart[21] documents this practice in considerable detail for traditional European societies and discusses briefly its occurrence in ancient Rome and parts of Asia. And it continues still in parts of Latin America. Incidentally, as a result of this norm, some lower-class businessmen may be able to purchase, through their wealth, respectable positions for themselves and their relatives and thus by-pass some of the restrictions ordinarily placed upon them.

A brief aside here is mandatory. The reader may wonder concerning traditional China, with its much-touted "civil service" examination system. At first glance, this seems to constitute a deviant case among preindustrial civilized societies. But compare it with personnel recruitment methods in other feudal bureaucracies and the supposed uniqueness of the Chinese system tends to evanesce. Although examinations were used by the Chinese ruling group for selecting personnel for bureaucratic posts, only a very small segment of the populace had access to the extensive formal education required to prepare for these examinations. Most people, poor as church mice, could neither read nor write, to say nothing of passing qualifying examinations in such esoteric subjects as poetry and philosophy. The examinations may have been public, but education was essentially private. In practice they were designed primarily not to determine an individual's technical competence for a position but to test the extent of his knowledge of the society's traditions and sacred writings and the orthodoxy of his interpretations of these. In keeping with this philosophy, the aesthetic qualities of the aspirant's handwriting constituted an important section of the test. Then too, in China, descendants of the topmost officials, most notably the sovereign, were exempt from these formalities. And examiners could occasionally be bribed, or, as elsewhere, bureaucratic posts were purchased outright, thereby opening up alternative channels to success.[22]

Returning to the principles of bureaucratic operation in feudal orders, we find that particularism is rampant in the selection of personnel, and it is fundamental to an individual's advancement and continuance in the system. The so-called "feudatory ties" of medieval Europe, treated at length by historians, are but a special instance of the interpersonal nexi that pervade all preindustrial civilized societies and are reflected in the day-by-day management of the bureaucratic structure.

The pre-eminence of particularism in the selection of personnel is seen in the comments presumably set forth by a onetime Chinese official under the Manchus.[23]

Now a magistrate must have someone whom he can trust working among the clerks, otherwise it is exceedingly difficult to find out what is going on outside of his own room. This is why some magistrates appoint no one except their relatives as chief clerks of the different departments.

Indeed, in most feudal bureaucracies leading functionaries have their personal retinues. In the event of a serious upheaval that results in the ouster of an official, his followers are likely to depart en masse as an expression of fealty, or, if not, their resignations will be forced by the incoming faction. In mid-century Latin America, relationships exemplary of these still come to the fore. A Latin American social scientist known to the author sought during his stay in the United States to establish close personal affiliations with visiting students from his own country so that when he returned to take up a prominent position there he could place these persons in strategic posts and thus be assured of faithful support in times of crisis. Loyalty is the price of sponsorship.

Particularism extends to the bureaucrat's handling of his "clientele." The layman who desires assistance gets action if he knows the right people or can offer substantial financial inducements. Ordinary persons in feudal cities, having no assets and strategic familial or friendship connections, are helpless in their dealings with officials—e.g., in seeking redress for over-taxation. In industrial-urban bureaucracies unfairness is present, but it is stifled by the norms calling for universalism and democracy. And the little man can pressure officials by complaining to congressmen, as in the United States, or writing to newspapers, in the Soviet Union.

What is viewed as graft—a term of opprobrium—in highly industrial-urban societies, is throughout the feudal world an accepted means of gaining a livelihood.[24] Functionaries do not receive an adequate or fixed salary, and tenure rights are few. The result: you try to get as much as you can while you can. In traditional Kabul, Cairo, Delhi, Peking, or Yarkand, an office-holder has been fully expected to supplement his income by extracting gratuities from those for whom he grants special favors. The bureaucrat who seeks from a superior a service for himself or a client is expected to pay for the favor and so extracts this from his subordinates in the hierarchy. It is in the realm of taxation that this rake-off is most extensive: from the lowliest official in the provinces on up the line, each subtracts his "cut." Yet, there are functional limits to how much each can take: excessive appropriation of funds by the lower officials would deprive those higher up of their share and swift reprisal would be the result.

The matter of "corruption" is particularly acute today in industrializing societies around the world—India, Latin America, southern Europe—for the traditional patterns seem to be "dysfunctional" to the realization of the industrial system; the impact of "honest graft" becomes accentuated when the government extends its range of services and controls into every nook and cranny of the social order. Again, not that industrial bureaucracies experience no malpractices; these, though grave relative to the ideal, are actually few compared to those in feudal systems.

We have alluded to the relationships between the level of technology and the bureaucratic apparatus, which, though its locus is the city, is a societal phenomenon. Unfortunately, writers of the caliber of Appleby and Berger[25] who concern themselves with underdeveloped societies fail to explore this functional nexus. When we do so, the preindustrial bureaucracy seems more rational than it might appear at first glance. The simple technology demands few highly specialized roles or complex hierarchies with well-defined tasks and duties, nor could these exist. One result is that feudal bureaucrats are notorious for their procrastination in decision-making, the city and the society being aligned against change. Moreover, the dearth of communication facilities within the bureaucracy and throughout the social order—most information is transmitted by word-of-mouth—enfeebles certain kinds of decision-making, certainly that demanding contact among bureaucrats in different communities. In the absence of record-keeping—in turn dependent upon the wide availability of paper, printing, typewriters, and the like—an efficient organization can never evolve, although these may not in themselves be sufficient conditions for efficiency. Record-keeping on a grand scale, although imposing obstacles to decision-making by inundating bureaucrats with red tape, nevertheless permits a minute detailing of duties and the stabilization of these over time.

A minimal level of technology is required if the rationalization of a bureaucracy through such a device as "cost accounting" is to be achieved. So too, if the hiring of personnel on the basis of firm technical competence were a desideratum in feudal orders, which it is not, such would be unachievable without adequate files on individuals detailing their work-records and educational histories; and without mass media and employment agencies, qualified persons can not be brought into contact with their potential employers. Under the circumstances, hiring someone you know personally is as efficient a system as any.

Control of graft is almost unattainable without effective record-keeping; the system of checks and balances so elaborated in industrial bureaucracies is inoperable in preindustrial cities. Lacking as it does an advanced technology, the recording of all transactions among bureaucrats and between bureaucrats and clientele is out of the question. After all, the preindustrial-urban populace is largely illiterate; their cooperation in maintaining records is patently impossible.

Examination of other interrelationships between the bureaucracy and technology must await a separate study.

Governmental Functions

The governmental apparatus in preindustrial civilized societies—on the local, provincial, and societal levels—fulfils three primary functions: social control or the maintenance of order, the provision of services, and the exaction of tribute from the populace to finance the operations of government and to underwrite the elite, or more narrowly the ruling group.

By now the reader is aware that the sovereign's tentacles of control extend outward to urban communities in the various provinces, where appointed officials, quite often related to the head of state by blood or marriage, represent the central government. But this apparatus would be totally ineffective without the backing of a loyal military arm that both protects the society from aggression from without and assists in maintaining law and order within. Besides the military (and the courts, discussed below), the central government utilizes special functionaries to preserve internal stability and check upon the loyalty of its servants. Not the least among these are informers or agents whose primary task is to uncover any elements that would subvert the authority of the divine ruler.[26]

We have already mentioned that the military plays an ambiguous role in feudal societies. Upper-class persons who are affiliated with the religious and educational bureaucracies find military leaders a threat to their own status. Far more than the political bureaucrat, the military man is by virtue of his role action-oriented, pragmatic, and anti-intellectual. On the other hand, the society, and especially the elite, of necessity rely upon the armed forces to protect them from enemy aggression. In the end, military leaders are accorded elite status, being customarily drawn from the upper stratum, although their position is generally not as exalted as that of their counterparts in the civilian hierarchy.[27] It is the lower echelons of the military that are staffed by recruits from the lower class and outcaste groups; the mercenaries of ancient Rome would fall into this category. But then, lower-class persons—among whom are caretakers, servants, and runners—also command the lowlier positions in the civilian governmental bureaucracy.

Army garrisons are usually found in or near large cities,

the most powerful forces being stationed in the environs of the capital to protect the sovereign and his court. Capital cities have historically been vulnerable to attack, for they are the prime target of any invading army. The surrender of the capital and the sovereign is tantamount to the society's collapse.

But armies are not sufficient to bring about law and order throughout all reaches of the realm. Concentration of the armed might in or about the major cities, along with the deficiencies of communication, make control of some of the more sparsely settled countryside difficult, if not well-nigh impossible. As a result the broad expanse between cities is likely to be subject to harassment by marauding bandits or criminal gangs who prey upon peasants, merchants, pilgrims, and other wayfarers. Travel between cities, throughout many parts of traditional China, Tibet, India, and Middle Eastern societies, has never been an undertaking for the fainthearted.

Turning to the local scene, often local urban officials have a small police force to search out lawbreakers. In addition, the wards, the guilds, and various ethnic groups, religious organizations, and extended families all assist the governmental apparatus in maintaining order on the local level. Thus elders wield stern control over other family members, leaders of minority groups superintend their followers, and the guilds punish violators of their codes. And religious courts often exist alongside secular ones, the ecclesiastics exercising broad powers of supervision. For example, in the Muslim Middle East, religious personnel have meted out physical punishment on the spot to persons they observe breaking a prescribed religious fast or who are unable to recite certain prayers on demand, women who are unveiled, and so on.[28]

Despite the vigilance of these varied agencies, criminals flourish in the cities, often aligning themselves into guilds for their mutual protection. What is criminal behavior as such is defined as violation of the "laws." Though some of these may derive from custom, most of the crucial norms can be traced to the sacred literature. The promulgation of new laws is limited to the sovereign and a few other topmost officials. Yet enactments of this sort are infrequent in the feudal order, for change is slow and reinterpretation of the existing precepts is usually sufficient to cover any new case that arises.

Feudal cities reinforce these norms through the courts. Although special judicial functionaries usually grace the urban scene, the sovereign or provincial governor or local magistrate often exercises judicial powers over his subjects.[29] But in actual practice, people avoid recourse to the courts; it is deemed far preferable to settle disputes privately, i.e., between families, guilds, and the like. Appearance in court is considered shameful, and hazardous as well, for one's fate is very often completely in the hands of a single functionary —the judge. Then too, the social order provides little protection for the accused: it is a principle of law that one is assumed guilty until proven innocent. Combine this with the fact that justice is a highly arbitrary matter. The poor may be thrown into jail, never to be brought to trial. Or if a trial is held, one's financial status often is a decisive factor, for bribery of judges and police, as with other bureaucratic officials, is an accepted norm in China, Japan, and elsewhere. Lane writes of nineteenth-century Cairo:[30]

The rank of a plaintiff or defendant, or a bribe from either, often influences the decision of the judge. In general, the Náïb and Muftee take bribes, and the Kádee receives from his Náïb. On some occasions, particularly in long litigations, bribes are given by each party, and the decision is awarded in favour of him who pays highest. This frequently happens in difficult law-suits; and even in cases respecting which the law is perfectly clear, strict justice is not always administered; bribes and false testimony being employed by one of the parties.

Another agent contributing to the inconsistent application of the law is the use of ordeals, or divining through magic, in cities in medieval Europe, the Middle East, Japan, China, India, and Tibet, as customary modes of determining guilt or innocence.

Punishment of religious or political offenders—those that

threaten the power and authority structure—is almost always exceedingly harsh; even minor offenses may be subject to violent retribution. In the medieval city of Prato, thieves and prostitutes were birched naked through the streets, and forgers and heretics were dragged behind carts, to be burned alive in the open square.[31] Traditional Middle Eastern, Chinese, and Japanese cities have employed flogging, torture, starvation, and life imprisonment in solitary confinement as common penalties, even for minor transgressions. Buddhist societies, wherein the religious norms prohibit extinguishing any form of life, have circumvented this stricture in varying fashions: as one instance, criminals in Lhasa were flogged so severely that most eventually died—yet the religious principles were not infringed, the ensuing death being viewed as a mere by-product of legitimate punitive measures.[32] According to Martin,[33] lawbreakers in Kabul at the turn of the present century were boiled in oil, had their hands or nose cut off, or were eaten by dogs; a butcher who was convicted of giving short weight was nailed by one ear to the door of his shop. Persons who flouted religious norms were stoned to death; the mulla threw the first stone and by-standers finished the job. In the preindustrial city even a jail sentence has meant often an early death, for conditions in them have often defied description.

The prior discussion forces us to explain not only the existence of crime in a social order where values are deemed sacred, but why punishment should take such harrowing forms. On the latter point, it appears that if the system is to bolster what is sacred, a "devil" or "devils" must be constructed. Violators of the norms receive, then, the brunt of the negative valuation—upon them can be heaped the blame for any malfunctioning of the sacred order. And strong negation justifies the severe treatment accorded offenders.[34] Moreover, in this city the abject poverty and ignorance of the populace permits harsher and more arbitrary measures than would be the case in an industrial center. Although violence is still the order of the day in societies entering the industrialization process, there is reason to believe that with mature industrialization—and the resulting mass literacy and the host of highly trained specialists who can not readily be replaced or manipulated—universalism will come to play a greater role in the judicial sphere. Accompanying this will be a break-up of the rigid class system and the special "legal" privileges enjoyed by the few. In industrialized cities, moreover, many persons fulfil roles that are divergent and contradictory; under such circumstances norms lose a degree of rigidity. Not that mature industrial-urban societies do not know injustices, but industrialization seems to be a necessary, though perhaps not a sufficient, condition for greater universalism and more "humane" treatment of lawbreakers in civilized societies. After all, laws come to be built more and more upon the consent of the governed.

Turning again to the preindustrial city, despite the strong negation of lawbreakers, these seem to thrive, and criminals have organized themselves into guilds in cities from Timbuctoo to Seoul. This anomaly is not readily explained. Evidently, crime will persist as long as there are laws to be broken; norms take on meaning because of their violation and the subsequent punishment of offenders. Moreover, in feudal cities, petty criminals, so long as they do not directly challenge the authority of political and religious leaders, come to be viewed as part of the natural order of things. A modus vivendi is usually achieved between the criminal guilds and the broader society. One writer comments as follows upon a rather traditional Chinese city:[35]

> Then, too, we were always expected to pay the annual tax to the Robbers' Guild! How, otherwise, could we have escaped petty thieving? . . . It was much easier to provide theft insurance by friendly subscription, each year, to the chief of the Robbers' Guild. He would then be on our side in case anything of value disappeared.

A second major function of the government is the provision of services to ensure the over-all functioning of the social order, and pre-eminently its cities, the abode of the elite. Nevertheless, in the matter of services the feudal government, whether societal, provincial, or local, is largely a passive agent, assuming only a minimum of responsibilities.

Yet some functions, like large-scale public works, can often be performed only by the government. Irrigation ventures, aqueducts to carry water to the cities (as in ancient Rome), the construction of roads between cities, or canals (as in traditional China) are largely societal undertakings. So too the societal, but at times the local, authorities have been responsible for the erection of many public buildings that grace the city. In each instance the government is in the most favorable position to exercise control over slaves or the corvée labor that is essential for realizing these projects. Muscle power being the prime form of energy, men must be conscripted in vast numbers.

The government in the feudal order may also support education to a degree, but generally only that on the advanced level. And the royal court, as mentioned earlier, is the chief patron of the arts—literature, music, painting, dancing, and the like.

The societal and local government seeks to wield some measure of control over the economic organization. The state may coin money and exert some efforts to standardize currency, as in China, as well as to regulate weights and measures —though often these meet with little success. Moreover, the government in many feudal societies, both ancient and modern, has interested itself in food storage, chiefly of grains, essential to the sustenance of the ruling group and to urbanites in general.

As to the city, the services it provides may include maintenance of the water supply, drainage, and garbage disposal; but where these are extant they are apt to be rudimentary indeed. It is, rather, the obverse of the coin that is apparent. Too, an entire gamut of services that industrial urbanites take for granted never receive attention from the local government in feudal societies. Public transportation is lacking, and fire-fighting often depends upon the activities of volunteers and on equipment hastily commandeered from householders. Few indeed are the ordinances that control the conditions of buildings or streets with an eye to the safety of the inhabitants.

Furthermore, except in a few cities, public hospitals and asylums for the aged or mentally ill have been non-existent. Welfare services of all kinds, aside from those provided by religious organizations, families, or guilds, are at an absolute minimum. Naive indeed is the comment of the historian, Wright,[36] that traditional China's government provided welfare services for the mass populace. Even assuming that it wanted to, it would have been impossible. The meager technology of the preindustrial city is sufficient only to support the elite in the style it expects. Were the latter to provide extensive services its members would quickly be reduced to poverty. Given the fact that the upper class is largely supported by the poor, who themselves produce little, any welfare services stemming from the upper class can be but few, unless one assumes that having the poor support the poor is public welfare. To be sure, the government might proffer a measure of relief in times of disaster, but only the most destitute could be aided. But then, for the poor, life from the cradle to the grave is one long crisis.

Ponder for a moment the industrial-urban world, wherein the government assumes an overwhelming share of the burden of providing services, ranging from support of the economic structure and mass education to the extension to individuals of benefits of all sorts. With the increased level of technology it is possible to add a wide range of services, which in turn sustain or generate further technological development. Then too, the science that underlies the new technology assumes that both nature and society can be rearranged; industrial man believes he can in large measure determine his destiny. Rather than wither away with industrial-urbanization, government becomes more all-pervasive.

The third function of government—one crucial to the survival of the leisured class—is the collection of tribute. The central government has its representatives in the various provinces, who in turn place their agents in the cities, towns, and villages. The abuses of the tax collector are a normal state of affairs. The lower class and outcastes, ignorant of the operations of the larger society, may have to pay exorbitant amounts to these hated and feared agents of the government.[37] The amount exacted by tax-gatherers in many societies depends largely upon the extent of their avarice; within very broad limits they are able to determine the tax-rate at will. They take a sizeable cut before remitting the tribute to their superiors, who in turn siphon off what they can, until finally it reaches the elite in the capital who command the greatest share of all.

Taxation of course takes varied forms. In some societies farmers and merchants who bring goods into the city to sell may have to pay a toll. Or merchants may be taxed on the amount of goods they sell—though this is difficult to regulate. But it is the peasants who carry the heaviest load, and, lacking currency, they frequently remit taxes in kind. Still another form of taxation is corvée: here the commoner must devote his time and labor to the state for specific periods.

As in the matter of justice, so in the realm of taxation, the upper class enjoys a highly favored position. The topmost officials are often exempt from taxation, and the upper class as a whole can evade it through bribery and other means.[38] Regressive taxation—a pattern whereby those who can least afford it are forced to carry the largest share of the tax burden —is well ingrained in the feudal order, firmly buttressing the existing class structure.

NOTES TO CHAPTER VIII

1. Heinrich Harrer, *Seven Years in Tibet* (London: Rupert Hart-Davis, 1953), p. 175.
2. Donald N. Wilber (ed.), *Afghanistan* (New Haven: Human Relations Area Files, 1956), pp. 99, 322; Herbert H. Vreeland (ed.), *Iran* (New Haven: Human Relations Area Files, 1957), pp. 246-47.
3. E.g., Walter B. Scaife, *Florentine Life During the Renaissance* (Baltimore: Johns Hopkins Press, 1893), p. 53; J. Duncan M. Derrett, *The Hoysalas, A Medieval Indian Royal Family* (Madras: Oxford University Press, 1957).
4. Ernest Landauer, "Aspects of Culture and Society in Modern South Central Turkey" (unpublished M.A. thesis, University of California, Berkeley, 1956), Chapter III.
5. Morton H. Fried, *Fabric of Chinese Society* (New York: Frederick A. Praeger, 1953).
6. Max Weber, *The Theory of Social and Economic Organization*, trans. A. M. Henderson and Talcott Parsons (Glencoe: Free Press, 1947), *passim*.
7. E.g., Joseph Needham, "Human Laws and Laws of Nature in China and the West," *Journal of the History of Ideas*, XII (January, 1951), 3-32, XII (April, 1951), 194-230.
8. "Burma," *Time*, LXXI (June 23, 1958), 29. Cf. "Thailand," *Time*, LXX (September 30, 1957), 29.
9. Eric Hoffer, "The Intellectual and the Masses," *Pacific Spectator*, X (Winter, 1956), 6-14.
10. Karl A. Wittfogel, *Oriental Despotism* (New Haven: Yale University Press, 1957).
11. S. N. Eisenstadt, "Study of Oriental Despotism as Systems of Total Power," *Journal of Asian Studies*, XVII (May, 1958), 435-46. Cf. W. Eberhard's review of Wittfogel's book in *American Sociological Review*, XXIII (August, 1958), 446-48.
12. E.g., Tsung-lien Shen and Shen-chi Liu, *Tibet and the Tibetans* (Stanford: Stanford University Press, 1953), pp. 44-46, 72.
13. A. D. Alderson, *The Structure of the Ottoman Dynasty* (Oxford: Clarendon, 1956).
14. E.g., A. H. M. Jones, *Athenian Democracy* (Oxford: Basil Blackwell, 1957), p. 46, *passim;* Stewart C. Easton, *The Heritage of the Past* (New York: Rinehart, 1955), p. 209.
15. Cecil John Cadoux, *Ancient Smyrna* (Oxford: Basil Blackwell, 1938), p. 186; Benjamin Farrington, *Science and Politics in the Ancient World* (London: George Allen and Unwin), pp. 72-73.
16. Milovan Djilas, *The New Class* (New York: Frederick A. Praeger, 1957).
17. Weber, *op. cit.*
18. For discussions of bureaucracies in semi-traditional societies that support many of these points, see, e.g., Paul H. Appleby, *Re-Examination*

of India's Administrative System (New Delhi: Government of India, 1956); Morroe Berger, *Bureaucracy and Society in Modern Egypt* (Princeton: Princeton University Press, 1957); William J. Siffin (ed.), *Toward the Comparative Study of Public Administration* (Bloomington: Department of Government, Indiana University, 1957).

19. E.g., Wilber, *op. cit.*, Chapters V and VI.

20. E.g., F. Spencer Chapman, *Lhasa: The Holy City* (London: Chatto and Windus, 1938), pp. 74, 82, 89; William Elliot Griffis, *Corea: The Hermit Nation* (8th ed.; New York: Charles Scribner's Sons, 1907), pp. 232, 275-76.

21. K. W. Swart, *Sale of Offices in the Seventeenth Century* (The Hague: Martinus Nijhoff, 1949).

22. Chung-li Chang, *The Chinese Gentry* (Seattle: University of Washington Press, 1955), pp. 174-209; Mary Clabaugh Wright, *The Last Stand of Chinese Conservatism* (Stanford: Stanford University Press, 1957), pp. 85ff.

23. Anon., *Reminiscences of a Chinese Official* (Tientsin: Tientsin Press, 1922), p. 75.

24. E.g., Mary Jean Kennedy, "Panjabi Urban Society," in Stanley Moran (ed.), *Pakistan: Society and Culture* (New Haven: Human Relations Area Files, 1957), p. 98; Wilber, *op. cit.*, pp. 98, 103, 115; Chapman, *op. cit.*, pp. 83-84, 93; Chester Holcombe, *The Real Chinaman* (New York: Dodd, Mead, 1895), pp. 216-20.

25. Appleby, *op. cit.;* Berger, *op. cit.*

26. Wilber, *op. cit.*, pp. 114-15; R. Ghirshman, *Iran* (Harmondsworth: Penguin Books, 1954), p. 144; Philip K. Hitti, *History of the Arabs* (3d ed. rev.; London: Macmillan, 1946), p. 325; Jones, *op. cit.*, p. 58.

27. Franz H. Michael and George E. Taylor, *The Far East in the Modern World* (New York: Henry Holt, 1956), p. 39; Majid Khadduri, "The Army Officer: His Role in Middle Eastern Politics," in Sidney Nettleton Fisher (ed.), *Social Forces in the Middle East* (Ithaca: Cornell University Press, 1955), pp. 170-72; Charles Dallet, *Traditional Korea* (New Haven: Human Relations Area Files, 1954), p. 35.

28. E.g., Frank A. Martin, *Under the Absolute Amir* (London: Harper and Bros., 1907), pp. 275-76; A. N. Kuropatkin, *Kashgaria* (Calcutta: Thacker, Spink, 1882), p. 45.

29. Harrer, *op. cit.*, p. 171; C. P. Fitzgerald, *The Tower of Five Glories* (London: Cresset Press, 1941), p. 72; Derrett, *op. cit.*, p. 181; Dan Fenno Henderson, "The Pattern and Persistence of Traditional Procedures in Japanese Law" (unpublished Ph.D. dissertation, University of California, Berkeley, 1955), pp. 101-02.

30. Edward W. Lane, *The Manners and Customs of the Modern Egyptians* (5th ed.; New York: E. P. Dutton, Everyman's Library, 1923), p. 118. Cf. Henderson, *op. cit.*, pp. 272ff.; Clifford Ernest Hodder, Jr., "Chinese Law: Principles and Characteristics of Pre-Reform and Modern Systems" (unpublished M.A. thesis, University of California, Berkeley, 1950), pp. 20-25.

31. Iris Origo, *The Merchant of Prato* (London: Jonathan Cape, 1957), pp. 59-60.

32. Harrer, *op. cit.*, p. 170.

33. Martin, *op. cit.*, pp. 168-70, 274-75. Compare the situation in tradi-

tional Europe: G. Vanel, *Une Grande Ville aux XVII⁰ et XVIII⁰ Siècles* (Caen: Louis Jouan, 1910), pp. 183ff.

34. Gideon Sjoberg and Leonard D. Cain, Jr., "Negative Values and Social Action," *Alpha Kappa Deltan*, XXIX (Winter, 1959), 63-70.

35. Edward H. Hume, *Doctors East: Doctors West* (New York: W. W. Norton, 1946), pp. 105-6.

36. Wright, *op. cit.*, pp. 145-46.

37. Kuropatkin, *op. cit.*, *passim*.

38. *Ibid.;* Chang, *op. cit.*, pp. 48ff.

CHAPTER IX

RELIGIOUS STRUCTURE

THE configurations of religious values and norms, it is frequently assumed, vary among cultures more perceptibly than other forms of social activity. Nonetheless, preindustrial cities share many traits in the religious realm that distinguish them from industrial-urban centers.

Class distinctions permeate much of the fabric of the familial, economic, and governmental organizations; and in this respect the religious order is no different. In feudal cities religion has its "high" and "low" forms, corresponding to the bifurcated nature of the system, and the sectarian groups reflect, at least in part, the existence of outcastes. Moreover, religion, as will become apparent below, pervades all facets of urban life, and religious ceremonies are crucial in integrating the individual into his community. A further aspect that demands attention is the web of relationships between magic and religion in the preindustrial city.

Class and the Religious Hierarchy

By now it should come as no surprise that the upper class in the feudal city commands the superior ranks of the religious bureaucracy. In the theocracies of ancient Sumer, Egypt, Cambodia, Ceylon, in various pre-Columbian cities of America, and until very recently in Tibet, the head of state was simultaneously the chief priest. Even in societies that could not be termed theocratic—and it is notable that the earliest cities were for the most part more theocratic than the later ones, reflecting the ever-expanding division of labor— the secular ruler and the top political officials have influenced, and in turn been strongly influenced by, the religious hierarchy. The priestly group in Europe is a familiar example. In late medieval Florence the union of church and state with respect to policy was a close one.[1] The secular government erected and repaired sacred edifices and supported the clergy; the latter in turn were entrusted with government documents and frequently disbursed state funds.

The clergy in some societies directly shape political policy, in others they serve as advisers to the ruling clique. The sovereign and top-level political bureaucrats look to religious leaders to legitimize their rule in the eyes of the people. This the priests do by appeals to tradition and to absolutes— embodied as these are in the sacred writings, of which they are the prime custodians and preceptors. The sacred literature is the chief source of the community and societal norms, legal or otherwise, that govern the actions of the people.

Although in general some separation does obtain between civil and canon law—between "secular" and "sacred" activities in the non-industrial city (even in theocracies)—the religious system still influences the scope and structure of civil law. The ecclesiastical courts, staffed by religious personnel and—in cities of medieval Europe, the Middle East, and Tibet—functioning more or less concurrently with the civil courts, exercise jurisdiction over a wide range of activities.

Religious personnel act in still other "political" capacities. In cultural settings as divergent as medieval Flanders and Kashgaria (Chinese Turkestan) they were entrusted, along with other police functions in the city, with checking weights and measures in the market place and the prosecution of all who falsified these in order to cheat their customers,[2] a pattern pointing up the lack of rigid separation of "church" and "state." (Incidentally, these limited economic controls do not vitiate our aforementioned thesis that in general the marketing process is relatively non-standardized and unregulated.)

The priestly group, some of whom may be governmental officers, controls the majority of the schools and provides most of the teaching personnel for these. Cairo's famed university, al-Azhar, functions in part as a mosque, the University of Fez functioned under the dominance of the city's ecclesiastical judiciary, Tibet's halls of advanced learning have been the monasteries, and many of the universities of medieval Europe were in one way or another intimately linked to the religious organization. Very often in preindustrial cities the elementary schools are adjuncts of religious edifices. In fifteenth-century York (England), as in late nineteenth-century Bokhara, practically all elementary schools were church-affiliated.[3] In cities where some of the teachers are not part of the priestly hierarchy, these are, notwithstanding, steeped in the sacred learning. The bulk of the literary tradition, after all, is of a religious-philosophical nature.

The religious functionaries' governmental and educational activities are supplemental to their more narrowly spiritual duties: interpreting the sacred writings, reciting the scriptures, delivering sermons to worshippers, performing special rites for families at marriages, death, and so on, and/or engaging in prayer and contemplation. As to the last, a number of the monasteries that provide the necessary seclusion are in or near the major cities; others are established in the countryside, though small urban communities tend to spring up about them.

Segments of the clergy within all the major religions—e.g., those in medieval Europe, the Muslim Middle East, Hindu India, the Buddhist Far East—have been distinguished by their emphasis upon contemplation and asceticism, including subsisting by begging alms, living as hermits, and/or engaging in self-flagellation or other forms of self-immolation. Olufsen describes the dervishes of Bokhara who abjured worldly goods, wandering almost naked and maintaining life through begging;[4] and mendicant priests have been an accepted part of the urban scene over much of Asia.[5] Although some cultural variations on this theme appear, the basic form is surprisingly general. Why should this be the case? One factor is the need to strike a balance within the system and fulfil certain contradictory functional requirements. Because some clerics enjoy positions of influence and privilege—a desideratum if the religious organization is to maintain its power and authority in the society or city—others in the system must indulge in extreme self-denial in order to sustain in the eyes of the populace the other-worldly ideals of behavior that are propounded by, and essential to, the religion.

But the specter of social class looms as always. The higher clergy are drawn from the elite and minister but to them, leaving the lower class and outcastes to recruit their religious functionaries from their respective groups. It is the lower rungs of the social order, for example, that provide the ascetic priests. At any rate, a yawning chasm, as in traditional China or medieval Europe, can be said to divide the clerics of the upper and lower classes. In Islamic cities the mullas who serve the lower class have little or no education; rarely, if ever, do they comprehend the meaning of the prayers they recite. In this and other respects the priests who minister to the ruralites and those who work among the lower classes in the city are basically identical.[6] Analogous situations can be found in India and elsewhere.

The upper-class clerics are those who acquire formal education, have a firm knowledge of the sacred writings, and wield influence in governmental affairs. The lower religious functionaries, largely illiterate, gain what knowledge they have through informal channels, perhaps by working alongside their superiors as assistants or apprentices. In any event, they have but a vague understanding of the ideal norms and pass on to the commoners a "non-standardized" body of knowledge and, in the view of the upper-level ecclesiastics, much "adulterated" lore. But clerics of all grades are accorded considerable deference by their followers through terms of address and personal mannerisms. Even the illiterate clergy possess some knowledge that the ordinary man lacks and, in the last analysis, are "representatives" of the divine.

But qualify we must our statements concerning the upper-lower class dichotomy within the religious system. Some evidence, limited to be sure, supports the hypothesis that the religious structure offers to persons of humble origin somewhat greater opportunities for advancement than does the governmental apparatus.[7] This pattern seems most prevalent in specific cultures like Tibet or Buddhist Southeast Asia or medieval Europe—it is by no means universal—where priests are required to be celibate. Under these circumstances the upper stratum can permit lower-class persons to enter the ranks and perhaps move up the social ladder, for these, lacking direct descendants, can not transmit to others the social advantages they acquire. Whatever the reasons for the relatively greater opportunities for commoners in the realm of religion, the basic dichotomy of an upper-lower class clergy is general. Contrast this with industrial-urban centers in some societies where, because of mass communication, a more flexible class system, and other factors, the ministrations of the clergy cut across divergent class and ethnic lines.

A word should be said about the religious hierarchy's source of sustenance. Although a wide range of alternative means are available in feudal cities, the emphasis given one or the other varies among cultures. The political organization may allocate to the clergy funds garnered through taxes. In a number of feudal societies the religious organization has owned considerable land—usually exempt from taxes—as well as other property. We have already indicated that large land-holding is associated with elite status. In some instances the clergy's control over property has led them to engage in business ventures that they would otherwise decry. Too, the lower clergy in many cities sell amulets, charms, and the like, and most priests are paid for a variety of services performed, including weddings and funerals. These sources of funds are supplemented by gifts bestowed upon the church by believers and, in a variety of cities, alms are obtained through begging.

Class and Religious Activity

The fundamental cleavage within the religious hierarchy has its counterparts in the religious beliefs and practices of the population: distinctly upper- and lower-class norms can be discerned. Consider Chan's comment on traditional China:[8]

> I have always argued that instead of dividing the religious life of the Chinese people into three compartments called Confucianism, Buddhism, and Taoism, it is far more accurate to divide it into two levels, the level of the masses and the level of the enlightened.

The abundance of treatises on the ideal norms in Hinduism, Confucianism, Buddhism, Islam, and other faiths—though exceedingly worthwhile—have riveted attention on these rather than on the wide divergencies in religious beliefs and practices as between the main strata of society.

The folk religious rites of the lower class, whether in country or city, may bear little semblance to the more formal observances of the upper stratum. Local deities and a panoply of spirits, at times in astounding numbers, dot the religious scene for the lower classes, and these vary greatly from one locale to the next. We do not wish to minimize the impact of "folk" beliefs, or the "little tradition," upon the elite; in point of fact, the sacred writings of Islam lend credence to jinns and the like, the Hindu scriptures to animism and belief in a host of supernatural beings.[9] Yet at the same time, the educated groups look with scorn upon the spirit- and demon-infested world of the common man.[10] Of course, women of the upper class, having little formal education, are likely to adhere to "non-intellectualized" beliefs and practices, but even these differ from those of the commoners.

A number of factors are responsible for the often striking divergencies in the religious behavior of the different classes. First of all, the sacred writings, repositories of the ideal religious beliefs and practices, are read and understood by a minute, howsoever influential, sector of the city and society; the religious behavior of this group is consequently standardized through time and displays striking homogeneity within and among cities. The uneducated, lacking acquaintance with many of the ideal norms, rely upon verbal interpretations of these by the priests. But they do not comprehend the elite clerics, who may speak a formal variety of the language or perhaps an entirely different tongue—as do the educated mullas in non-Arabic cities. And the lower-class priests do not fully understand the formal style of the upper-class functionaries. Both the lower clergy and their followers are cut off from direct communication with the elite learning; the knowledge they do possess is at best a distorted form of it.

Another reason for the contrasting activity of the elite and the commoners in the spiritual realm is the heavy expenditure of time, effort, and financial resources required if one is to fulfil the exacting religious requirements set forth in the sacred writings. To cite an instance: it is one of the tenets of Islam that a devout Muslim must make a pilgrimage to Mecca, Islam's most sacred city. But the cost of such a journey, the time consumed, and the discomforts attendant upon it for persons who live in cities far removed from Mecca—say in Afghanistan and the remoter reaches of Central Asia or Southeast Asia, all areas of sizeable Muslim populations—are so prohibitive, given the poor transport and low economic surplus in feudal orders, that few outside the urban elite can fulfil this requirement.

The periodic public ceremonies and family-centered rites

like marriages or funerals, too, are highly costly ventures; the commoners can hardly indulge in the pomp and circumstance so emblematic of the upper-class way of life.

Sects and Minority Religions

Although sects are a prominent feature of preindustrial cities, American sociologists concerned with religious structure have ignored them; one result is that we have few analytical tools at our disposal for their analysis. The rift between the two principal sects of Islam—the Sunnites and the Shiites —has long been a pressing politico-religious issue in Muslim cities and societies. In some areas one sect tends to maintain power and authority, while in others the situation is reversed. For many generations Tibet has had its "Red Hat" and "Yellow Hat" sects of Lamaism, among others, Cambodia its Thommayut and Mohanikay sects of Hinayana Buddhism. A wide panorama of sects illumines the Indian social scene, though the main ones are devoted to the worship of Vishnu or of Śiva.

Sectarian groups seem to arise first in the cities, thence to diffuse to the rural areas. Although the preindustrial city is quite stable compared to the industrial one, it nonetheless has its moments of crisis and internal dissension. It is during these periods that new sects emerge and take hold, often around a charismatic leader. Historically, many of these separatist movements have been reformist in character: in Tibet, the Middle East, medieval Europe, and elsewhere.

Significantly, once a sect experiences a degree of success it tends to crystallize and eventually becomes as tradition-bound as the religious body it broke away from. (The sects we refer to in non-industrial cities are not loosely organized groups, as are those in some industrial cities, but rigidly structured entities.) Often the membership of a sect displays distinctive dress and personal mannerisms, in addition to special ceremonial patterns.

Evidence suggests that sectarian groups in at least some feudal orders are constituted along class lines. In Cambodia, the Thommayut sect caters to the royal family and nobility, whereas the Mohanikay sect seems oriented to the lower class.[11] But the power and authority of a minor sect can be dramatically revised if the ruling elite, notably the sovereign, embraces it.[12] The Emperor Constantine's acceptance of Christianity and Aśoka's conversion to Buddhism radically changed the fortunes of these hitherto obscure, generally lower-class, bodies, setting them on the road to full-fledged status as religions on a par with the older "great faiths."

Sects are at once a divisive and an integrative force. Though they compartmentalize a society, the existence of "competition" between segments of a single religious system strengthens credence in the tenets of the faith. Each side, through negation of the other, comes to adhere more strongly to its own values and norms: in effect each "keeps the others honest."

Up to now we have commented upon the divisions within or offshoots of a particular religious system. But quite disparate minority religions may exist within the society—practiced largely by outcastes, some of whom have their own literate religious elites. It is in the cities, the nodal points of communication, that these minority groups—products of conversion, migration, or political conquest—tend to congregate.

Early Christianity was spread by conversion, by the proselyting efforts of the Apostles who, as foreigners and outcastes, carried it to cities bordering on the Mediterranean. On the other hand, Zoroastrianism was introduced into Indian cities by immigrants from Persia whose descendants, the Parsis, exist today in India as a highly urbanized minority group engaged in manufacturing and commerce. The Jews have since the diaspora spread to cities in almost every corner of the world. And note the movement of Hindus into Central Asia or Muslims into China, there to serve primarily as outcaste merchant groups.

Because these minorities provide an indispensable function they are permitted to flourish. And inasmuch as they are focal points of community negation, they are symbols for integrating the devotees of the majority religion: the latter's clergy can point out to the populace what is most abjured and the outcaste state that is the bitter fruit of heterodoxy.

Prescriptive Nature of the Religious Norms

The clergy, in the dominant religion and in the sects, preside over a system characterized by a well-defined value orientation; the latter supports and is supported by religious norms that govern a wide range of action patterns. Many of these norms are highly prescriptive, spelling out precisely the desirable and undesirable kinds of behavior. One's daily activities are pervaded by religious injunctions. The orthodox Hindu says certain prayers before arising, performs a set of ablutions in a fixed order, and only then prepares or consumes the first meal of the day. Furthermore, for the devout Hindu,[13]

every day has some religious significance and the whole day and night can be turned into a round of religious duties. The number of deities to be worshipped are numerous; every day is under the influence of some planet which may be propitiated and the reading of the sacred texts is always recommended.

Islam propounds a host of specific rules for persons to follow in their daily activities; the urban upper class, particularly the men, indoctrinated into the sacred writings and having the means to fulfil the ideal norms, tends to set the pace for society. For example, the scriptures require that the individual pray at appointed times: 1) in the morning (preferably after dawn and before sunrise), 2) in the early afternoon, 3) in the late afternoon, 4) immediately after sunset, 5) at night (preferably before retiring, so that it becomes the last act of the day). Each prayer has its specified number of raka'āt, or acts of devotion, requiring standing, bowing down, prostration, and sitting in a prescribed manner and in a designated order.

Mandatory for Muslims as preparation for prayer is wuḍū', or partial ablution. The sacred writings—e.g., the Ḥadīth—enumerate the steps in this "outward purification" process. According to Muḥammad 'Alī,[14] the main steps are: first, the hands are washed up to the wrists, next the mouth and nostrils are cleaned with water; the face is then washed; the right hand and then the left are cleansed from the wrist to the elbow; the head, including the ears, is wiped over with wet hands; finally the right foot, then the left, are washed up to the ankles. (If socks, stockings, or boots are worn and have been put on since a recent ablution, it is necessary only to pass the wet hands over them.) General ablution (bathing) is required for Friday prayers and in some other special situations.[15]

Much of the religious ritual, including prayers, is of a repetitive nature, frequently expedited through mnemonic devices. Devout Muslims have their rosaries (similar in function to those of the Catholics of medieval Europe and the present day) ever at hand while walking or sitting and say the name of Allah as they move each bead. Pious Hindus finger their rosaries and chant verses from the Vedas a fixed number of times. Urbanites in Tibet turn prayer wheels a selected number of revolutions and tell their beads.[16] Rosaries are used in Japanese cities as well. The name of one's god or pious verses from the scriptures are supposed to be constantly on the lips of the devout practitioner of the faith in preindustrial cities.

Although upper-class men perpetuate the ideal norms of the religious organization, the women, especially the older ones, while generally lacking knowledge of the intellectual bases of their religious beliefs, are zealous in fulfilling the prescriptive norms in the ritualistic sphere. In many societies, urban homes, notably the wealthier ones, are apt to contain private shrines for worship of the household gods or favorite saints. Cities in China, Japan, Korea, Tibet, India, or Latin America, and ancient Babylonia, Egypt, Greece, or Rome for that matter, have all evinced this pattern. Some upper-class persons in medieval European, Indian, Tibetan, and other cities have gone so far as to hire priests to perform rites periodically in their homes. Private worship among the elite stems in part from the pattern of cloistering women in this stratum, in part from the desire for seclusion on the part of the privileged element.

Furthermore, frequent periods of fasting are supposed to fix people's attentions upon the divine. Various dietary injunctions govern one's day-by-day behavior. Those of Judaism and Catholicism are known to most readers. To a Muslim, be he a resident of Timbuctoo or Fez or Cairo or Kabul, it is forbidden to consume intoxicating beverages, carrion, blood, pork, and meat from animals not killed in a prescribed fashion and over which any other name than that of Allah has been pronounced at the time of slaughtering. The scriptures of Islam, moreover, set forth the proper modes of eating—as an instance, one is forbidden to take food with the left hand. In some sects of Hinduism animal foods of all kinds are prohibited, in others just those that involve the taking of life.

All this ritual serves to reinforce belief in the primacy of religious values; furthermore, deviation from the norms leads to punishment—either in this life, in the shape of illness or disaster, or in the "hereafter," whatever form the latter may take: hell or purgatory in Islam, or the multitude of hells in Tibetan Buddhism. Even the ancestor-worship of Confucianist China implied punishment of relatives in the hereafter for one's failure to adhere, e.g., to "filial piety."[17]

Our commentary on the prescriptive religious norms in preindustrial cities should in no way imply that the specific content of these is identical across cultures. It is in their basic form and function that they evince such striking similarity.

Moreover, we reiterate that it is the educated urbanites who adhere most closely to the ideal norms concerning daily behavior. Even in India, with its deep-seated heterogeneity, the upper class—because it is the most Sanskritized element of the society and the bearer of the "great tradition"—displays far greater communality of behavior than does the lower class; e.g., the dietary restrictions could hardly be followed by the very poor. Contrary to the views of sociologists that the city everywhere is a secularizing force par excellence, the feudal city, seat of the upper class, is at one and the same time a center of orthodoxy and a focus of change.

Business activity itself, which might be considered the most secular of any and is usually rejected by the religious leaders and other elite as beyond the pale of respectability, is not immune to the impact of spiritual values. Businessmen, whether of upper, lower, or outcaste status, are all heavily influenced thereby.

The description of the religious orientation of a business-man in the medieval Italian city of Prato could be duplicated, except in specific cultural details, in other preindustrial centers throughout the vast expanses of Eurasia and North Africa.[18]

Francesco was not, and did not consider himself, a virtuous man; but he never questioned the necessity or the efficacy of these devout customs. His business contracts, like his private letters, began and ended with a pious formula; the Ten Commandments stood at the head of his ledgers; a fresco of St. Christopher guarded his front door. In Lent and on other fast-days both he and his wife fasted . . . , and if he sometimes worked on a Sunday, he blamed himself most severely in the year in which he had attended only *six* Lenten sermons! Though he often scoffed at priests and monks, he went regularly to confession, and, in sickness, called five Franciscans to his bedside; though ungenerous by nature, he gave alms freely, paid his tithes regularly, built shrines and chapels. There was hardly a rich man of his time who did not do the same, and the few who failed to fulfill these duties were considered wicked men.

Or, consider a preindustrial-like urban merchant group, of the Jain community, in twentieth-century India.[19]

The Marwari believe fervently that . . . they will gain the good will of the gods who will . . . make them more prosperous. A . . . religious act of most Marwari is to hire a Pundit to chant Ram Ram thousands of times. . . . The Marwari donate huge sums to temples, hospitals, and schools . . . to gain grace.

Artisans also appeal to the supernatural to protect and assist them in the fulfilment of their tasks. Moreover, various guilds have been potent forces in promoting religious activity. Though primarily economic organizations, each has its own tutelary deity or patron saint and carries out periodic religious observances in which other elements of the community occasionally participate. One writer comments as follows about the Guild of the Blind in Peking in the 1920s.[20]

The worship of the gods of the gild was the first business of the meeting. On the raised platform at the upper end of the hall an altar had been arranged for the God of Heaven, the God of Earth, and the God of Men, from whom the gild gets its name of the "Three Emperors Associations." On the wall were hung the pictures of the three gods, the Emperor of Heaven being in the middle and slightly higher than the other two. In front of them, on a table, was spread a feast of chicken, pork, fish, wine, vegetables, fruit and rice. On the edge of the table burned two large candles and the incense offered to the gods. The members of the executive committee came up two by two, to offer to the gods their obeisance and thanks for the prosperity of the past year.

Religion not only influences the life-ways of those who participate in the economic sphere but leaves its imprint upon the ecology of economic activities. Markets and fairs, for example, spring up in or about religious edifices. For this, we could cite pre-Columbian and later Latin American cities, or those of medieval Europe, the Middle East, Tibet, and China. Christ in his day had to chase the money changers from the temple. One explanation for this recurrent phenomenon is that the church, mosque, or temple is a focus of perambulation, and given the difficulties of travel to and fro within the city, the religious center is a convenient spot for interchange between buyer and seller. That religious holidays are also the chief market days is in keeping with this pattern.

More potent than these positive effects are the negative influences on economic behavior emanating from the majority
group's religious values. The most apparent are the proscriptions against money lending for interest in medieval Europe
and in Islamic cities. The religions of most feudal societies
inveigh, in one way or another, against profit-making as a
false "god." The sacred writings are also likely to embody
proscriptions in matters of weights and measures, the drawing
up of contracts, and the like.

The impact of religious values and norms is no less apparent in the realm of political behavior. The very structure of
government in preindustrial civilized societies, i.e., defining
what the ruling clique can and can not do, is shaped by the
religious orientation. Indeed, most of the laws enforced by
the secular governing bodies either find support or have their
origin in the sacred literature.

In light of the foregoing, it is no source of wonder that
religion forms the very marrow of the normative structure of
education in the feudal city. What men study, what they
think about, what they seek to create are intimately related
to the spiritual values of the city and the society.

Art forms such as poetry, painting, drama, music, and
dancing are laden with religious themes. Once more the religious values define what is acceptable and what is not. A
dramatic instance of their impact upon art is the general absence of human and animal motifs in the architecture, painting, tapestry, mosaics, etc. of Islamic cities: representation
of animate beings is forbidden by the religion. The intricate
beauty of the world-renowned mosques and palaces of Samarkand or Granada or Isfahan, calling forth as they did
supreme artistic ingenuity, is indirectly a product of this religious injunction.

With the advance of industrial-urbanization, the impact of
religion slackens perceptibly: its all-pervasiveness and rigidity
diminish. It is true that a number of scholars in certain preindustrial cities of the past—the ancient Greek ones are an

outstanding case in point—challenged some time-honored religious views. Yet the basic social structure was never greatly affected thereby. It takes industrialization to spark dramatic changes. The traditional religious system is no longer able to prescribe norms to fit every possible situation in the industrializing city. Constructed as it is upon the appeal to tradition and to absolutes, it tends to view the world as a fixity. The sacred writings can be reinterpreted to fit new conditions only where social change is relatively slow. Once it becomes intense, and men of exalted and humble rank witness upheaval before their very eyes, they find it difficult to conceive of immutable and everlasting laws. And the new technology creates unprecedented conflicts that can not be handled merely by appeal to the older sacred writings. The ecclesiastical body's power and authority is thereby undermined, one reason for the resistance on the part of tradition-oriented religious hierarchies to the industrial-urbanization process, as in parts of southern Europe. Then too, science, the basis of modern technological advance, has by its very nature been a threat to traditional religions: it develops mainly by questioning the accepted ways of looking at the universe. It is no easy matter for the ecclesiastical structure to sustain belief in absolutes in the face of the incessant revisions in the natural order effected by science, and the clerics have lost ground in the face of the growing knowledge and authority of the scientific expert.

Added to the secularization of knowledge is the fact that as urbanites come to play multiple, and often inconsistent, roles in the complex industrial city, rigid adherence to time-honored norms is detrimental to personal organization. The traditional religious beliefs do not necessarily disappear (they may in fact have definitive functions in the industrial city), but permissiveness rather than prescriptiveness is the order of the day—although this very liberality creates conflicts of its own.

Ceremonial Activities

Implied in the foregoing is that ceremonial life in the pre-industrial city is shot through with religious considerations, as indeed it is. The frequent domestic religious rites serve to integrate the family, and an analogous process is at work in the guilds. Moreover, the quarters, or wards—above all where these are organized along ethnic lines—often have their own religious rites.

But much more prominent are the periodic ceremonies that involve the entire community, excepting possibly the out-castes. A recurrent pattern in preindustrial cities are the community-wide festivals in honor of the city's patron saint or god. In parts of traditional China the city-god was considered a personification of the city, occupying in the spirit world a position analogous to that held by the city's supreme officer in this world. Under the Manchu dynasty the officials regularly reported to the city-god concerning current happenings in the community and offered up prayers for the latter's welfare. The ancient Mesopotamian and Phoenician cities each had their tutelary deities, as did the cities of ancient Greece and Rome. According to a description of Florence in 1333, the preparations for the celebration of the city's patron saint, San Giovanni, occupied a whole month, and companies of volunteers were formed in order to foster hilarity throughout the community. The city of Fez puts on an annual festival in honor of its patron saint, Moulay Idris, and the more traditional cities of Latin America continue similar practices still.[21]

Besides these festivals honoring the city's god or patron saint, a year-round panorama of ceremonies, primarily religious in character, occupies much of the attention of urbanites. Many of the religious festivals involve colorful and lavish processions and a variety of public entertainments. The latter may include religious dramas (as in Tibet and medieval

Europe), dances performed as an act of devotion (in much of Asia and in some Mexican cities today), or games or sports held in honor of the gods (in ancient Crete and Grecian cities, in Rome, or cities of pre-Columbian America).[22] In Muslim cities the most salient of the annual rites is that of Ramadan, where a whole month is devoted to worship in the form of fasting. During this entire period no one is permitted to eat, smoke, or drink (even water) between sunrise and sunset. Only small children, old people, and the infirm are excepted. The tempo of life in the city is drastically altered, and today with the introduction of better lighting, many daily activities are carried out at night. The month of fasting, not surprisingly, culminates in enthusiastic feasting and merriment.

Bear in mind that though certain religious fêtes are confined to a particular city and its hinterland—the surrounding ruralites being drawn to the urban center on these occasions —certain large-scale religious observances like Ramadan in Islamic societies or Holi and Divali in India are held concurrently in cities across a broad geographic expanse. However, the capital city is often the focus of special ceremonial activity. Here the sovereign may perform certain religious rites that have significance for the entire society, as occurred, for example, in China and Japan.

Ferreting out the functions of these periodic ceremonies, we see that, first and foremost, they reinforce the religious norms and values of the urban populace. Certain rites serve to instill in one a worshipful attitude—as is the case with fasting during Ramadan. And the dazzling processions highlight the significance of the religious organization and remind people of the role of the gods. Likewise, the authority of the ruler is reinforced through his association with religious festivals. In Lhasa, the Dalai Lama was borne on a litter through the streets amid the thronging crowds on the occasion of certain religious fêtes, a situation duplicated in many another pre-industrial city—from traditional Japan all the way round the globe to pre-Columbian America, where Moctezuma II was carried on a palanquin by bearers through the Aztec city of Tenochtitlan. Rulers in all feudal societies—not just theocratic ones—use these types of mechanisms to fortify their position.

Public ceremonies and festivals also provide entertainment for the populace in this urban community where voluntary associations are few, mass communication and entertainment are absent, and most people lack the means to travel elsewhere to observe new wonders. For the very poor these provide opportunities to witness dancing, to hear music, and to enjoy other diversions.

These periodic ceremonies, moreover, lend cohesion to the urban community (though the outcaste groups may be excluded as always) by enabling the populace to join in city-wide activities. They are among the few occasions when the elite and the commoners participate on a more equal basis. Furthermore, such ceremonies, though basically religious in orientation, permit the populace to relax temporarily some of the rigid strictures upon relationships between the sexes. Thus are dissipated some of the strains generated by the ordinarily severe injunctions upon social behavior. The following commentary on a Chinese New Year Festival, essentially a religious observance, in the sixth century bears this out.[23]

I have seen . . . in the capital, and elsewhere, each night of the full moon of the first month (fifteenth day), streets and lanes full of people, where the noise of the drums deafens heaven and where the torches illumine the earth. The people wear masks depicting animals; the men dress as women; singers and jugglers disguise themselves strangely. Men and women go jointly to the spectacle and are found together without avoiding one another. . . . It isn't a question . . . of nobles or commoners; men and women mix in this disorder and clerics and laymen are confused. Inhibitions are lost and it is also the occasion for thefts and banditry.

Granted that the foregoing may exaggerate the actual circumstances somewhat, the observer evidently was struck by the lowering of traditional class and sex barriers, just as Sahagún was respecting an Aztec city some centuries ago. More narrowly, in Lhasa, certain ceremonies have been accompanied by behavior that sharply contrasts with the usually rigorous norms of boy-girl morality. Timbuctoo's young women who are ordinarily cloistered go out into the streets to celebrate community religious festivals, and in Cairo over a century ago a religious holiday was one of the few occasions when men and women intermingled in the mosques.[24]

Although ceremonies in preindustrial and industrial cities are similar in some respects, fundamental differences obtain. Those in the industrial-urban environment are at times completely divorced from the traditional religious sphere. Here some of the more meaningful ceremonial occasions are those devoted to nationalistic issues. Nationalism, as with science itself, comes to substitute, at least in part, for the traditional religious values, functioning in effect as a secular "religion" and as a key integrative mechanism in modern industrial cities. (However, this opens the way for political leaders during crisis situations to take on charismatic, "god-like" qualities, countervailing some of the otherwise democratic forces that appear to inhere in industrial systems.)

Magic

Magical practices, like religious ones, flourish in the preindustrial civilized society—among the lower-class urbanites and ruralites and the elite as well. Theoretically, religion refers to those beliefs and actions concerned with "ultimate" matters, whereas magic is more "empirical," being directed to the solution of everyday, mundane problems. Although, analytically, magic and religion are separable entities, the two merge, or overlap, in the real world; it is almost impossible to determine where one begins and the other ends. Actually, magical rites are frequently given justification in the sacred writings—as in the Hindu Vedas.

The prevalence of magic in the preindustrial city is attested to by the wide range of special functionaries, some of whom also provide religious services; certainly the division of labor with respect to magical practices is far more complex than in folk societies. Priests, magicians, diviners—astrologers, oracle-priests, geomancers—and others, each with their own body of knowledge, embellish the urban scene. These functionaries are in turn subdivided into those who cater to the upper class and those who serve the lower class—just as in the religious hierarchy, and still other magical specialists serve the outcastes.

The statements above are generally accepted and understood. But we must proceed a step further in our analysis. Preindustrial man, as we suggested earlier, does not seek to control or to remake his social and physical environment. Instead he takes this as a given, as part of the natural or divine order, something not to be tampered with. As will be emphasized in the succeeding chapter, the preindustrial civilized world has had a science of sorts (magic overlaps both with religion and with science), but unlike the science that underlies modern industrial technology, the former has relied mainly upon observation and has shunned experimentation (which involves manipulating the social and physical order). Of course, a functional requirement that runs contradictory to this is the artisan's need to experiment to a degree with the physical world in order to improve his craft, but this is far from the dominant orientation in the feudal technological realm.

Magic comes into play by assisting man in adjusting to the social and physical world: i.e., the natural and/or divine order. Unlike modern science, magic does not, theoretically at least, seek to control or reshape the functioning of the universe. It is hardly compatible with modern technology; the advent of the latter spells the demise of the former.

Three types of magic, we argue, are employed by preindustrial urbanites: *protective, restorative,* and *predictive.*

One utilizes protective magic to ward off evil, to keep the social or natural order in the proper equilibrium. But malevolent spirits or gods or other forces may upset the balance in nature by causing illness or some other social or physical disaster. This disharmony the preindustrial city dweller seeks to redress through restorative magic. And he may use predictive magic, i.e., divinatory methods, the better to adjust to the natural/divine order and to avoid the adverse consequences of any violation, albeit unintentional, of the "correct" modes of behavior.

We need not tarry long in discussing *protective,* or preventive, magic. Certainly it is almost universally employed. In Muslim cities it is common to dress a child unattractively to discourage jinns and other hostile beings, and thus to ward off illness. In Chinese cities, wearing red clothes, and in Bokhara, sewing variegated strings of beads onto children's clothing, was thought to repel the hostile supernatural. Amulets, obtained from clerics or fortune-tellers, have been worn in city after city for a similar reason.

Restorative magic is employed where the forces of evil have upset the natural and/or divine order—where, for example, a person commits an evil deed, at least from the point of view of the victim, or one falls ill, or a famine or plague is afoot in the land. Restorative magic is intended to reestablish the "correct" balance of forces in nature. Thus one seeks to exorcise the evil spirit (or spirits) who may be responsible, most usually by calling upon good spirits to overcome the malevolent agents. For whatever the specific cultural content of feudal orders—and this can vary widely—there is always a dichotomy between the good and the bad, i.e., between a god and a devil, or good and evil spirits or deities, as the case may be. Sociologists fail to perceive the generality of this phenomenon and of the basic means, though the details vary among cultures, by which imbalances in the natural order stemming from hostile forces are avoided or redressed. Restorative magic, for instance, has prevailed in feudal orders from the most ancient ones in the Near East to those in the Greek and Roman periods, in Central and Eastern Asia, in medieval Europe and pre-Columbian America, down to those that survive today. Still, it must be kept in mind that just where religion ends and magic begins is not readily determinable on the empirical level.

The illustrations of restorative magic are legion. We can cite only two here. One is contained in Doolittle's commentary regarding health practices in Foochow, China, in the nineteenth century:[25]

> Should any one who has had general good health be suddenly and mysteriously taken with dizziness in his head, pain in his eyes, or with inability to use his hands or feet as usual, his illness is not unfrequently ascribed to the influence emanating from some one of seventy-two malignant spirits or gods. Immediate measures must be taken to counteract or expel this evil influence. A table is placed in the lightest part of the room in which the sick man is. On it are arranged three cups of wine, a platter having on it five kinds of fruit, and a censer, and a pair of candlesticks. A quantity of mock-money is also procured, ready for burning. A Tauist priest is hired to recite the proper formulas, in order to secure expelling of this malignant influence from the sick man. Sometimes he invokes the aid of a certain headless demon in this important work. The priest provides himself with a small bell, which he rings while he repeats his formulas; and with a bowl of water which he sprinkles or snaps with his fingers on the articles offered, and on the sick person. He has also a bundle of various kinds of paper charms for use when needed, and a small stick of wood, with which he strikes the table at intervals during the recitation of his formulas.

True, there is occasional recourse to one kind of demon to overcome other evil forces, but in most instances the curing rites performed seek to invoke the good to counteract the bad.

It is not unusual for the chief officers of feudal societies to hire special functionaries to perform restorative magic. In Tibet in the 1940s the Dalai Lama and other governmental officials called in the Oracle of Gadong, the most famous rainmaker in the land, to alleviate the prolonged drought in the Lhasa area and thereby save the harvest. The rainmaker, a monk, fell into a trance, during which a divine spirit entered his body, heard his plea for rain, and spoke through the mouth of the oracle-priest, granting rain—so say the chroniclers of the event.[26]

Predictive magic is an attempt to foresee the future, or more usually to determine the proper course of future action, through analysis of various objects and events so as to discover their "meaning." In theory, then, one must act in accordance with that which is predestined to occur: the pre-industrialite accepts the inexorability of his fate.

Specialists in divination functioned in the ancient cities of the Near East and persist still in numerous Asian and North African cities. Astrologers or astrologer-priests have been adjuncts of the royal courts in almost every feudal order. Few weighty decisions are made by the sovereign or major public ceremonies held until a diviner is consulted as to the most auspicious day for such action. In medieval Europe, astrologers were resorted to even on military matters, serving on occasion as key strategists.[27]

Perhaps the most dramatic example of the prominence of divination in the administration of the feudal society and its cities is the traditional method of selecting the supreme ruler in Tibet. Harrer[28] describes how the fourteenth, or most recent, Dalai Lama—reincarnation of the Living Buddha, the patron god of Tibet—was discovered. Some time before his death in 1933, the thirteenth Dalai Lama had given intimations as to the manner of his "rebirth." After his body had sat in state for awhile it was noted that his head had turned to the east. The State Oracle was consulted and went into a trance during which he flung a white scarf in the direction of the rising sun. For two years nothing more definite was indicated until the acting governmental head journeyed to a certain lake and after protracted prayers saw in the water a vision of a three-storied monastery with golden roofs, near which stood a little Chinese peasant house with carved gables. In 1937 search parties were sent out, and after long wanderings one group found a monastery and house resembling those envisioned by the Regent. In the house was a two-year-old child who recognized the identity of one of the Lamas disguised as a servant. The group examined the child, who correctly chose the rosary of the thirteenth Dalai Lama, as well as other pertinent objects, out of a number shown him. And he had the marks on his body that the incarnation was supposed to bear. Thusly, according to Harrer, was the fourteenth Dalai Lama selected.

Businessmen in preindustrial cities often consult astrologers before undertaking a new venture or concluding a business transaction. In Indian cities today the Marwari,[29] a merchant caste, also seek the advice of astrologers before they start on a journey connected with their business. If the astrologer names a certain day as auspicious for the trip and the merchant is disinclined to leave on that day, the latter will "go through the motions" of doing so by checking a bag at the station or leaving it at a friend's house and will avoid sleeping at home until he is ready to undertake the journey; in this way he seeks to avoid upsetting the natural order and experiencing the adverse consequences of this.

A special cultural development among diviners are the geomancers of the traditional Far East—specialists in directions and geographical environment who "read" the lines or surface character of the earth and are consulted by businessmen and others. For each spot of ground has had its own spiritual forces that are sensitive to any change in the condition of the locality and may be hostile to some types of activity while friendly to others. Businessmen have hired these divinators to determine the propitiousness of establishing a particular kind of business in an area.[30] Similarly, geomancers have determined the proper sites for homes and graves. According to Gray,[31] rows of houses and shops in nineteenth-century Canton were rarely arranged in a direct line or built to the same height, for if they were, so said the geomancers, disaster would surely result: the natural order would be disturbed.

Families and individuals consult diviners of various persuasions on matters of illness, the meaning of dreams, auspicious names for children, the proper time for marriage and funerals, or whether a couple should be married at all. Of course, the diviners who serve the elite have had formal training in the complex body of literature on astrology, hepatoscopy, and so on, while those who work with the lower class and uneducated outcaste groups pick up their knowledge through informal channels like apprenticeship.

Finally, certain forms of magic are practiced by the preindustrial urbanite without the intervention of specialists. The ordinary person predicts events according to predetermined norms. In Middle Eastern cities from Cairo to Kabul one learns to gauge his actions according to certain "lucky" or "unlucky" days or months. In Lhasa certain days have been considered propitious, others not, for undertaking a journey, while in traditional China every day of the month was lucky or unlucky in varying degrees for specific activities.[32] Again, though cultural variations exist in the specific application of predictive magic, a recurrent structural theme is apparent throughout the preindustrial-urban world: magic is employed to help one accommodate to the day-by-day struggle for existence.

Obviously magic is not confined to preindustrial cities. It is practiced in the industrial milieu—but to a much lesser extent. As the traditional religions lose their effectiveness, magic itself becomes less pervasive, for the two tend to buttress each other. And industrial man comes to use science, rather than magic, to achieve his ends. Unlike the non-industrialite, he purposively seeks to control, manipulate, and revise many features of the physical and social order, seeking to overcome, not merely to adjust to, his environment. Such a transformation in thought-ways is a necessary condition for industrialization.

We conclude this chapter on the note with which we began it: that most observers of preindustrial civilized societies and their cities overlook the uniformities these display in the realm of religion, stressing rather the differences among traditional Hinduism, Buddhism, Christianity, Islam, and so on. Not for a moment do we wish to minimize the divergencies, intellectual and otherwise, among these faiths! But neither can it be denied that some recurrent themes appear in religious behavior, and in magical practices as well, and that these have been slighted. The uniformities in the magico-religious sphere emerge most dramatically when the preindustrial-urban forms are contrasted with the developing ones in industrial-urban systems, where science and nationalism have arisen as competing "religions," having supplanted some of the traditional religious beliefs. Nevertheless, it may be that certain of the more traditional religious values and norms must be salvaged if stability in the industrial-urban context is to be maintained.

NOTES TO CHAPTER IX

1. Walter B. Scaife, *Florentine Life During the Renaissance* (Baltimore: Johns Hopkins Press, 1893), p. 138.

2. John H. Mundy and Peter Riesenberg, *The Medieval Town* (Princeton: D. Van Nostrand, 1958), p. 145; A. N. Kuropatkin, *Kashgaria* (Calcutta: Thacker, Spink, 1882), p. 45.

3. Edwin Benson, *Life in a Mediaeval City* (New York: Macmillan, 1920), pp. 59-67; O. Olufsen, *The Emir of Bokhara and His Country* (London: William Heinemann, 1911), pp. 385-91.

4. Olufsen, *op. cit.,* p. 397.

5. William M. Masters, "Rowanduz: A Kurdish Administrative and Mercantile Center" (unpublished Ph.D. dissertation, University of Michigan, 1954), pp. 177ff.; J. J. M. de Groot, *The Religious System of China,* VI (Leyden: E. J. Brill, 1910), 1270.

6. E.g., Herbert H. Vreeland (ed.), *Iran* (New Haven: Human Relations Area Files, 1957), p. 247.

7. Thomas Fitzsimmons (ed.), *Cambodia* (New Haven: Human Relations Area Files, 1957), p. 258; F. Spencer Chapman, *Lhasa: The Holy City* (London: Chatto and Windus, 1938), p. 206; Luigi Villari, *Italian Life in Town and Country* (New York: G. P. Putnam's Sons, 1902), p. 156.

8. Wing-tsit Chan, *Religious Trends in Modern China* (New York: Columbia University Press, 1953), p. 141. Cf. Jacques Gernet, *Les Aspects*

Économiques du Bouddhisme dans la Société Chinoise du V au X* Siècle* (Saigon: École Française d'Extrême-Orient, 1956), p. 2.

9. E.g., Kenneth W. Morgan (ed.), *The Religion of the Hindus* (New York: Ronald Press, 1953), especially Chapter III.

10. E.g., G. Morris Carstairs, *The Twice-Born* (London: Hogarth Press, 1957), p. 26.

11. Fitzsimmons, *op. cit.*, p. 299.

12. E.g., Tsung-lien Shen and Shen-chi Liu, *Tibet and the Tibetans* (Stanford: Stanford University Press, 1953), pp. 28ff.

13. P. Thomas, *Hindu Religion, Customs, and Manners* (2d ed. rev.; Bombay: D. B. Taraporevala Sons, 195-) p. 33. Cf. Shen and Liu, *op. cit.*, p. 132, who stress the daily religious rites of the upper class in urban Tibet.

14. Maulānā Muḥammad 'Alī, *The Religion of Islām* (Lahore: Aḥmadiyyah Anjuman Ishā'at Islām, 1950), pp. 406ff.

15. *Ibid.*, pp. 395ff.

16. For the use of rosaries in various cultures, see, e.g., Frank A. Martin, *Under the Absolute Amir* (London: Harper and Bros., 1907), p. 267; Jean Kennedy, *Here is India* (New York: Charles Scribner's Sons, 1954), p. 4; Chapman, *op. cit.*, pp. 162-63; L. Austine Waddell, *The Buddhism of Tibet* (2d ed.; Cambridge: W. Heffer, 1934), p. 205.

17. E.g., Waddell, *op. cit.*, pp. 89-92; Francis L. K. Hsu, *Under the Ancestors' Shadow* (New York: Columbia University Press, 1948), p. 146.

18. Iris Origo, *The Merchant of Prato* (London: Jonathan Cape, 1957), pp. 306-7. Cf. H. Lapeyre, *Une Famille de Marchands: les Ruiz* (Paris: S.E.V.P.E.N., 1955), pp. 130, 133. The latter lays considerable stress upon the role of religion in business activities.

19. Harry Millman, "The Marwari: A Study of a Group of Trading Castes of India" (unpublished M.A. thesis, University of California, Berkeley, 1954), pp. 47-49.

20. J. S. Burgess, *The Guilds of Peking* (New York: Columbia University Press, 1928), p. 104.

21. E.g., John K. Shryock, *The Temples of Anking and their Cults* (Paris: Privately printed, 1931), pp. 98ff.; Li-ch'ên Tun, *Annual Customs and Festivals in Peking*, trans. and ed. Derk Bodde (Peiping: Henri Vetch, 1936), p. 25; M. Cary and T. J. Haarhoff, *Life and Thought in the Greek and Roman World* (London: Methuen, 1957), p. 307; Scaife, *op. cit.*, p. 203; Roger Le Tourneau, *Fès: Avant le Protectorat* (Casablanca: Société Marocaine de Librairie et d'Édition, 1949), pp. 301-2, 363.

22. E.g., G. Vanel, *Une Grande Ville aux XVII* et XVIII* Siècles* (Caen: Louis Jouan, 1910), pp. 245-75; A. H. M. Jones, "The Cities of the Roman Empire," in *La Ville*, Recueils de la Société Jean Bodin, VI (Bruxelles: Éditions de la Librairie Encyclopédique, 1954), 160; G. C. Vaillant, *The Aztecs of Mexico* (Harmondsworth: Penguin Books, 1956), pp. 192-98; Edward W. Lane, *The Manners and Customs of the Modern Egyptians* (5th ed.; New York: E. P. Dutton, Everyman's Library, 1923), Chapters XXIV-XXVI; Jukichi Inouye, *Home Life in Tokyo* (2d ed.; Tokyo: Tokyo Printing Co., 1911), pp. 286-88; Tun, *op. cit.*, passim.

23. Gernet, *op. cit.*, pp. 231-32. The quoted passage is a translation from the French version of part of a Chinese document.

24. Fr. Bernardino de Sahagún, *Historia General de las Cosas de Nueva España*, I (México, D.F.: Pedro Robredo, 1938), Book 2, 97, 168; Tsewang

Y. Pemba, *Young Days in Tibet* (London: Jonathan Cape, 1957), p. 115; Horace Miner, *The Primitive City of Timbuctoo* (Princeton: Princeton University Press, 1953), p. 124; Lane, *op. cit.,* pp. 432-36.

25. Justus Doolittle, *Social Life of the Chinese,* ed. Paxton Hood (London: Sampson Low, 1868), p. 105.

26. Heinrich Harrer, *Seven Years in Tibet* (London: Rupert Hart-Davis, 1953), p. 172.

27. E.g., Lynn Thorndike, *A History of Magic and Experimental Science,* III (New York: Columbia University Press, 1934), Chapter XXXIV; T. Lobsang Rampa, *The Third Eye* (London: Secker and Warburg, 1956), p. 147; Martin, *op. cit.,* p. 84; Gernet, *op. cit.,* p. 84; Vaillant, *op. cit.,* pp. 231-32.

28. Harrer, *op. cit.,* pp 267-70. Cf. Pemba, *op. cit.,* pp. 88-90.

29. Millman, *op. cit.,* pp. 51ff. Cf. data on Persia: Napier Malcolm, *Five Years in a Persian Town* (New York: E. P. Dutton, 1905), p. 120.

30. Chester Holcombe, *The Real Chinaman* (New York: Dodd, Mead, 1895), pp. 146-53.

31. John Henry Gray, *Walks in the City of Canton* (Hongkong: De Souza, 1875), pp. 27, 284, 492.

32. E.g., V. R. Burkhardt, *Chinese Creeds and Customs,* II (Hongkong: South China Morning Post, 1955), 6.

CHAPTER X

COMMUNICATION,
EDUCATION, AND
THE NATURE OF KNOWLEDGE

ONE fundamental structural arrangement in the feudal city and society remains to be considered: to wit, the formal educational apparatus and the system of knowledge it perpetuates, features that set the preindustrial civilized society off so dramatically from the primitive, or folk, order. But before we can attempt this, we must investigate the modes of communication in the non-industrial city upon which the dissemination of knowledge depends.

Communication

People who live in industrial-urban surroundings take mass communication media—radio, TV, newspapers, magazines, and books—pretty much for granted. Industrial man may find it impossible to imagine a city without mass communication. Yet, some cities of the mid-twentieth century—like Andkhui and Mazar-i-Sharif in Afghanistan or Katmandu in Nepal—are largely lacking in mass communication media, and cities of this sort were far more numerous a scant half century ago.

The lines of both communication and transport in pre-industrial civilized societies are few and rather tenuous, providing only a modicum of contact among cities, and to an even lesser degree between urban and rural areas. Railroads, motor vehicles, telephones, telegraph, radio, and so forth are lacking in the typical feudal society, vastly minimizing contacts among people and the diffusion of knowledge and ideas. Most persons communicate with one another through oral, face-to-face methods—and because of the poor transportation, the number of such contacts is highly restricted, even within a city. The small, but powerful, educated element employs writing as well. It is this latter medium that is so meaningful for our definition of the city and of civilization.

Oral Communication

Given the limited technological mechanisms for diffusing knowledge in the typical feudal city, it should come as no surprise that even the literate upper class is dependent in high degree upon word-of-mouth communication for the fulfilment of many functions, including the governing of society. Despite the incalculable impact of writing upon the feudal society, the ruling elite can not make wide use of this tool in the community; even where mechanical techniques of printing and paper-making have existed these have been highly laborious and costly. More than this, the mass populace is illiterate and can not be reached except through oral communication. Aside from a few literate outcaste elements, the humbler strata of society depend upon face-to-face communication in the performance of their daily tasks.

Because the city must have some system of communicating to the broad citizenry news of special events or crisis situations, special functionaries exist to serve this end. Town

criers station themselves at central gathering points to an-
nounce to the assembled populace special items of news or
to read official proclamations. Others may circulate through
the community warning of enemy attack, fire, or other impending disaster. In Fez, as in other cities, these criers have
been organized into a guild.[1] Various of their functions are
illumined by the following commentary on the Italian city
of Prato,[2]

> The town crier, *il banditore*, hurried from one street corner to the
> next, to spread the day's news: births and weddings and deaths,
> bankruptcies and emancipations, lists of lost property and lost cattle,
> even applications for wet-nurses—while more important official
> news was imparted by three trumpeters on horseback, dressed in the
> colours of the Commune, who blew a treble blast on their trumpets
> before announcing the sentences of the courts of law—banishments
> and fines, and sometimes executions.

Sometimes each quarter in a city has its own special crier.
In Kabul the Uzbek minority hires a *xabarče* to spread
tidings of births, deaths, festivals, and the like to members
of this ethnic group in their own language. A female *xabarče*
conveys news to the women in their homes.[3]

More influential than any of these in diffusing knowledge
and information in the city are story-tellers, street singers,
and actors, each group being organized into a guild, or its
functional equivalent. Typically urbanites, some of their
members nonetheless wander over the countryside from city
to city or from village to village, being special frequenters of
market towns on market days. (Priests, astrologers, and
magicians, already considered in the chapter on religion,
also disseminate information orally to a broad public.) A
prominent part of the repertoires of the story-tellers are
selections from the society's most revered literature: the
religious writings, the sagas of traditional heroes, and the
great poets. Many of the songs of the wandering bards and
the dances and dramas put on by professional entertainers
are strongly religious in their content or origin. The role of
entertainers, especially story-tellers, in the functioning of the

traditional city has been noted for Tokyo, Peking, Cairo, and Kabul, to cite but a few localities.[4]

Singer[5] comments upon these professional entertainers in Madras, India, of the mid-twentieth century. Here story-tellers, particularly, spread some of the learning in the ancient Sanskrit writings to the man-in-the-street, for though Madras is undergoing industrialization, a large body of illiterate persons still lacks any formal instruction in the society's sacred learning. Admittedly, the smatterings of traditional knowledge that pass through these functionaries, who themselves have often acquired it from second- or third-hand sources, are inevitably corrupted by lower-class ideas and beliefs. Yet, with the limited mass communication, this is the only way the society's religious traditions and history can be transmitted to the non-literate segments of the populace. And such dissemination is essential if the lower class is to grasp, albeit imperfectly, the norms that govern the social order, and some degree of community, or societal, cohesion achieved.

While it is true that scholars and other high-ranking priests may in some cultural settings give recitations from the sacred or highly revered writings, their audiences are most usually members of their own class; the temples, mosques, or other places where these meetings are held are typically allocated to upper-status groups. And the formal style spoken there is incomprehensible to the bulk of the populace, given the wide divergencies between upper- and lower-class speech in most feudal orders.

Professional raconteurs, troubadours, actors, and the like, though they help diffuse the upper-class traditions to the populace, occupy a low position in the status hierarchy. Most usually, they come from outcaste groups. The more privileged among these professional entertainers serve the elite, but usually their audiences are commoners who gather in special halls or temples or on street corners in the poorer quarters of the city. The intellectuals look upon them with scorn, not simply by reason of their humble or outcaste origins and the fact that they usually sustain close contacts with the lower class, but also because these professional story-tellers are apt to introduce distortions into their renditions of the sacred lore. This results in part from their illiteracy, which forces them to rely upon memory, in part from their efforts to dramatize a story to gain more listeners and thereby increase their earnings. So the epics recounting the society's past glories become more legendary than historical, the heroes more warlike, and the tales of love more romantic. Nevertheless these functionaries play a vital function in diffusing knowledge, forming a tenuous bridge between the educated elite and the illiterate mass populace.

Despite the aforementioned functionaries, most oral communication is effected through more informal means; the market place in fact is a center for the dissemination of much news. Traveling merchants are frequently sought after, for they bear tidings from other cities and from distant lands. Several writers have commented upon this phenomenon, noting, for example, that the caravan driver in Middle Eastern cities has been an unofficial medium of communication between all parts of the society, conveying especially news of prices and goods from bazaars in remote cities and villages.[6] Besides the market, the guild halls and places of worship are centers where people can assimilate gossip and other news of the day.

In several of the previous chapters we treated some of the results of this heavy reliance of the populace upon oral communication media. As an instance, the prevalence of haggling in the market place is partially a product of the inadequate knowledge of the current state of supply and demand. Moreover, the selection and advancement of governmental and other bureaucratic personnel on the basis of particularistic, rather than universalistic, criteria stems in large measure from the dearth of record-keeping and of communication media. Without these, prospective personnel can simply not be evaluated on anything but personalistic grounds.

Communication and the Written Word

As previously stressed, despite the narrow utility of writing in the preindustrial city, its very existence has made civilization and city life possible. To this day, many sociologists fail to appreciate the impact of writing upon society. At once a conservative and a revolutionary force, it opened the way for the development, transmission, and perpetration of knowledge on a far grander scale than could ever be achieved through oral methods alone. It could now be spread more easily across cultures and societies and down the corridors of time. Writing, then, permitted the accumulation of a vast store of learning and promoted, among other things, further developments in the technological sphere which eventually resulted in the Industrial Revolution.

On the other hand, writing fixes—even stultifies—ideas, beliefs, and behavior patterns over time and space. For with permanent records, feudal orders can perpetuate traits that might evanesce within a merely verbal tradition. Furthermore, in societies like those in the Muslim Middle East, India, and China, writing has standardized action-patterns over broad geographic regions. The elite, inculcated in a narrow set of sacred writings and in the norms enunciated in these, have tended to display considerable homogeneity, in striking contrast to the illiterate urban lower class and the ruralites, who have been far more influenced by local customs and thus differ among themselves in numerous ways. And the homogeneity of the ruling elite has had the major consequence of permitting the expansion of empires.

Because writing has been the medium for publishing abroad and perpetuating the sacred norms, and inasmuch as its use has been the exclusive property of the leisured class, it has taken on a special status in preindustrial civilized orders. Calligraphy is the focus of considerable attention in the schools. Writing has been considered one form of art. As the recording media of the sacred literature, the traditional scripts are highly elaborate and formalized and tend to continue so through time. Gray[7] observed that in Canton in the latter part of the nineteenth century writing was greatly revered because it was a medium for disseminating the "wisdom of the sages." It was a sacrilege to trample under foot any fragment of paper upon which Chinese characters were written or printed. And in some Chinese cities—e.g., Peking—the literati placed receptacles at street corners and in shops reminding people to "respect the written character" and to deposit therein any scraps of waste paper containing writing. At stated intervals the contents of these boxes were conveyed to a temple, to the accompaniment of band music and processions, there to be burned with much ceremony in a special shrine.[8]

Books are often treated as holy. Olufsen[9] witnessed this in Bokhara at about the turn of the present century. His servants handled reverently, even kissed, his Russian dictionary and nautical almanac. Such is understandable if we recall that the feudal city's writings are devoted largely to philosophical-religious matters: the most sanctified values, those deemed most estimable by the elite, are recorded therein; in turn their preservation in writing ensures their pre-eminence over competing values. By extension, all books come to acquire a "sacred" character. That only a select few can read enhances the prestige of the incribed word. The mere ownership of books—if yellowed with age, all the better—is a status-marker: the owner is thereby endowed with a degree of learning quite apart from his actual familiarity with the contents of the volumes.

Little wonder, in light of these practices, that writing is thought to have magical properties as well. Urbanites in China and in the ancient and modern Middle East have worn amulets containing a slip of paper inscribed with a few words from the sacred writings to cure illnesses or ward off evil spirits.[10]

Printed matter, as such, is scarce. Where mechanical means of reproducing literary works are non-existent, the distribution of writings has had to be effected through laborious copying of manuscripts by hand, the reproductions being available just to a privileged few. Historians of medieval Europe have oft remarked upon the extraordinary degree of time and effort expended by certain monastic orders in the hand copying of literary works. As noted earlier, even in preindustrial cities that have utilized some printing techniques, books and pamphlets have been costly and relatively scarce; the widespread illiteracy and the dearth of libraries have meant a minuscule market for any book. Many of the surviving printed works from Europe of only a few centuries ago are collector's items, primarily because of the insignificant number of copies issued.

Apart from books and pamphlets, brief written communications—reports, proclamations, and letters—are employed for special purposes in the bureaucratic apparatuses, primarily between offices in different communities. And the larger merchants—these are the ones who engage in intercity commerce—may place orders and draw up contracts in writing; the small urban shopkeeper or merchant, of course, is as illiterate as the vast majority of his customers.

Many feudal orders, including older ones like ancient Rome and the early Arab empires, as well as traditional China, Korea, and Central Asia, have had a postal system of limited proportions for transmitting official dispatches. Also in non-industrial cities, private individuals—only the wealthy qualify—utilize their own servants as couriers. In some instances merchants band together to support a private messenger service. Merchants in Fez[11] hired couriers to deliver messages within the city and between Fez and other urban centers, these agents being reimbursed in accordance with the season, the urgency of the mission, and the distance traveled. Caravan-drivers, porters, itinerant merchants, and assorted travelers supplement the courier system in many preindustrial civilized societies, affording thereby tenuous links among urban centers.

Quite apparent is the overturning of all of this under industrial-urbanization, demanding as it does rapid and widespread dissemination of information. Today oral communications are amplified and reproduced many times over, say by radio and television, and so reach the mass populace. Written data are speeded on their way by telegraph and proliferated widely through printing and a variety of other duplicating techniques. In its firm dependence upon the written word, modern industrial civilization rests upon a magnificent foundation of paper held together with "red tape."

Script

We have reserved one aspect of communication for special treatment; this is the matter of writing systems per se. It is of some moment that in most preindustrial cities the scripts, though admittedly varying among cultures, contrast in their complexity with the simpler ones of industrial cities. Pre-industrial Europe has been a definite exception in its use of relatively efficient alphabetic scripts such as the Greek and the Roman, wherein each meaningful "phonetic" entity in the language is marked, more or less, by a distinctive symbol—in linguistic terms, these alphabets are "pseudo-phonemic." Still, even the traditional European scripts have been more elaborate than those employed in most advanced industrial societies.

Ordinarily the writing system in feudal cities is so complex that it actually hinders the advancement and diffusion of knowledge (though the very existence of writing permits the accumulation and extension of learning on a scale undreamed of in the preliterate order). Learning these scripts demands of one considerable time and effort, a luxury obviously limited to the diminutive leisure class. Especially is this the case with the traditional writing system for Chinese. The number of ideographic signs it employs staggers the imagination. Facility in reading the highly elaborate characters is attained only after years of assiduous effort; loosely, each of the characters must be memorized as a separate entity. They are, moreover, rather difficult to execute, so that proficiency in writing requires endless practice. Small wonder that the highly educated alone ever really master the traditional Chinese writing system.

Simpler than the aforementioned were the hieroglyphic scripts of ancient Sumeria, Egypt, and Meso-America, which contained both ideographic elements and signs standing for "phonetic" sequences, usually syllables. Yet these scripts literally swarmed with complicated symbols, each one of which had to be painstakingly executed and memorized as a somewhat distinct entity.

Other writing systems have generally eliminated ideographic, or non-phonetic, characters, representing instead sequences of sounds. Such syllabaries include the later Assyrian, the early Persian, the Hittite, the Japanese kana, and others. Since the number of distinctive syllables in a language can be rather great, a writing system that contains separate signs for the majority of its syllables is obviously highly cumbersome.

The invention of an alphabetic script, where ideally each letter stands for a single phoneme, was a monumental breakthrough for communication. Yet the earliest alphabets, those developed for the Semitic languages, had many imperfections, as do their latter-day representatives, the Hebrew and the Arabic. The Arabic is also the medium for Persian and Urdu and, until recently, Turkish and its related languages as well. These scripts for the most part include some signs that are quite elaborate and others that are all too similar to one another, slowing the learning process perceptibly, and the usual practice of omitting vowel markers, except in selected instances, demands of the reader a fair degree of education before he can determine the meaning of the words he reads. The number of signs in the Arabic writing system is further swelled by the fact that most of the sounds are rendered in from three to four distinctive fashions according as they appear initially, medially, or finally in words or stand alone. The list of symbols required in the printing process is thereby multiplied appreciably.

So too, type-fonts for the various alphabetic scripts of India, scripts evidently derived from the early Semitic ones, include a veritable army of symbols. Granted that some Indian languages are marked by an extraordinarily full set of distinctive sound-classes, many of these latter are represented by varying symbols depending upon the letters with which they are combined. Consequently, the number of separate signs used in printing, as in Telugu or Tamil, can run into the hundreds.[12]

The nexus between the writing system and the sacred literature in feudal orders has tended to conserve the elaborateness of the scripts. And the definition of calligraphy as a fine art has in many instances induced a further embroidering of the symbols. Scholars in traditional China passed many an hour in perfecting their brush techniques for drawing the characters of Chinese, concern with the aesthetics of one's handwriting being a mark of the learned man. Arabic is another script that has lent itself admirably to artistic fancy. Even the Roman alphabetic script has not evaded extensive elaboration on this account.[13] Throughout medieval Europe the Roman letters were shaped into various intricate forms. Viewing the problem from a different angle, we see that the Cyrillic alphabet of pre-Revolutionary Russia has been simplified as the Communists have pressed for greater simplicity in the writing system, seeking thereby to break the tie with the past and to promote industrial-urbanization.

The aforementioned obstacles to communication that writing systems in literate preindustrial societies present are further compounded by the fact that often the script represents a form of the language—viz., the formal style—that differs strikingly from the various colloquials. As an instance, in areas of Arabic speech, Classical Arabic, the language of the Koran and other sacred works, has usually been that "reduced" to writing. Partly as a consequence of this, Classical Arabic has changed little over time, whereas the colloquial idioms—whether the informal tongue of the elite, or those of the people—rarely committed to writing, have been allowed to go their separate ways.

It can readily be seen that a complex script reinforces the authority of the upper class. It means that few persons have access to the "sacred" knowledge, for alone among the populace the leisured class has the time and the funds to devote long years to achieving mastery of this tool. An intricate writing system is, moreover, a stumbling-block to communication, not merely because of the difficulties of learning it, but because it inhibits the development of technological devices that permit the printing and distribution of mass quantities of inexpensive literature.

Many of the old scripts are simply not amenable to mechanization. Typewriters made for Japanese, Telugu, or Arabic are exceedingly cumbersome machines with their vast array of symbols. Hsia[14] observes ". . . the Chinese typewriter is a very bulky machine with a total of 7,792 characters (2,380 often-used and 5,412 rare ones)." Under these circumstances, typing proceeds at a snail's pace and is a highly costly operation. Yet without typewriters that permit extensive correspondence and record-keeping, large-scale business or governmental enterprise flounders. Printing, too, becomes expensive —for one thing, typesetting by hand may be the only practical method when the number of symbols runs into the hundreds or thousands. Newspapers, magazines, and the like are thus placed financially beyond the reach of the common man.

To see this issue in better perspective, let us examine more closely what has been transpiring in industrializing societies. In almost every sector of the "underdeveloped" civilized world the argumentation over what to do about the traditional scripts has waxed ebullient. China, Japan, India, the Middle

East, parts of Europe—few areas have been exempt. The battle has raged in China over decades, for the resistance to change has been strong. But the Communists, determined that industrial-urbanization must proceed at any price, now seem intent upon overhauling the writing system in one way or another. As one of the first steps toward industrialization, or what is loosely termed "Westernization," Turkey replaced its Arabic script by the much simpler Roman, and today in Soviet Central Asia the Arabic script—the traditional medium of Uzbek, Kirghiz, Kazakh, and other languages—has been supplemented by the more efficient Cyrillic.[15] There is more than Russianization involved here, though that too is operative.

The clash between the old and the new in the matter of script reform has, however, been bitter in some transitional societies. The adoption of a new script means cutting off most of the new educated class from the society's historic traditions. If China effects a thoroughgoing script reform, only a handful of persons will in the future be able to read the traditional writings in the original medium.

Understandably, the old intellectuals are reluctant to give up a writing system that has through the ages been deemed sacred and aesthetically pleasing. They are not oblivious to the fact that with script reform they relinquish the chief basis of their monopoly of the traditional learning. Simplification of writing induces mass literacy and, ultimately, universal access to most of the society's knowledge. Then too, the older literature forfeits its sanctified status as literary works, both old and new, become disseminated throughout the industrializing society.

The Educational Structure

As expected in a social order with few mechanisms for diffusing knowledge via the written word and none for achieving oral communication on a massive scale, instruction for most urbanites is gained through direct, face-to-face contacts. Children learn from family members at home, by observation in the streets and markets, and in their place of work. Those fortunate enough to gain a foothold as apprentices to shopkeepers or artisans receive specialized, albeit informal, training in a specific occupation. And everywhere story-tellers, street singers, and actors diffuse some knowledge through oral or visual means.

Formal education for the favored few is a distinguishing characteristic of this city. Moving from the urban center to the countryside, we encounter fewer and fewer people who can read and write, and the isolated soul who does is a poor practitioner of the art.

That formal education is the province of the upper class should be qualified: only males are deemed eligible. Few girls ever learn to read and write, and those who do, receive this training at home and for a few years at most.

Most schools on the elementary level are supported privately rather than publicly. Persons of means hire tutors for their children or send them to private schools established by groups of urban families, the teachers being paid in money or in kind. Respecting primary schools in Bokhara in the nineteenth century, Khanikoff writes:[16]

. . . the Mullah stipulates with the parents or relatives of the child intrusted to him, for a fee, which averages generally from one to three tillas per annum. Independently of this, the students, on entering school, must present their tutor with a khalat, a shirt, a pair of boots, slippers, &c., likewise a tray with dried fruits, a pound of tea, and nine loaves of bread, and over and above, each school-boy must bring to his master on Thursday a loaf of bread, whilst the parents make him a present of a khalat, as soon as their child begins to read the Kúran. For such as are in more easy circumstances, it is customary to present a Khalat to the teacher for every *sureh* (or chapter) of the Kúran.

Some public support of schools might be said to exist in various societies, especially theocratic ones, where governmental leaders or others of the elite subsidize religious organizations, for these in turn organize schools. Schools in feudal cities have in one way or another been interrelated with and supported by the religious apparatus. With education and religion so intermeshed, and formal learning being defined primarily as inculcation in the sacred lore, the religious personnel are those deemed best qualified to instruct the young. In medieval York, Benson contends, the church sought to control all education in the city, and the priests were the elementary-school teachers.[17] In earlier Japanese and Chinese cities, elementary-school instruction outside the family schools was carried out in the temples;[18] so too, primary-school teaching in Middle Eastern cities has had as its setting the mosque, or a building adjacent to this, with the mulla, or priest, functioning as educator.

Moving on to advanced education, we still find the religious system closely linked with and supporting much of what passes for higher learning. But now, direct governmental support is more common. For example, during at least some phases of traditional China many institutions of higher learning were subsidized by the government, and an analogous situation existed in Fez in the 1900s.[19] At this stage the government can afford to take a greater interest in advanced education, for a mere fragment of the total population is involved; except for rare individuals, the socially ineligible have been eliminated from the race through their inability to acquire primary-school learning.

Mass education is deemed non-essential, often undesirable, by the upper strata. The simple technology of the feudal city and the broader social order demands little in the way of education from the common man; no complex body of technical knowledge need be elaborated and perpetuated. More than this, it is patently impossible for the society to support many persons, or for these to sustain themselves, for lengthy periods of study. Children of the poor must early take up the never-ending search for sustenance. Besides, the barriers to social mobility are so formidable that little motivation for improving one's skills is kindled within the commoner group. And were the schools to produce a large body of educated persons, not all of these could find employment in positions commensurate with their training.

Despite the alleged profusion of primary schools in Bokhara at the turn of the present century, only about one-twentieth of the populace was estimated to be literate.[20] This is perhaps higher than the percentage attained in most pre-industrial cities. Yet it is minute compared to the proportion of literacy in highly industrialized cities, where almost all urbanites can read and write; mass education is essential to the maintenance of the complex, scientifically oriented industrial system.

The exclusiveness of the educational process now made apparent, we examine the system itself. The primary schools or private tutorial methods offer the student a narrow curriculum, one that serves to glorify and to perpetuate the society's traditions, not to develop intellectual curiosity and creative thinking. Reading, writing, and simple arithmetic, occasionally some geography and history, are taught in the beginning stages of elementary education. Students are early introduced, first superficially through memorization, later through the modicum of explanation, to the sacred writings—the scriptures, the works of the revered poets, and so on—that embody the society's hallowed traditions, and these constitute the bulk of the reading matter throughout the remaining years of study.

The schools of higher learning, roughly comparable to the colleges and universities of industrial cities, provide a much broader offering than the aforesaid. Nonetheless, humanistic studies—theology, law (usually canon law), history, philosophy, and literature—form the core of the curriculum. Advanced grammar, calligraphy, rhetoric, logic, mathematics (including geometry and algebra), astronomy (considerably admixed with astrology), occasionally medicine and music,

are other fields that students can savor. It is usually understandable that theology, philosophy, history, and literature
(including a heavy dose of poetry), should be given strong
play; they socialize the student into the basic values of the
social order and serve to buttress the already concrete-like
authority structure. The prime purpose of higher education,
and in China the governmental examination system for bureaucratic positions, is to ensure that the rising officialdom
is fully indoctrinated into the society's ideal norms.

Concerning the other university offerings, grammar is essential to an understanding of law and of logic, and it serves
to keep the upper-class formal spoken language free from
the impurities that characterize the colloquials—forms of
speech that to the educated man's ears seem highly "corrupted." Logic is basic to philosophical and religious disputation. Mathematics is a vital tool in astronomy, and the latter
in turn is linked to the religious system in preindustrial civilized orders. Formerly in a city like Fez, mysticism and divination were part of the university curriculum, exemplifying the
close relationships between magic and religion and the respectability accorded certain aspects of magic.[21] Astrology was
taught at the University of Florence[22] and other medieval
European institutions as well. Significantly, except for logic,
mathematics, and astronomy, branches of science that do not
demand experimentation in order to advance, medicine is
often the only "practical," scientific subject offered in feudal
universities. But, we argue farther on in this chapter, the
medical knowledge expounded, while foreshadowing modern
medicine, is of a very different order than that in the present
industrial world.

Often in schools of advanced study there is a lack of any
fixed program for a specific degree, and the time devoted to
any one subject may vary greatly among students. In Bokhara
some reportedly remained in the university for as long as 20
years, and Tucci says of Tibet that often a student would
graduate in theology only after about 25 years of study,

examinations, and public disputations.[23] In part the indeterminacy of the length of study for a degree in the feudal city is related to the irregularity of attendance at classes and of the conduct of the courses themselves. It was common practice in many an Islamic university for a professor to seat himself in a corner of the mosque or special hall and wait for students to collect. If some showed up he might lecture; if pupils were too few in number on that day he abandoned the idea. In addition, the academic year, whether in primary schools or institutions of advanced learning, is interrupted frequently by vacations, some rather lengthy, and many of them geared to the never-ending round of religious festivals in the city. Nor should one exaggerate the diligence of university students; they engage in their share of horseplay along with their studies.

Notwithstanding the lack of a rigid schedule in the typical urban school, the academic atmosphere is a spartan one. Schoolrooms are often makeshift affairs, poorly lit, ill ventilated, and almost devoid of furniture and of teaching aids of any kind. Very often, even in the universities, students sit on the floor.

From the standpoint of the industrial-urban community, a minimum of ordering of students according to ability and stage of progress obtains. Students of varying ages and competence work in the same room with a single teacher.

With respect to the learning process itself, religious ritual forms part of every school day. As an instance, primary-school pupils in China, on entering the schoolroom, bowed to the tablets of Confucius and of the God of Letters before which burned incense sticks.[24] And because creative thinking is strongly de-emphasized, rote learning is the rule from primary school on through the university. To further memorization—the key learning device—the whole class recites lessons aloud. Often long poems, selections from traditional works, or whole books are committed to memory. In Bokhara:[25]

All those [primary schools] . . . were arranged in the same way; they consisted of one single room where the light penetrated but sparingly through a loop-hole in the wall. . . . Platforms were used by the pupils as tables for the books, and they all read aloud at once, the upper part of the body being always bent to and fro. One reads his alphabet, another verses by Khodsha Hafis, one the Koran in Arabic, in shocking confusion.

Whereas in Lhasa:[26]

On several occasions I visited the school kept by the monk telegraphist. One day the children were all reading aloud, but no two seemed to be reading the same thing. Sometimes they repeated prayers. Usually they were sitting cross-legged on the floor writing from memory passages of the scriptures.

So too, memorization was central to the learning process in ancient Rome.[27]

Though the curriculum is a narrow one—in Bokhara, so says Khanikoff, memorization of passages from eight books comprised the entire elementary-school offering; in China it was the "Four Books," and after that, others of the "Thirteen Classics," all conceived within the framework of Confucianist thought[28]—students are likely to have no real comprehension of the words they parrot. This is especially apparent in Muslim cities where Arabic is not the language of the people —e.g., in areas of Turkic or Persian speech. The instructors themselves may not know enough Arabic to fully understand the Koran or the other sacred books being taught. But then, even native speakers of Arabic may comprehend little of the sacred writings they memorize. Hurgronje says of a Meccan school of higher learning:[29]

No one may attend the *tafsîr* lectures [on exegesis] who has not several times recited the Qur'an from end to end according to the rules of *tajwîd,* and most of those who attend know the Qur'an by heart. It is interesting to observe, how such students now hear for the first time the sense of the mysterious words which they have been reciting. . . . But even for the "knowers by heart" the Holy Book as a whole remains closed with seven seals until the high science of the *tafsîr* has been studied by them or until learned friends have expounded to them separate passages.

Besides memory-work in schools of advanced learning, much attention is given to the development of verbal skills and to disquisitions into minor passages in the texts. This last adds little to knowledge, its aim being merely refinement in the interpretation of the traditional writings so revered by the society.

Why should learning in the schools—elementary and advanced—be achieved primarily through memorization? The technology, once again, offers a partial explanation. Books and writing materials are scarce, forcing persons to rely upon memory. And in the feudal order the classical writings are the receptacles of the true, and absolute, knowledge, and "mastery" of the latter is defined as total and undeviating inculcation in it. In China, "All knowledge resided in the classical writings; the well-informed man was the one who could point his finger at the place in the classics where a particular gem of knowledge was hid,"[30] just as in traditional Cairo:[31]

Those who have committed to memory the whole, or considerable portions, of the Kuran, and can recite two or three celebrated "kaseedehs" (or short poems), or introduce, now and then, an apposite quotation in conversation, are considered accomplished persons.

In schools of higher learning, exegesis, or commentary, on the doctrinal literature forms a legitimate part of the curriculum and verbal disputations are permitted, but the basic validity of this knowledge remains unquestioned.

Lest we be misunderstood: occasional ruptures in the aforementioned patterns did occur prior to the Age of Enlightenment in Europe. Certain intellectual advances set the stage for the Industrial Revolution, and preindustrial cities were the focal points of the accumulated learning. But from the vantage point of the industrial-urban world, most intellectual "revolutions" in preindustrial cities were mere waves upon a vast ocean of tradition. Learning in Classical Greek cities, though evincing much creativity, nonetheless resembled that of other feudal cities in its reliance upon humanistic theory for interpreting the world, not empirical verification, and upon oral disputation far more than methodical accumulation of data. More of this shortly.

We come now to the student-teacher relationship. Discipline in the schools is exceedingly strict, and corporal punishment is meted out with little hesitation, not surprising in an educational system that emphasizes moral deportment, indoctrination in the ideal norms, and the suppression of intellectual curiosity. The instructor's authority is unquestioned by either students or their parents; he is, after all, the perpetuator and disseminator of knowledge, much of which, as we emphasized, is of a sacred character. Though the teacher's prestige is high and his power in the schoolroom considerable, his economic rewards are rarely lucrative. In many preindustrial cities he has had to hold several jobs concurrently.[32]

Our generalizations raise an interesting theoretical problem. A number of historians of ancient Greece and Rome[33] have concluded that teachers there occupied a low status. Again the matter of reference points rears its ugly head. Historians seem to argue for the low status of teachers on the basis of their poor pay, gained chiefly from serving as tutors to rulers and the wealthier elite (a pattern common to other preindustrial cities). Except with respect to some societies' special outcaste teachers, such reasoning is highly questionable, if not downright false. True enough, set against the upper echelons of the elite their status was low, but to place teachers and other intellectuals, as these writers implicitly do, with the abysmally poor and ignorant is dubious, sociologically. Taking the urban community as a whole, teachers and intellectuals had much more in common with the elite than with the lower class. Many of the problems of interpreting the social structure of ancient cities stem from a complete disregard of the real conditions of the lower class, and also at times from the failure to recognize that the ideal legal norms do not necessarily reflect the actual social structure.

Learned men in all feudal orders are accorded respect

through special terms of address, often embodying references to their academic status, and well-defined personal mannerisms. The following description from a school of higher learning in Mecca is indicative of the patterns of deference toward professors (though obviously the particular cultural content varies from one feudal order to the next).[34]

. . . some recite before each lecture the prescribed form of praise of the study which is in hand. . . . In the end the professor closes the book, and whispers a prayer. . . . Then as a sign of conclusion he gently rubs his hands over his face. The students rise, go up to him as he sits, and kneeling down on his right give a parting kiss to his right hand. He however gets up for the older students as it would be arrogant to receive their kiss sitting; . . .

The respect the teacher enjoys endows him with considerable authority. His students are expected to lend him absolute obedience and not to contradict him in any way. Social distance between teacher and pupil is usually wide, and when a close relationship does develop, it is a hierarchical one, where deference is always shown by the student to the professor. One becomes a disciple of his mentor. This master-student relationship continues long after one completes his formal schooling. Throughout the history of India, devotion to one's *guru* has been a highly valued norm. Japan has had its genealogies of successive generations of masters and their disciples. In China, not infrequently, wealthy families paid homage in the domestic ancestral shrines to the memory of teachers of family members. Finally, students of the same teacher are apt to maintain ties in later years, forming cliques in the governmental bureaucracy and other non-academic realms.[35]

To clarify further the educational process in the feudal city and society, we examine the nature of knowledge itself.

The Nature of Knowledge

As the curricula of the formal educational institutions aptly demonstrate, learning of the intellectual sort—as opposed to that developed on the practical level by unlettered persons in the arts and crafts—is primarily of the humanistic variety, focusing upon theology, philosophy, literature, and juridical matters. In working out rationales for man's ultimate existence, the preindustrial civilized society attained heights unmatched in the industrial milieu. We are not interested in evaluating the soundness of these philosophical and theological notions. Suffice it to say that the literature of preindustrial societies, that of the Chinese, the Indians, the Persians, the Hebrews, the Greeks, the Romans, and others, will long be sources of inspiration to man in his strivings to cope with the world, even the new technology.

But looking back over the history of feudal societies, we see that this knowledge has tended to ossify, for orthodoxy of interpretation, rather than critical valuation or discovery, has been the badge of the learned man. Moreover, the humanistic literature of feudal cities, including Athens during its intellectual florescence, displays other recurrent characteristics:

An obvious trait is an absorption with problems having little relevance for the lives of the common people. The modern social scientist must piece together mere fragments of data if he is to gain any understanding of the lower class and outcaste groups in older feudal orders—e.g., ancient Athens, Rome, and even medieval European cities. This is one reason I have relied heavily upon more recent descriptions of feudal city life for illustrating the generalizations of this book. Occasionally, concrete issues like the mechanics of government have been examined by some writers, say in China or ancient Greece, but these have tended to be couched in abstract terms. Histories in preindustrial cities, where they exist, are, with some exceptions, discussions of local happenings in a particular community or province, or are the panegyrics of royalty, or the nobility, or other leading families. Objective description of his own social order is not the goal of the feudal intellectual. Nor has he displayed any real interest in foreigners. Consequently, the occasional commentaries of travelers to these cities are invaluable to social scientists, for they allow fleeting glimpses of life as it was lived.

In seeking to explain this disregard by intellectuals of the lower class and outcaste groups, we find that the authority structure does not rest upon the consent of the governed; the ruling clique need pay little heed to the desires of the disadvantaged groups. Deriving its authority from tradition and absolutes, the governing element can close its eyes to the condition of the general populace. Objective description, moreover, is superfluous in a social order that is not concerned with purposive planning, with revising the existing order.

Another reason is that the intellectuals, as moralizers, are absorbed with what men must do to adjust to the divine will or the forces of "nature." Emphasis is on what ought to be, not on what is. Had the intellectuals brought themselves to explore the latter in detail, attempting descriptions of the lower strata, they would certainly have experienced some degree of secularization. Concern with what is tends to expose the ideal to critical reflection, for the discrepancies that always exist call for explanation.

By way of contrast, look closely at the industrial world. The class structure has become more fluid, and the government, inasmuch as it derives its authority from the consent of the governed, must indirectly or directly concern itself with the problems of the mass populace—it must be attuned to what people think and how they act. But other forces are at work. With the emergence of mass education, oriented increasingly to the natural sciences, and an expanding body of experts who believe man can control and revise the social order, we find government and business and other bureaucracies collecting data on a wide range of social phenomena. Purposive planning presupposes certain basic information on the social system. Not unexpectedly, one of the first items on the agenda for underdeveloped countries seeking to industrialize are better censuses. And if the past and present course of events in the Soviet system is any indication, a long-run trend there—interrupted by periodic reversals on political accounts—apparently will be the collection of more and more empirical data on the economy and related areas.[36]

But what about knowledge in the physical and natural sciences, on the technological order in general? A fundamental thesis of this work is that this sort of knowledge is, with rare exceptions, perpetuated in feudal cities by the lower class, not by the educated elite. The artisan, the merchant, the herbologist, the barber-surgeon, have all attained a degree of technological know-how. Metal workers, weavers, dyers, potters, and others often possess rather detailed empirical knowledge, garnered through the centuries of hit-or-miss observation. But this empirical knowledge has been passed on through informal means; it has rarely been put down in writing.

The data from myriad feudal orders—traditional India, Tibet, medieval Europe, traditional China, the Middle East —indicate that the abstract thinking, or theoretical framework, of the intellectuals or learned men has not been related to the technical knowledge amassed over time by the common man; the two have been almost completely disjunct. This harks back to our earlier statements about the structure of the feudal city. Practical knowledge, being obtainable largely through work with the hands, has been devalued, often most strongly by highly literate, educated men. Intellectuals' concern with everyday matters is limited mainly to the ceremonial aspects of religion or to the political arena. Least of all are the literati interested in effecting technological change in the city.

Actually, that activity of the learned which might be considered "scientific" has more often than not been intermeshed with the religious and magical beliefs of the upper class. Thorndike[37] says of Europe in the late Middle Ages that wisdom and astrology were considered almost synonymous. So the latter was esteemed by the church. Medical men had a lively interest in astrology and, to a lesser degree, alchemy. All of these patterns have been duplicated in other preindustrial orders.

Stepping back in time, we see that mathematical knowledge, as against the simple arithmetic that the merchant or artisan utilizes, has been closely tied to religious activity. For instance, precise mathematical knowledge was applied in the construction of religious edifices in ancient Egypt and the Maya cities, though in different ways. And it has been crucial in astrology and astronomy, for calculating the concourses of the planets, etc. Not all mathematics has been functionally related to religion, but it must be conceded that priests and mathematicians have worn the same hat in many preindustrial cities, although not all members of the priestly group have been mathematicians.

Time and again we are forced to the conclusion that the feudal system has utilized its knowledge not to change the natural and/or divine order, but rather to promote man's adjustment to unseen forces in the universe. The reader will recall comments in previous chapters that the magician seeks to influence the spirit realm. But this is merely to restore harmony in nature and to facilitate man's *adaptation* to the world about him; it is not an attempt to revise it.

Not that feudal cities have witnessed no scientific development. Needham[38] sees the germs of modern scientific thought in early Chinese civilization, contending that certain scientific notions conceived in the West were anticipated much earlier by the Chinese. The reader may be so transported by Needham's arguments that he fails to recognize the wide chasm between the scientific thought of the past few centuries and that in feudal societies. Other historians have glorified the science of ancient Greece. Clagett,[39] for one, presents a highly favorable picture of scientific progress in Greek cities. But he is comparing it not with that in industrial-urban orders but rather with the science of prior antiquity and of the Roman and medieval European cities that followed. Obviously, from these angles of observation, the progress in Greece is impressive; but Clagett's reference points are not ours. Seen in contrast to the scientific attainments of the modern industrial world, those of the Greeks look paltry indeed.

Among the ancient Greeks, as with other traditional urbanized peoples, the scholarly activities of learned men were, with rare exceptions, divorced from everyday, mundane existence. While some intellectuals in Athens and other cities made observations of the world around them that added to the store of data in astronomy, biology, physics, and other fields,

their general attitude toward life resulted in many cases in a positive aversion against increasing knowledge by experiment. In the ordinary affairs of life, they esteemed mental activity far more highly than physical, which they thought unworthy of freemen and fit only for slaves. . . . As Xenophon said: "The mechanical arts carry a social stigma, and are rightly dishonoured in our cities. . . ."[40]

The abstract thinking of the learned men, evidenced for example in the classification systems of the Greeks with respect to natural phenomena, was based upon observation and speculation, only rarely upon experimentation; nor were their theories conjoined with the practical knowledge of the lowly artisans. This latter would have required work with the hands and identification, or at least closer contacts, with the common man. So it has been in other feudal cities as well.

Yet, contrary forces operating in preindustrial cities have demanded a modicum of application of theoretical knowledge. Astronomy and mathematics, we noted, developed largely by the priestly group, have provided the data for calendrics and, in some societies, for temple-building as well, although the resulting "scientific" progress has usually been an unanticipated by-product of these developments whose purpose has been overwhelmingly ceremonial. The prime objective has been adjustment to the natural-divine order. Thus, astronomical calculations, dependent in large part upon progress in mathematics, have served mainly the ends of astrology, being widely employed in divination—in government, in the economic sphere, in the realm of family and personal affairs—for widespread in feudal cities is the conviction that man's destiny is in many ways controlled by the stars.

As Charles Singer[41] and others recognize, it was only in the seventeenth century that the happy combination of theory and practice occurred and modern science was born. Theories now were tested pragmatically, and intellectuals began to classify and evaluate the practical knowledge of the artisans. Admittedly, such empirical findings had been accumulating over several millennia, but this was far from sufficient. The two strands of scientific thought—the theoretical and the practical—had to be fused, possible only within a social system whose class structure, relative to that in the past, was more fluid and which embodied a value system that did not deem it shameful for scholars to test their theories through experimentation—i.e., through manual work involving the handling of heavy or perhaps grimy instruments and materials. Learned men's acceptance of the need for questioning the time-honored modes of thinking, and for verifying their own theories as well, was a radical departure from tradition. More, the interplay between theory and experimentation enhanced the possibility of man's dominion over nature, thereby profoundly affecting the attitude toward the natural-divine order. Indeed, planned experimentation per se effects some revision in the latter.

Make no mistake about it: modern science has immensely altered the pace of urban living. The saying, "The more things change the more they remain the same," was proved false by the Industrial Revolution. The comments of Cohen[42] upon Charles Singer's five-volume work on the history of technology (summarizing the accomplishments in primitive societies, the most ancient empires, the Mediterranean civilizations, medieval Europe and the West up to 1900) are instructive. He observes that comparable coverage of the developments since 1900 would require just as many volumes or more.

A half-century compared with some millennia! The wedding of scientific theory and practice a few centuries ago led to the Industrial Revolution. And the new technology breeds further technology, resulting in a never-ending concatenation of scientific achievements. Current scientific advances are inextricably interwoven with the behemoth industrial system that makes certain vital economic resources available to the scientist.

But back to the preindustrial city. To clarify our arguments and treat more fully a neglected aspect of the preindustrial city's social structure, we examine a special field of applied natural science, medicine.

All the evidence—for Chinese, Korean, Indian, Tibetan, Middle Eastern, and medieval European cities—points to a differentiation between "higher" and "lower" medicine, whose practitioners are drawn from the urban upper and lower strata (including outcastes), respectively; this schism has over many centuries blocked any substantial progress in the field. One kind of medicine, that practiced mainly by the priests or other literati, has taken the high road; the other has been plied by the generally illiterate diviners, herbalists, midwives, bonesetters, and "surgeons," many of the last doubling as barbers, who engage in blood-letting, cupping, pulling teeth, and the like. These lower-class and outcaste practitioners lack a standardized body of knowledge and a scholarly orientation. Contrariwise, the literate medical men evince these latter but eschew dissection, surgery—anything that involves contact with "blood and guts," a source of ritual or physical "defilement" (a pattern deviating sharply from that in industrial cities). Bullough[43] has shown that even in late medieval Paris, when "surgeons" sought to elevate their status through formal education, they gave up their manual techniques, leaving these to the uneducated barbers. Practitioners who engage in surgery may treat rich and poor alike, whereas the formally educated upper-class physicians, many of whom belong to the priestly group, serve but the elite.

In many non-industrial cities the religious values specifically enjoin against mutilation of the body, most of all by cutting; only lower-class people can flout the resulting norms. These religious prohibitions, added to the disdain for physical labor, explain why scholarly medical men in feudal cities rarely bother to verify their theories about human physiology through minute inspection of the human body. Pertinently, the Hippocratic school of medicine, though it rejected "supernatural" forces as a cause of disease and concentrated upon the interaction of "humours" in the body, nonetheless based its theories primarily upon crude observation, the classification of phenomena, and a high degree of speculation; actual examination of the human body through dissection of cadavers was almost unknown.[44] The empirical anatomical studies of Galen, mainly through dissection of animals, and those conducted in late medieval Europe at the medical school in Bologna have been singularly rare exceptions to the patterns of medicine in the preindustrial world whereby the elite avoid any empirical inspection of the physiology of humans or animals.

The upper-status, educated physicians in feudal cities display a curious admixture of anatomical knowledge (advanced over that in folk orders but illusory from the viewpoint of modern medicine) and indoctrination in the operation of the supernatural forces that are considered to be the cause of much illness. Both kinds of knowledge may be used in the diagnosis and treatment of disease.

As to the first type, in traditional Tibet, Waddell[45] observes, the higher schools taught that the heart of a woman is in the middle of the chest, the man's on the left, that blood circulates on the right side of the body and yellow bile on the left, and that by feeling the six pulses on the wrists (the three red on the right and three yellow on the left) one can diagnose a malady, for each pulse is associated with a specific organ. Chinese medical treatises present, among other notions, a highly complex theory of pulses, a number of which supposedly indicate approaching death, and recommend the use of acupuncture (based upon an imaginary system of canals in the body) to restore within the patient equilibrium between the two vital principles of life, Yang and Yin.[46] The ancient Ayurvedic system of Indian medicine, part of the sacred, "revealed" knowledge, and still much practiced today,[47] is essentially a humoral theory of human physiology, unique in its details but akin in form to the theories of medicine that have flourished in other preindustrial civilized orders. The humoral theory, like the Yang-Yin concept of pathology in China, considers disharmony between or among certain fundamental elements in the body one cause of illness; treatment consists in re-establishing equilibrium. In much of the Middle East, for example, constitutional "balance" is restored by giving patients "hot" or "cold" foods, depending upon the classification of the ailment—e.g., fever, a "hot" ailment, is treated with "cold" foods.

Intermixed with this empirical body of medical knowledge—much of it unsound by modern standards—is the concept of supernatural forces as agents of disease.[48] Part of the formal training of the educated medical man is indoctrination in divinatory rites for establishing the specific nature of an ailment and determining the proper cure. For example, certain treatments are "effective" only when the stars are in proper position, regardless of the disease in question. It is meaningful that almost everywhere in the feudal world astrology is part of medical education in schools of higher learning. The elite physicians also resort to incantations, charms, and spells to exorcise or propitiate the offending evil spirits, or gods of disease, or to prayers and sacrifices to enlist the aid of healing deities, saints, and the like to overcome the forces of evil.[49] Curing consists not in revising the natural or divine order but rather in adjusting to it, as basically immutable, or of restoring equilibrium in it through systems of medicine that are essentially rigid, closed bodies of knowledge.

The lower-class (or outcaste) medical practitioners, too,

exhibit this combination of scientific, or pseudo-scientific, knowledge and magico-religious belief. Barbers-surgeons and midwives, almost invariably of low status, do have some specialized empirical knowledge of human physiology and provide services of a manual and defiling nature that are shunned by the elite physicians; nevertheless, as with other practitioners, their concepts of the etiology of bodily ills are interlaced with magico-religious notions. Alongside them in the city function lower-class medicine men of various trades, including many illiterate priests who have acquired some of the medical learning that trickles down from above; these may diagnose and treat illness according to the stellar configurations, sell amulets containing fragments of the scriptures—used to ward off disease—prescribe magical potions, and so on. They use preventive, restorative, and predictive magic intermixed with religious practices.

Unlike his preindustrial counterpart, industrial man seeks attainment over, rather than attunement to, the divine and/or natural order. Nowhere are the results of the new purview of the universe more visible than in the field of modern medicine. In the preindustrial city, morbidity and mortality rates are exceedingly high, and the urban panorama is marred by the ranks of the infirm, the maimed, and those made destitute by disease. The new orientation to medicine that characterizes the industrial city, while not inimical to all magical beliefs, does effect some dramatic changes. One is a shift in the age and sex structure in the city, due to the increased life-span, with far-reaching effects upon social organization.

Finally, allow us to comment briefly upon the nature of knowledge in the industrial city. In our attempts to assay the divergencies between industrial and preindustrial cities, technology is everywhere our key explanatory variable. But unlike many other writers who utilize the concept of technology, we see science as indisputably part of it.

In contrast to the absolutistic orientation toward knowledge in the preindustrial city, modern science by its very nature destroys many of the "old gods." Negation lies at the very heart of experimentation: indeed, the history of modern science is but a graveyard of hypotheses discarded as false. An intriguing question—as yet unanswered—is: What will be the long-run, over-all impact of this negation process upon the industrial-urban system? The scientific method has been a secularizing force, tending to undermine credence in absolute values and norms in the religious, educational, governmental, and other spheres. A functional relationship, not fully understood, appears to exist between science and democracy. Science thrives best in an atmosphere that encourages dissent and the exploration of alternatives. And an industrial society, if it is to survive as such—and this is true even of one ruled by a dictator—must permit considerable give and take, i.e., democracy, in many areas of activity affected by the scientific approach. But contradictory forces operate as well: the instabilities created by the negative orientation of science may be antithetical to the effective functioning of a democratic order. And science itself may become another absolute.

Science leaves its impact in other ways. The scientific method calls for the use of objective, universalistic criteria in the selection of hypotheses. It follows that scientists, the carriers of the method, must themselves be selected and promoted on a similar basis if science is to prosper. Inasmuch as a profusion of bureaucracies in the industrial city tend to be staffed by experts socialized into the scientific method, and insofar as these organizations are committed to advancing the cause of science, these are driven to hire and promote personnel on the basis of universalistic criteria. Not that this ideal is ever really achieved, for contrary forces operate, but that this is a dominant orientation can not be doubted.

This brief discussion is intended merely to suggest that the particular system of knowledge that underlies the industrial technology has a built-in value system that has a major, though little appreciated, impact upon the industrial city's social structure, differentiating it from that of the feudal city, whose formal learning is anti-experimental and insulated from the functioning of the workaday world. The conjunction of highly abstract thought with practical knowledge has had untold repercussions for modern urban living.

NOTES TO CHAPTER X

1. Roger Le Tourneau, *Fès: Avant le Protectorat* (Casablanca: Société Marocaine de Librairie et d'Édition, 1949), pp. 258-59.

2. Iris Origo, *The Merchant of Prato* (London: Jonathan Cape, 1957), p. 59.

3. Babur Çağatay and Andrée F. Sjoberg, "Notes on the Uzbek Culture of Central Asia," *Texas Journal of Science,* VII (March, 1955), 97.

4. E.g., Jukichi Inouye, *Sketches of Tokyo Life* (Yokohama: Torando, 1895), pp. 3-12; Wilhelm Grube, "Zur Pekinger Volkskunde," *Veröffentlichungen aus dem Königlichen Museum für Völkerkunde* (Berlin), VII (1901), 99ff.; Edward W. Lane, *The Manners and Customs of the Modern Egyptians* (5th ed.; New York: E. P. Dutton, Everyman's Library, 1923), pp. 449, 480-81; Donald N. Wilber (ed.), *Afghanistan* (New Haven: Human Relations Area Files, 1956), pp. 6, 383-84.

5. Milton Singer, "The Great Tradition in a Metropolitan Center: Madras," *Journal of American Folklore,* LXXI (July-September, 1958), 347-88.

6. Dalton Potter, "The Bazaar Merchant," in Sydney Nettleton Fisher (ed.), *Social Forces in the Middle East* (Ithaca: Cornell University Press, 1955), p. 103. Cf. Edwin Benson, *Life in a Mediaeval City* (New York: Macmillan, 1920), pp. 69-70.

7. John Henry Gray, *Walks in the City of Canton* (Hongkong: De Souza, 1875), p. 192.

8. Chester Holcombe, *The Real Chinaman* (New York: Dodd, Mead, 1895), pp. 121-23.

9. O. Olufsen, *The Emir of Bokhara and His Country* (London: William Heinemann, 1911), p. 389.

10. E.g., Yan Phou Lee, *When I Was a Boy in China* (Boston: Lothrop, Lee, and Shepard, 1887), p. 10; Horace Miner, *The Primitive City of Timbuctoo* (Princeton: Princeton University Press, 1953), pp. 87-89.

11. Le Tourneau, *op. cit.,* pp. 406-11.

12. Some idea of this can be gained from A. H. Arden, *A Progressive Grammar of the Telugu Language* (4th ed.; Madras: Christian Literature Society, 1955), Chapter III. Arden's work does not include all the symbols in current use, however.

13. E.g., Austin Lane Poole (ed.), *Medieval England,* II (Oxford: Clarendon Press, 1958), 542; Wilber, *op. cit.,* p. 379.

14. Tao-tai Hsia, "The Language Revolution in Communist China," *Far Eastern Survey*, XXV (October, 1956), 151.

15. E.g., "The Writing Reform," *China News Analysis*, No. 214 (January 31, 1958), pp. 5-6; Stefan Wurm, *Turkic Peoples of the USSR* (London: Central Asian Research Centre, 1954), pp. 45ff.; W. Norman Brown, "Script Reform in Modern India, Pakistan, and Ceylon," *Journal of the American Oriental Society*, LXXIII (January-March, 1953), 1-6.

16. Khanikoff, *Bokhara: Its Amir and its People*, trans. Clement A. De Bode (London: James Madden, 1845), p. 275.

17. Benson, *op. cit.*, pp. 56-68. For Europe in general, see Sidney Painter, *A History of the Middle Ages: 284-1500* (New York: Alfred A. Knopf, 1956), pp. 466-72.

18. E.g., R. A. B. Ponsonby-Fane, *Kyoto* (Kyoto: Posonby Memorial Society, 1956), pp. 417-18; Lee, *op. cit.*, p. 52; Justus Doolittle, *Social Life of the Chinese*, ed. Paxton Hood (London: Sampson, Low, 1868), p. 303.

19. Doolittle, *op. cit.*, p. 304; Le Tourneau, *op. cit.*, p. 456, cf. pp. 214, 260-62.

20. Olufsen, *op. cit.*, p. 388.

21. Le Tourneau, *op. cit.*, p. 455.

22. Walter B. Scaife, *Florentine Life During the Renaissance* (Baltimore: Johns Hopkins Press, 1893), p. 108.

23. Khanikoff, *op. cit.*, p. 280; Giuseppe Tucci, *To Lhasa and Beyond* (Roma: Instituto Poligrafico dello Stato, 1956), p. 103.

24. Victor Purcell, *Problems of Chinese Education* (London: Kegan Paul, Trench, Trubner, 1936), pp. 18-19.

25. Olufsen, *op. cit.*, p. 388.

26. F. Spencer Chapman, *Lhasa: The Holy City* (London: Chatto and Windus, 1938), p. 108.

27. Jérôme Carcopino, *Daily Life in Ancient Rome* (New Haven: Yale University Press, 1940), p. 112.

28. Khanikoff, *op. cit.*, pp. 275-76; Chiang Yee, *A Chinese Childhood* (New York: John Day, 1952), p. 83.

29. C. Snouck Hurgronje, *Mekka in the Latter Part of the Nineteenth Century*, trans. J. H. Monahan (Leyden: E. J. Brill, 1931), pp. 190-91, 197-98.

30. Purcell, *op. cit.*, p. 23.

31. Lane, *op. cit.*, pp. 222-23.

32. Carcopino, *op. cit.*, p. 104; Wilber, *op. cit.*, p. 359; Le Tourneau, *op. cit.*, pp. 458-59.

33. M. Cary and T. J. Haarhoff, *Life and Thought in the Greek and Roman World* (London: Methuen, 1957), pp. 281-82; Ernst Pulgram, *The Tongues of Italy* (Cambridge: Harvard University Press, 1958), p. 354.

34. Hurgronje, *op. cit.*, pp. 190-91.

35. E.g., C. P. Fitzgerald, *The Tower of Five Glories* (London: Cresset Press, 1941), p. 149; Edwin O. Reischauer, *The United States and Japan* (Cambridge: Harvard University Press, 1957), p. 159.

36. E.g., Harrison E. Salisbury, "Soviet to Start Full Inventory of its Resources," *New York Times* (May 24, 1959), pp. 1, 3.

37. Lynn Thorndike, *A History of Magic and Experimental Science*, III (New York: Columbia University Press, 1934), Chapters I, III, and XXXIV.

38. Joseph Needham, *Science and Civilisation in China,* II (Cambridge: Cambridge University Press, 1956).

39. Marshall Clagett, *Greek Science in Antiquity* (London: Abelard-Schuman, 1957).

40. James Jeans, *The Growth of Physical Science* (2d ed.; Cambridge: Cambridge University Press, 1951), p. 41.

41. Charles Singer *et al.* (eds.), *A History of Technology,* III (Oxford: Clarendon Press, 1957), v-vi; Charles C. Gillispie, "The Natural History of Industry," *Isis,* XLVIII (December, 1957), 398-407; especially 402.

42. I. Bernard Cohen, "Review of Charles Singer *et al.* (eds.), *A History of Technology,* Vols. IV and V (New York: Oxford University Press, 1958)," *New York Times Book Review* (February 1, 1959), p. 6.

43. Vern L. Bullough, "The Development of the Medical Guilds at Paris," *Medievalia et Humanistica,* XII (December, 1958), 33-40. For a discussion of upper-lower class divisions in medicine in Seoul, Korea, see J. B. Busteed, "The Korean Doctor and His Methods," *The Korean Repository,* II (January, 1895), 188-93.

44. E.g., Arturo Castiglioni, *A History of Medicine,* trans. and ed. E. B. Krumbhaar (New York: Alfred A. Knopf, 1941), pp. 160-62.

45. Austine Waddell, *Lhasa and its Mysteries* (New York: E. P. Dutton, 1906), pp. 376ff.

46. Castiglioni, *op. cit.,* p. 105.

47. Efforts to maintain the old system are continually discussed in Indian newspapers. See, e.g., *The Hindu* (Madras), "Ayurvedic and Unani Systems" (September 25, 1956), p. 4; "Indigenous Medicine" (October 19, 1956), p. 4. Cf. "Where East Meets West," *Time,* LXXII (August 18, 1958), 65.

48. E.g., Francis L. K. Hsu, *Religion, Science and Human Crises* (London: Routledge and Kegan Paul, 1952).

49. For a discussion of the "supernatural" and medical practice in certain cities of antiquity, see, e.g., Walter Addison Jayne, *The Healing Gods of Ancient Civilizations* (New Haven: Yale University Press, 1925). For medieval Europe see, e.g., Douglas Guthrie, *A History of Medicine* (Philadelphia: J. B. Lippincott, 1946), pp. 98-99.

CHAPTER XI

A BACKWARD GLANCE:
A FORWARD LOOK

THROUGHOUT this work the burden of our argument is that preindustrial cities and the feudal societies that support them, whether past or present, or in divergent cultural settings, share an imposing number of structural characteristics. Similar in many facets of their ecology, as well as in their class, familial, economic, political, religious, and educational structures, they differ dramatically from industrial cities and societies. Although we are cognizant of the variations among preindustrial cities through time and across cultural boundaries, our task has been the search for similarities in these communities, particularly in those features that set them apart from industrial cities.

No claim is made that every preindustrial city displays each one of the traits delineated in the preceding chapters. Nevertheless, non-industrial, or feudal, cities evince a startling degree of communality. Remember, we have introduced into our "constructed type" only those traits for which empirical evidence is at hand for cities in at least several divergent cultural systems.

Although empirical illustrations are offered throughout to buttress our generalizations, these are merely suggestive of the wide range of supporting data available! Complete documentation of each proposition would have resulted in a set of volumes of unmanageable proportions, our theses smothered in a welter of technical details.

Granted that the materials on preindustrial cities are of uneven quality, and that hiatuses exist, they are nonetheless more extensive than most readers might assume. Those who desire further particulars, as well as a fuller picture of specific cities, should examine the cited works; these serve as an introduction to a voluminous body of literature.

We undertook this research in the belief that systematization of existing data, and their interpretation into some meaningful whole, is a desideratum in American social science, geared as it is to absorption with particulars. The fundamental premise of this work is that social science in general, and sociology in particular, to fulfil the requirements of a science, must seek to isolate the common elements in societies and cultures. It is only by abstracting out the universal, or near-universal, traits in preindustrial cities that one really discovers and explicates what is unique. The more materials on cities around the world that I examine, the more I am convinced that too many social scientists assume uniqueness where such does not exist.

Our primary intention has been to analyze feudal cities and their societies and thereby to provide a perspective for a clearer understanding of modern industrial orders. But we are jumping slightly ahead of ourselves. We need first to synopsize the structure of the non-industrial city, and then restate the theory underlying our work. After this we consider the possible utility of our typology for future research, most perceptibly in underdeveloped countries. Lastly we pose the query: What is transpiring in contemporary preindustrial cities and what will be the possible end result as these are swept up in the tidal wave of industrialization?

The Preindustrial City in Capsule Form

Cities of this type have been with us, present evidence indicates, since the fourth millennium B.C., when they first began their development in the Mesopotamian riverine area. Before long, in response to the growing technology and a variety of political forces, city life proliferated over a broader area. To an astonishing degree, preindustrial cities throughout history have prospered or floundered, as the case may be, in accordance with the shifting tides of social power.

In terms of their population these cities are the industrial city's poor relations, few ranging over 100,000 and many containing less than 10,000 or even 5,000 inhabitants. Their rate of population growth, moreover, has been slow and variable as well, in accordance with the waxing and waning of the supportive political structure. Yet throughout the shifting fortunes of empire, and the concomitant oscillation in population growth and decline, certain persistent structural characteristics signalize preindustrial cities everywhere.

As to spatial arrangements, the city's center is the hub of governmental and religious activity more than of commercial ventures. It is, besides, the prime focus of elite residence, while the lower class and outcaste groups are scattered centrifugally toward the city's periphery. Added to the strong ecological differentiation in terms of social class, occupational and ethnic distinctions are solemnly proclaimed in the land use patterns. It is usual for each occupational group to live and work in a particular street or quarter, one that generally bears the name of the trade in question. Ethnic groups are almost always isolated from the rest of the city, forming, so to speak, little worlds unto themselves. Yet, apart from the considerable ecological differentiation according to socioeconomic criteria, a minimum of specialization exists in land use. Frequently a site serves multiple purposes—e.g., it may be devoted concurrently to religious, educational, and business activities; and residential and occupational facilities are apt to be continguous.

As to class, one is born into a particular stratum and usually must live out his life in accordance with the rights and duties of his position. Few aspects of daily activity escape the pervasive influence of class. A small urbanized, privileged group commands the local community and the society and is nourished by the lower class and an outcaste group; this last, by performing functions considered defiling and beyond the bounds of respectability, is ostracized by both the lower and upper strata. Social mobility in the city, at least as viewed over several generations, seems, relative to the industrial norms, inconsequential. The small upper class, immediately identifiable by its dress, speech, and personal mannerisms, controls the key organizational units of government, religion, and education in the city and society. Distinctive familial arrangements and clear avoidance of economic activity mark the elite as well. Of course, as earlier emphasized, there are contrary forces at work that disturb these neat arrangements.

The preindustrial urbanite functions within a family system and subordinates himself to it. One consequence is that, typically, marriages are arranged by families, not by individuals. The large extended family, with numerous relatives residing in a single "household"—i.e., one that is a functioning social unit—is the ideal toward which all urbanites strive, though a sizeable, closely knit family is generally attainable only by the upper class. Economic circumstances prevent the urban poor and the peasantry alike from maintaining large households; for them the famille souche is more normal.

The men in the family lord it over the women; but though the latter are relegated to a humbler position, they are protected to a degree by the rigid sexual division of labor. Upper-class women, moreover, are isolated from most aspects of community life. Those in the urban lower class, like the rural women, play a rather more salient role in family affairs and are accorded wider freedom and responsibility in the community than are the elite womenfolk, though by no means to the degree permitted the males, nor to the extent enjoyed by the industrial city's women. Added to the profound status differentiation by sex in the feudal city is the sharp age-grading; the older family members dominate the younger, both as between generations and between siblings.

The family is the key socialization agency in the community and serves, for the women and children, and men to a lesser degree, as the focus of leisure-time activity. But more than this, given the low level of social mobility, a man's family is the chief determinant of his future career, be this in the topmost levels of the governmental, educational, or religious bureaucracies or, in the case of the commoners, in the lower-status jobs. Personnel are recruited according to kinship or personalistic criteria far more than on objective, universalistic grounds.

Economic activity is poorly developed in the preindustrial city, for manual labor, or indeed any that requires one to mingle with the humbler folk, is depreciated and eschewed by the elite. Except for a few large-scale merchants, who may succeed in buying their way into the elite, persons engaged in economic activity are either of the lower class (artisans, laborers, and some shopkeepers) or outcastes (some businessmen, and those who carry out the especially degrading and arduous tasks in the city).

Within the economic realm the key unit is the guild, typically community-bound. Through the guilds, handicraftsmen, merchants, and groups offering a variety of services attempt to minimize competition and determine standards and prices in their particular spheres of activity. Customarily also, each guild controls the recruitment, based mainly on kinship or other particularistic ties, and the training of personnel for its specific occupation and seeks to prevent outsiders from invading its hallowed domain.

The production of goods and services—by means of a simple technology wherein humans and animals are almost the only source of power, and tools to multiply the effects of this energy are sparse—is accomplished through a division of labor which is complex compared to that in the typical folk order but, seen from the industrial city's vantage point, is surprisingly simple. Very commonly the craftsman fashions an article from beginning to end and often markets it himself. Although little specialization exists in process, specialization according to product is widespread. Thus each guild is concerned with the manufacture and/or sale of a specific product or, at most, a narrow class of products.

Little standardization is found in prices, currency, weights and measures, or the type or quality of commodities marketed. In the main, the price of an item is fixed through haggling between buyer and seller. Different types and values of currency may be used concurrently within or among communities; so too with weights and measures, which often vary as well among the crafts. The marketing procedure is further complicated by the extensive adulteration of produce, forcing the buyer to be wary in every transaction; the quality of commodities is rarely, if ever, guaranteed.

The expansion of the economy is limited not only by the ruling group's negation of economic activity, the lack of standardization, and so on, but very largely also by the meager facilities for credit and capital formation.

Turning from the economy to the political structure, we find members of the upper class in command of the key governmental positions. The political apparatus, moreover, is highly centralized, the provincial and local administrators being accountable to the leaders in the societal capital. The sovereign exercises autocratic power, although this is mitigated by certain contrary forces that act to limit the degree of absolutism in the political realm.

The sovereign, and the societal leaders in general, along with the bureaucracies they control, base their authority upon appeals to tradition and to absolutes. The political bureaucracy, and the educational and religious systems as well, are characterized by rigid hierarchical arrangements; notwithstanding, the lines of authority in decision-making are most imprecise. The result is that decisions are arrived at not according to impersonal rules but rather with reference to the "persons" involved. Bureaucratic personnel are selected mainly on individualistic grounds—i.e., according to whether they have the correct community, kinship, and friendship ties. Clientele are served on a similar basis, which means that the elite determine policy to their own advantage. These patterns, combined with the lack of a fixed salary system, are conducive to graft and, from the point of view of industrial-urban systems, marked inefficiency. Nevertheless, as we have sought to show, this bureaucracy can, from the perspective of the preindustrial system, be considered quite rational in its operation.

Like the political structure, that pertaining to religion is a potent force making for order in the preindustrial city. The religious personnel, as well as religious beliefs and practices in general, are rent by the same upper-lower-outcaste divisions that prevail in other areas of activity. Upper-class persons occupy the topmost positions in the hierarchy; furthermore, the elite's religious norms conform most closely to those enunciated in the sacred writings, understandable only to this literate group, whereas the values and norms of the lower strata, most notably those of the outcastes, are apt to deviate considerably from the ideal.

The religious norms, deriving from the religious values and in turn reinforcing them, are highly prescriptive. One's day-by-day behavior is largely governed by religious injunctions, and few areas of activity—be these family life, politics, economics, education, or whatever—escape their pervasive influence. Moreover, the periodic religious ceremonies, in which a large segment of the community may participate, are one of the few mechanisms the city possesses for integrating disparate groups in an otherwise segmented community.

Strong reliance is placed upon protective, restorative, and

predictive magic for assisting the individual in adjusting to the natural-divine order, something taken as an absolute, a given. The elite itself, lacking as much as the common man the means to manipulate and revise the social and physical world, employs magical practices freely. And a good part of the magic is integrated into the religious body of knowledge.

Relative to the industrial-urban community, communication in the feudal city is achieved primarily by word-of-mouth, specialized functionaries serving to disseminate news orally at key gathering points in the city. Members of the literate elite, however, communicate with one another to a degree through writing. And the formal educational system depends upon the written word, the means by which the ideal norms are standardized over time and space.

Only the elite, however, have access to formal education. And the educational and religious organizations, with few exceptions, are interdigitated. The curriculum in the schools, whether elementary or advanced, is overwhelmingly devoted to predication of the society's traditional religious-philosophical concepts. The schools are geared not to remaking the system but to perpetuating the old. Modern science, wherein abstract thought is coherent with practical knowledge and through which man seeks to manipulate the natural order, is practically non-existent in the non-industrial city. The emphasis is upon ethical and religious matters as one is concerned with adjusting to, not overcoming, the order of things. In contrast, industrial man is bent upon revising nature for his own purposes.

Theoretical Orientation

Inasmuch as preindustrial cities in numerous divergent cultural milieu display basic similarities in form, some variable other than cultural values, in the broad sense, must be operative; regularities of this sort are not the result of mere chance.

Here technology—viz., the available *energy, tools,* and *know-how* connected with these—seems the most satisfactory explanatory variable.[1] This mode of reasoning should not commit us in any way to credence in technological determinism or unilinear evolution; indeed we firmly reject these stands. In point of fact, we make frequent reference to social power in accounting for the fluctuating fortunes of cities and the fate of technology and give due recognition to its role in producing organization in the society. Nor do we ignore values. These, we have remarked in a number of contexts, account for certain divergencies from our constructed type; too, some values tend to be correlated with a specific level of technology; as a notable instance, the scientific method has built-in values that must be diffused, along with the energy-sources, tools, and requisite know-how, to underdeveloped areas if these are to industrialize. Further, we see the city per se as a variable to be reckoned with; rural and urban communities are in many ways intrinsically different. Although we lend priority to technology, we can not dispense with the other variables enumerated.

With these qualifications (and we hope the reader will keep them ever in mind), it seems clear that the transition from the preliterate to the feudal level, i.e., to the preindustrial civilized order, or from the latter to the industrial-urban society is associated with certain crucial advances in the technological sphere. The very emergence of cities is functionally related to the society's ability to produce a sizeable surplus; and the orientation, quite late in history, to an industrial base made possible a kind of city never before imagined. To minimize technology, as to ignore the value system, would be poor procedure.

As has been asseverated time and again, we have been searching for similarities among cities in feudal societies, rather than areas of cultural divergency. Our primary vantage point has been the industrial city—though we have maintained awareness of the relations between folk and feudal orders as

well. Our hypothesis that preindustrial and industrial cities
are fundamentally distinctive entities is unmistakably borne
out by the existing data.

Having taken technology as the dominant variable for
explicating the divergencies between preindustrial and industrial cities, and their respective societies, we then proceeded
to set this analysis within the context of contemporary structural-functionalism—with one outstanding modification: we
introduced the concept of contradictory functional requirements, or what are termed "imperatives," "prerequisites,"
"necessary conditions," and other sociologisms.[2] Eschewing an
excessive preoccupation with staticism and neatly integrated
wholes, the proclivity of so much structural-functional analysis, we perceive the operation of contradictory structures,
each "essential" to the system, yet at odds with one another.
This is obviously the source of some of the strains that pervade even the relatively static non-industrial civilized society.
Phrased differently, it is not just societies in some stage of
transition from one fundamental form to another that undergo
strain and tension; so-called "non-transitional" orders, either
feudal or industrial, are plagued with self-inconsistencies.

As an illustration of our recourse to structural-functional
analysis, may we briefly review certain aspects of the class
system in the preindustrial city. Some segment of the populace must be freed from food production or other physical
labor so that it can devote its time to governing others. The
labor force must be controlled and integrated, goods must be
siphoned off from the hinterland to feed the city, political
stability must be maintained, and so on. A leisure class can
be considered a "requirement" if the city is to operate with a
limited technology. And at the same time, this privileged
element is created by the technology (advanced as it is over
that in the folk order), though the size of this group is firmly
restricted, for in the absence of machines the populace must
labor long and hard to support even a few in leisured status.

We can go a step farther and state that if this stratum is to persist it must bar ingress into its ranks from below; the result is an overwhelming tendency toward autocratic rule and a rigid class system wherein one's status is generally ascribed by birth. The political, religious, and educational hierarchies all intensify this by staffing the key posts on particularistic, primarily kinship, grounds. More, the elite legitimizes its dominance by appeal to absolutes and to tradition. Just as the existence of this class is made possible by the prevailing technology, so too, its autocratic rule and obstruction of social mobility for others are fostered by the technology which permits, and requires, few experts, no mass education, and so forth.

Nevertheless, in the matter of exclusiveness, though a considerable amount of it is permitted the elite, such can not be fully achieved, for contradictory forces are at work. On the one hand the elite scorn, and attempt to ostracize, businessmen on a number of counts—most notably the fact that the latter's field lends itself to the amassing of wealth, and therefore possible upward mobility, by commoners who possess special talents for manipulation. This is an obvious threat to the elite's position, based as it is on kinship and reinforced by appeals to absolutes and to tradition. Yet because the city, to be a city, must allow for commercial activity, and because the upper class itself requires wealth if it is to maintain eminence, successful businessmen, if not from outcaste ethnic groups, can occasionally utilize their monetary gains to purchase upper-class status. Because the elite require the services of merchants, they nurture them, paving the way for a partial undermining of their own position. Although the preindustrial city's, and the society's, internal structures reinforce one another to a high degree—a "circularity" that actually makes exposition difficult—the component parts are at times at odds with one another, generating stresses within the system.

When comparing the preindustrial and industrial city-types,

bear in mind that while each generates its own dominant patterns—e.g., the preindustrial city emphasizes class rigidity and particularism, the industrial city class fluidity and universalism—countervailing forces operate within both cities. Neither absolute rigidity nor extreme fluidity is achievable. Most writers ignore this, choosing to analyze systems in terms of fictional types; we have selected a more empirical orientation despite a resulting degree of muzziness; indeed the latter is characteristic of reality itself.

An ideological issue looms before us. Most treatments of feudal orders are essentially moralizations as to the merits or demerits of these societies' world outlook. "Conservatives" look back in praise on what they consider to be a glorious past and lament the expansion of industrialization.[3] The "liberals" look back in shame and anger. We have attempted to tread a narrow line between these extremes. Although continually contrasting the feudal city with the industrial type, we do acknowledge the former's contributions to man's heritage. But we shun the interpretations of writers of Mumford's persuasion, who glamorize the medieval European city, or of some social scientists who, incredibly, are unaware of the stark poverty of the lower classes in ancient cities.[4] It is preferable to accept the preindustrial city for what it is, realizing its positive contributions but noting its deficiencies as well. We shall not cheer, neither shall we weep, as it fades from the scene.

One final comment on our theoretical approach. Throughout, recognition has been given to the theoretical distinctions between a city and a society. But empirically these fuse—our efforts to analyze one force us to treat the other. In practice, the city is our starting point, but we have branched outward from it to encompass the total feudal order. This work is, in the end, a survey of the preindustrial civilized society with special emphasis upon the city, the hub of all major activity therein.

Utility of This Typology for Research and Analysis

The ultimate test of our constructed type, of course, is its long-run utility for interpreting empirical phenomena. It does seem to enlarge one's purview of preindustrial cities and feudal societies. For this reason the typology should prove useful to historians, anthropologists, and archeologists attempting to reconstruct the social arrangements in cities long since dead. Certain aspects of their life-ways lie forever beyond our grasp. The only reasonable alternative is extrapolation to the past from data on more recent feudal cities, utilizing in the process, recent advances in the social scientist's knowledge of social systems. Knowing "what to expect" in earlier cities imparts fuller meaning to written records and permits more satisfactory reconstructions where gaps exist in the data. A salient weakness in much historical research is the tendency to assume uniqueness for much of the social phenomena encountered; all manner of false interpretations ensue. Such is "historicism," ultimately a denial of objective generalization as the goal of social science. A considerable proportion of sociologists, bound as they are to the American social scene, are unwitting proponents of this myopic approach.

This study will perhaps encourage some scholars to focus attention upon the preindustrial cities that survive today; in turn, the data amassed on these can be used to refine our constructed type. Such need not be an end in itself. Acute awareness of the social structure of preindustrial civilized societies and their cities is essential for anyone who hopes to understand current processes in societies now changing over from feudal to industrial modes of organization. In this connection, it is instructive that some writers see regularity in form across industrial systems yet implicitly deny uniformities of structure for preindustrial civilized societies. But that such regularities abound should be apparent to any observer of these societies who attains a broad space-time overview. It is these uniformities that provide a "yardstick" for measuring and interpreting across cultural boundaries the significant social changes that are occurring. So much of the analysis of social change in India, China, the Middle East, and other underdeveloped areas thus far has been accomplished with no real effort to isolate the underlying structural themes that run through these varying cultures. Surprising, yes, but nonetheless true. Only through the use of some kind of "standard," like the one offered herein, against which to measure change, can we determine whether one society (with its cities) is relinquishing its traditional forms more rapidly than others. For as statistics on industrializing societies become quantitatively and qualitatively more adequate, firmer generalizations concerning these fundamental processes should become possible.

It is high time sociologists in general, not just the few, began to deal with the industrial-urbanization process in underdeveloped countries. The repercussions of this revolution throughout the world are devastating. And the impact of these changes on social science theory, sociological theory in particular, bids fair to be revolutionary as well.

Scanning the history of sociology, we see that sociologists today who are attempting to understand the nature of change in "underdeveloped" countries (by no means a satisfactory term) are more closely akin theoretically to the German social thinkers than to the typical French, English, or American social scientists.[5] The explanation seems to be that Germany in the latter part of the nineteenth century experienced a rather sudden transition from (to employ the terminology of those who wrote about it) "feudalism" to "capitalism." Most German social scientists, including Max Weber, Sombart, Tönnies, and a host of others, were concerned with the breakup of the old and its replacement by the new. But lamentably, their analyses in general were Europe-bound. Yet how could it have been otherwise? They were writing in an era before industrialization had taken firm hold in Japan, before the Communists' will to industrialize Russia and China, before the upsurge of movements intent upon adopting the new technology in societies the world over. The future of social science theory—the ethnocentrism of urban sociology notwithstanding—lies in its long-run ability to explain the current processes on the world scene. Our effort is a step in this direction.

The Preindustrial City in Transition

The heydey of the preindustrial city is past. A few cities of this type persist in almost pure form, but in the face of industrialization they are fast relinquishing their special characteristics. The dissolution before our very eyes of a city-type that has existed for fifty-five centuries or more is deserving of some attention. Contrarily, the traditional social structure does not evanesce as rapidly as might be imagined. Unlike the folk society, it possesses remarkable capacities for stemming, at least for a time, the tides of change; its complex institutional apparatus—above all its literate elite—are potentially powerful forces of resistance.

Preindustrial-urban forms continue to dominate the cityscape in India, the Middle East, in sections of Latin America, and elsewhere. Even where industrialization is well advanced, as in Japan, survivals of traditional forms crop up on every hand, and efforts by the old elite to maintain the past in the face of a veritable avalanche of industrializing influences continue strong. More impressive is the formidable opposition the Soviet Union, with its police-backed instruments of change, has encountered in its attempts to wipe out the preindustrial-urban carryovers in Muslim Central Asia. Some recent commentaries of Soviet social scientists frankly acknowledge the failure of the Russian state to eliminate many of the traditional religious, economic, and familial patterns in the cities of Central Asia—in Uzbekistan, Tadzhikistan, Kirghizia, Kazakhstan, and Turkmenistan—despite decades of concerted effort in this direction.[6] A number of writers are clamoring for study of these communities, not so much to gain objective scientific knowledge as to acquire information that will enable the governmental apparatus to root out these survivals more effectively.[7]

That preindustrial structural arrangements endure in many parts of Europe should not be ignored. In Spain the traditional social structure continues to ward off the advances of industrial-urbanization on many fronts. France and Italy preserve many feudal city forms as well. Nor are England and Germany completely shorn of their preindustrial-urban structures. Failure to recognize this, however, is widespread. In a recent study of the ecology of Oxford,[8] for example, the data point to the maintenance of traditional patterns; yet the authors betray a lack of perspective on England and the rest of Europe, to say nothing of world cities, while contrasting Oxford with the American city.

Here we should point out that the United States is unique in many respects. It started down the road to industrialization and urbanization without a firmly entrenched feudal elite— in government (including the military), religion, or education—to slow its pace. Its industrial forms, consequently, appear more strongly developed than those in any other sector of the globe. This is a compelling reason for exercising caution when generalizing from the United States to other societies.

What we are getting at is that in industrializing societies the clash between those who seek to revive the feudal order —e.g., in the area of politics the monarchists have been quite vocal in some societies—and those who insist the old must go has periodically waxed intense. For over a century, France has been struggling in vain to achieve a compromise between the proponents of these opposing views. Italy has been rent by a similar political schism, and its effects have been felt in every city throughout the land. The conflict between the traditional and the modern is now manifest in cities in India —in the realms of marriage and family life, in religion, in medicine, and so on—as a perusal of Indian newspapers will confirm. Inasmuch as many Indian cities show only a thin veneer of industrialization, the worst is yet to come.

Implicit perhaps in our reasoning has been the assumption that industrialization is more or less inevitable. We need to qualify this somewhat. Other alternatives are theoretically possible. The preindustrial civilized order could reject industrial-urbanization completely. But several compelling factors make this unlikely. First, if the traditional elite is to sustain itself as a "dominant" group it must industrialize. Pressure for industrialization stems from both internal and external sources, although we contend that the latter exert paramount influence. The traditional elite in most underdeveloped countries—India or those in the Middle East, for example—is promoting industrialization in large part to overcome its own and its nation's colonial status, although this process encourages class fluidity and threatens the elite's authority. Even the ideological pressures upon these systems to industrialize —say, to ameliorate the lot of the common man—come primarily from their efforts to emulate their more highly industrialized neighbors.

At one time the author envisioned the possibility of an eventual modus vivendi between feudal and industrial forms, at least in some societies. An industrial-urban system could, theoretically, be superimposed upon a feudal order without necessarily obliterating the latter: both could function concurrently. France and Italy have displayed this pattern over decades. Despite the industrial aspect of many cities in France, it still remains a society of many small shopkeepers, handicraftsmen, and peasants. In Italy the preindustrial-industrial split has in large part coincided with the regional distinctions between north and south.

No longer do we regard a "dual" society as a possible "stable" end result for most underdeveloped countries today.

One reason is that, possessing as they do a relatively large population base, they must industrialize and urbanize in order to effectively curb the vast population expansion and keep it from cancelling out any "gains" resulting from their industrial efforts. Even assuming improved birth control practices could be introduced without concomitant industrialization, an unlikely eventuality, the power variable is still to be considered. Because world power is so closely tied to advancing industrialization, and consequently urbanization, new ruling elements will take shape in some societies and will do their utmost to further this process—if necessary, seeking to erase the traditional order through violence. Nevertheless, smaller countries, far less preoccupied with becoming world powers and amenable to domination by the larger societies, appear less likely to industrialize and may well over time retain many of their feudal ways. Yet, of course, the long-run world trend is toward ever larger, more complex industrial societies.

The result of the drive to industrialize and urbanize will not be a path studded with bliss for all. The stronger the pressures the more bitter will be the fruits. So we find police methods being used to impose industrial-urbanization in the Soviet Union and in Communist China; in the latter, the government would like to extirpate the old order in one fell swoop. Even where force of such proportions is not involved, the strains and stresses are nonetheless intense.

One means of alleviating the internal conflicts is the creation of "devils," usually outsiders, upon whom the blame can be heaped for the shortcomings of the leaders and the intransigencies of factions in the society. Communist China and various Middle Eastern societies can be seen resorting to this "out."

Contemplating the scene, we do not see, as some writers do, a panacea for the world's ills in the industrialization and urbanization of underdeveloped countries, at least not over the shorter run. Not that we oppose these efforts. But the history of the industrial-urbanization process so far offers little encouragement in this regard, and the blossoming of negative values as a means of stabilizing internal arrangements and rationalizing a society's failures are explosive forces that can set off intersocietal conflicts if not handled with care. Viewing certain European societies or Japan in retrospect, one can assume that global strife will multiply with the spread of industrialization and urbanization.

Before turning from this subject, we must emphasize that the end product, the industrial system, will not be the same in India, for example, as in China or England or the United States. Each society's cities will retain much of their own special cultural flavor, but the recurrent theme throughout will be the industrial-urban social structure, to which we now turn.

The End Product [9]

Aside from its distinctive ecological features, as contrasted with the non-industrial-urban forms, the industrial city-type displays a fluid class system, status being based primarily upon achievement rather than ascription. In part this latter reflects the requirement that occupational posts be filled more according to universalistic than to particularistic criteria. Sociologists who perceive the industrial city's class system as rigid and well defined undoubtedly gain this impression from their penchant for contrasting reality with the ideal of absolute fluidity which, after all, given the contradictory demands of the industrial-urban order, is quite utopian.

The industrial city is also characterized by a loosely organized familial unit, primarily conjugal in form, with comparatively few superordinate-subordinate relationships with respect to age and sex. A family system of this nature, permitting and encouraging the exercise of individual choice in the realms of marriage and occupation, is compatible with the high degree of social and spatial mobility encountered in the industrial order.

The economy is mass-production oriented. And it is dominated by large-scale enterprises whose networks of relationships, extending across cities and societies, link the ever-expanding numbers of highly educated, specialized experts who are steeped in the scientific tradition that lies at the vortex of the industrial system. The progress attained in communication and transport, moreover, is associated with wide standardization of currency, prices, and the manufacture and marketing of goods—all acting to sustain the new industrial-urban complex.

In the realm of government we find a rather loosely defined power structure, reflecting the fluid class system. Social power in the industrial city is translated into authority chiefly through appeal to the governed and appeal to experts; reliance upon traditions and absolutes is de-emphasized. Paradoxically, the conservative elements in industrial cities and societies seek the consent of the governed to justify their credence in tradition and absolutes. In all, the industrial system with its proliferation of experts, of mass education, and of the scientific orientation—which lays stress upon negation of traditional thinking—lends support to the new kind of authority structure.

In the governmental bureaucracy, as in business, the emphasis is upon formal rules rather than the primacy of the "person" in the decision-making process, upon clear-cut lines of authority, and on universalism in the selection of personnel and the handling of clientele. Other patterns include fixed salaries and full-time occupancy of bureaucratic posts.

Anent the religious sphere in industrial centers, its norms are generally permissive. Actors play divergent, and often contradictory, roles, and the new technology ensures a continuous cycle of change, all of which requires flexibility in the norms. Though elements of the traditional religion remain strong in some industrial cities, "secular religions" like science and nationalism are looming more significant.

Mass education, where selection tends to be according to ability, is interlinked with the fluid class and family systems; it is a must if the industrial city is to prosper. At the same time, only a highly industrialized system can educate all of its members. Education in the industrial city is geared primarily to emphasizing experimentation and change, negation, and man's ability to manipulate and revise the natural order. Not only has the availability of formal education reached monumental proportions, but knowledge is becoming ever more widely diffused through mass communication media.

As in the preindustrial city, the apparent circularity in the industrial system—the interlinking and mutual support among all of its structures—is interrupted at intervals by the presence of contradictory elements that are, apparently, both essential to the system and at odds with one another. Though the patterns enumerated for the industrial city are the dominant ones, their complete fruition is often precluded by the opposing functional demands of societal forces. Earlier we chanced the observation that although the trend is toward fluidity in the class system, countervailing forces operate. For example, the industrial city requires well-developed status hierarchies in the governmental and economic realms. Although its bureaucracies emphasize universalism and reward individual achievement, persons at the apex of the pyramid can circumvent these norms and ensure, say, special advantages within the system for their children. Then too, concurrent with the demands for permissive religious norms is the need for societal "integration." The dilemma is that the latter may be approached more readily through the medium of traditional religious systems than through more secular ones. Or consider the fact that people's upward striving for success is essential if the educational, scientific, and occupational systems are to prosper; yet emphasis upon upward mobility generates strains, for those who fall by the wayside, particularly during periods of crisis, will perhaps unite behind some charismatic leader to revise the legitimate authority structure. A cataloging of the internal contradictions in industrial cities, to say nothing of the opposition between "external" and "internal" demands upon the industrial-urban order viewed as a whole, requires another treatise.

In another context we set forth some of the problems involved in isolating the structural requirements, or correlates, of industrial-urban centers.[10] We shall not review these issues here but will simply mention one or two of the more compelling ones. The United States, we reiterate, is taken as the prime basis for generalization. This is all right up to a point. But most of the world is only now beginning to industrialize and urbanize on a massive scale, and nowhere has this process reached its peak (even in the United States), nor has it become stabilized in place and time. Of necessity we must extrapolate from incomplete information.

During the next few decades close watch must be kept on cities in, for example, the Soviet Union[11] to determine whether these are drifting toward the type here delineated. Existing evidence seems to indicate that the trend is in this direction, though more noticeably in some spheres than in others. The political arena is especially perplexing. Some social scientists, as well as certain newspaper columnists, perceive a definite trend toward appeals to the consent of the governed and enlarged authority on the part of the vast array of highly trained technical experts in the Soviet Union. This does not mean that countermovements may not arise, or that democracy as defined and cherished in other industrial societies has (or will) become the norm. Certainly the Soviet system has not yet institutionalized any democratic process for transferring authority from one existing leader to his successor. Even so, the Soviet system seems to have moved toward the point where its political system perhaps has more in common with other industrial societies than with strictly feudal orders. In the end, we must keep an open mind to new or contradictory evidence.

Whatever the final result, and its attendant problems, the city is man's own creation. He passed thousands of years within it, more or less satisfied with its preindustrial form, but now is intent upon its drastic reorganization. By the end of the present century, barring an atomic holocaust, the industrial city will be the dominant community form throughout the world. The pattern for the future is set: there is no turning back. The tidal wave of industrial-urbanization, conjoined with the on-going technical revolution and the rapid population growth, will lead to cities of gargantuan dimensions. We believe sociologists' objective understanding of this process may help to ease the inevitable stresses that will follow. Our fervent hope is that the transition will be as painless as possible and that man, adaptable being that he is, will achieve a more satisfying existence through the "monster" he alone has fashioned.

NOTES TO CHAPTER XI

1. For other sociologists who have given attention to the technological variable see: Francis R. Allen *et al.*, *Technology and Social Change* (New York: Appleton-Century-Croft, 1957). Unfortunately, some sociologists tend to drift into a materialistic interpretation of technology, something we have tried to avoid.

2. The terminology of structural-functionalism is by no means satisfactory. We perhaps favor the term, "requirements," but we have utilized it more or less synonymously with those listed in the text as well as introducing the concept of "correlates." We can, obviously, be called to task for this "looseness," but we believe the context will aid the reader in defining the terms. This approach seems preferable to repeating the terms, "requirements" or "necessary conditions" ad infinitum—when these concepts themselves are subject to misinterpretation.

Concerning the label, "contradictory functional requirements," we emphasize that this must not be confused with the concept, "dysfunction." The latter, as employed by sociologists, still stresses the internal harmony of social systems, quite at variance with our approach.

3. E.g., Friedrich Georg Juenger, *The Failure of Technology* (Chicago: Henry Regnery, 1956).

4. E.g., Lewis Mumford, *The Culture of Cities* (New York: Harcourt, Brace, 1938). Pulgram, for one, leaves the impression that Italy under the Romans was more prosperous than it is today—disregarding completely two millennia of technological progress. Ernst Pulgram, *The Tongues of Italy* (Cambridge: Harvard University Press, 1958), pp. 34-36.

5. The dominant concern in present-day American sociology is comparing the real with the ideal norms (the informal with the formal), not contrasting the past with the present. Undoubtedly a reflection of the growing maturity of the urban industrial society, such an orientation is of little value in studying underdeveloped countries.

Because of these differing emphases among sociologists, there is a good deal of unnecessary polemic. Writers concerned with the real vs. the ideal often attack the past-vs.-present, or the developmental, theorists on spurious grounds. Many recent criticisms of Weber's ideal-type formulation of bureaucracy, for example, stem from sociologists' failure to realize that Weber was not studying deviations from the ideal, but rather contrasting traditional society with his so-called "capitalist" one. To play the record over again: keep clearly in mind what is being compared!

6. "The Survival of Religious and Social Customs in Uzbekistan," *Central Asian Review,* VI (1958), 5-15.

7. A. Bennigsen, "Traditional Islam in the Customs of the Turkic Peoples of Central Asia," *Middle East Journal,* XII (Spring, 1958), 227-33. Of course, in all these efforts to rid the Turkic peoples of their traditional patterns, the Soviets are seeking to do more than merely revise the social structure; they seem intent upon Russifying these Muslims—i.e., imposing a new culture upon them.

8. Peter Collison and John Mogey, "Residence and Social Class in Oxford," *American Journal of Sociology,* LXIV (May, 1959), 599-605.

9. Marion Levy, "Some Sources of the Vulnerability of the Structures of Relatively Nonindustrialized Societies to Those of Highly Industrialized Societies," in Bert F. Hoselitz (ed.), *The Progress of Underdeveloped Areas* (Chicago: University of Chicago Press, 1952), pp. 113-25; Kingsley Davis, "Social and Demographic Aspects of Economic Development in India," in Simon Kuznets *et al.* (eds.), *Economic Growth: Brazil, India, Japan* (Durham: Duke University Press, 1955), pp. 293ff.; Bert F. Hoselitz, "Social Structure and Economic Growth," *Economia internazionale,* VI (1953), 52-77.

10. Gideon Sjoberg, "Comparative Urban Sociology," in Robert K. Merton *et al.* (eds.), *Sociology Today* (New York: Basic Books, 1959), pp. 334-59.

11. For one perspective on this issue see: Alex Inkeles and Raymond A. Bauer, *The Soviet Citizen* (Cambridge: Harvard University Press, 1959). Some will contend that the authors exaggerate the similarities between the Soviet Union and other industrial societies, but they make a strong case for their position.

INDEX

Absolutes, appeal to, 183, 221, 225-27, 230, 239, 257, 271, 308, 331, 340; *see also* Authority, bases of, Divine right
Achievements, 124, 134; definition, 109; *see also* Economic structure, Educational structure
Age grading, 175-77, 339
Agrarian societies; *see* Feudal society, peasantry
Agriculture: earliest cities, 28-30, 36-37, 41, 44; grains, 10, 29-30, 34-38, 41-42, 44, 46, 250; Meso-America, 29-30, 46, 48; *see also* Irrigation, Surplus, agricultural, Technology
Agriculturists, 36-37, 48, 81, 83, 89, 100, 112, 122, 161-62, 187-88, 200, 207, 211, 252; *see also* Agriculture, Peasantry, Rural-ites, Villages
Alderson, A. D., 139
Alphabet; *see* Writing
Appleby, P., 243
Artisans; *see* Handicraftsmen
Arts; *see* Fine arts
Asceticism, 258-59
Astrology, 70, 119, 155, 230, 276, 279-81, 287, 300, 309-12, 315-16; *see also* Magic
Authoritarianism, 235-36; *see also* Despotism, Dictators, Political structure, Power, social
Authority, 109, 119, 124, 221-22, 224-31, 233, 271, 273-74, 305-6, 308, 340, 342; bases of, 224-31; *see also* Absolutes, appeal to, Divine right, Power, social

Bacon, A., 169
Beggary, 160, 187-89, 192, 195, 203-4, 258-59, 261
Bell, C., 126
Benson, E., 299
Berger, M., 243
Botero, G., 3
Bowen, H., 188
Braidwood, R., 32
Bribery; *see* Graft
Bromehead, C. N., 40
Bullough, V. L., 313
Bureaucracy, 14, 118, 120, 139, 233, 237-44, 290, 308, 317, 325, 340-41; characteristics of in feudal society, 239-44; China, 138, 240-42; and technology, 240, 243-44; Weber's concept of, 238; *see also* Political structure
Burgess, E., 2
Businessmen; *see* Merchants

Caillé, 94
Capital cities, 38, 69, 70, 73, 86-88, 115-16, 131, 203, 220-21, 234, 246, 252, 273
Capital formation, 149, 193, 197-98, 201, 203, 214-17
Capitalism, 228, 237-38, 334, 344 fn.5
Caste, 118, 127, 148, 189, 211-12; *see also* Outcastes
Chan, W., 261